MW00879124

Copyright © 2023 b

This publication is designed to provide accurate and authoritative information in regard to the subject matter covered. While the author has used his best efforts in preparing this book, he makes no representations or warranties with respect to the accuracy or completeness of the contents of this book and specifically disclaim any implied warranties of merchantability or fitness for a particular purpose.

Book Cover by Censored Anon. You can find more of his work at https://www.arbalestediting.online.

1st Edition 2023.

Table of Contents

Acknowledgments

As the saying goes, this book was made possible only by "standing on the shoulders of giants." Those who addressed these topics before me put in massive amounts of work that I can scarcely begin to imagine; if I have been able to synthesize their ideas in a new way, it is solely because they already did so much of the research. I am deeply indebted, and deeply grateful, to everyone - living and dead - whose work helped me put this book together.

I am also profoundly thankful to those people in my life who have helped encourage and shape my own thinking and spiritual growth. Such forward motion has been just as necessary to this book's completion as those who helped me collate its content. I'd also like to thank Reader Stephen Crawford for editorial feedback and Censored Anon for the beautiful book cover. The countless people with whom I've discussed or debated these topics, each of whom helped to sharpen my mind in one way or another, deserve no less credit simply because I have not had the room to name them all.

I'd also like to thank *you* for your interest in this book and for picking up a copy for yourself. The opportunity cost of the necessary research is likely incalculable and your purchasing this book goes a long way toward helping me recoup the price of those late nights and long hours. I hope that you find this book worth your investment and that you learn something new and meaningful from it.

Finally and most importantly, I'd like to thank my wife Dymphna for her gentle encouragement and support as I wrote this book. There were many times when I came home from a 10-hour workday and, in my obsessive urge to work on <u>Fascism Viewed From The Cross</u>, was unable to spend as much time as I'd have liked with her. I'm sure there were times when this was not her preference, but God's timing is not our timing and I am eternally grateful for the space she provided for my creativity and productivity to flourish. All of my work, from the manual labor to this book, has been made worth the effort by her smile and embrace.

Preface

At this moment I've been Baptized Orthodox for just over five years, and I still don't know far more than I do. I have not read all the Fathers, all the Councils, or all the Saints. I continue to struggle with passions, the enduring existence of which is a source of endless frustration. I say all this to highlight my lack of experience and spiritual growth, which doubtlessly affects my writing and the way I conceive of all these topics. As I set out to expound the Orthodox view of various subjects, my aim is to reflect that eternal Light of which - at my best - I possess but one small Ray. It seems unavoidable that I will make mistakes, draw wrong conclusions, and otherwise distort the holy teachings of our Church if I dare take a step off the path laid down by our Saints. Therefore, before I begin, I beg your forgiveness for whatever errors this book contains and encourage you with my whole heart to reject whatever is not of God.

I have done my best to transmit what has been taught by our Saints and our Church, if perhaps organized here for a new purpose. I intend for this book to be a work-in-progress, a living tome updated with new editions as necessary, as I'm exposed to both new information and new spiritual horizons from which to perceive the bigger picture. For that reason, I invite any and all constructive criticism; if you have good reason to believe that what I've set out here is wrong, I ask you to contact me and let me know. If I've misinterpreted what I've read, or misrepresented our Church, then I seek to update this book in continued realignment with our Faith. In this manner, the book may perhaps become a collaborative testament on a subject which evades all attempts at simplification. Lastly, as you'll discern from the many footnotes, this book relies very heavily on both firsthand sources and research compiled by others. I am incredibly grateful for those whose work has helped form the foundation of this one - and God willing, the present volume will contribute in the future to someone else's research as well.

This book is separated into two major sections: the first is *Orthodoxy* and the second *Fascism*. Though its contents can be used as a reference guide on various subjects, I recommend that you read it start-to-finish. It is an edifice built brick-by-brick, and the second part relies on the foundation of the first. I pray that you find my small contribution to this topic helpful, and that reading it will spare you the years of research that went into it. I set out to write a book that I wish had already existed; only God and time will tell whether I've succeeded. May He bless, guide, forgive and save us all.

In the name of the Father, and the Son, and the Holy Spirit.

Amen.

Introduction

Readers of my previous books are aware that I do not like to spend time on long introductions; I like to get to the meat of the matter as quickly and efficiently as possible. However, given the complexity of today's topic, a brief preface will simply not suffice. In fact, it will take me a significant portion of this book to chop through enough weeds just to see the path clearly in the first place. But it's my hope that in doing so, I am able to present you with a book that I pray can help guide you toward Truth.

Thus far, this book has been my hardest to write. I knew what I wanted to say in On The Masons And Their Lies[1]: that Freemasonry and Christianity are incompatible. I knew what I wanted to do with Theopoetica[2] as well: write and comment on poems and the state of poetry in general. Writing Fascism Viewed From The Cross, however, has proven a monumental task. I had to not only deep-dive into the history of Orthodox politics and theology, but to search with equal diligence into the very heart of Fascism. Each of these was difficult enough on its own, requiring my reading many books and doing my best to make sense of them - but it wasn't until I tried to synthesize what I'd learned that I realized what a tall mountain I'd have to climb.

This book's purpose is to examine, as dispassionately

---

[1] Witcoff, M. (2018). *On the Masons and Their Lies*. Createspace Independent Publishing Platform.

[2] Witcoff, M. (2020). *Theopoetica*. Createspace Independent Publishing Platform.

and objectively as possible, the phenomenon of Fascism from a traditional Orthodox Christian perspective. I cannot think of a topic more shrouded in propaganda or more charged with emotion, and in writing this book I must battle against even my *own* psychological programming. I aim simply to present the facts to the best of my ability.

My first task thus becomes the definition of the terms "traditional Orthodox Christianity" and "Fascism." I must do both of these before I can proceed, since making an educated comparison of one to the other relies on an accurate understanding of both. As I'm sure you can imagine, this is no small undertaking; if you ask a hundred Christians about the proper Christian view of politics, you will likely hear a hundred different answers. If you ask those same Christians what Fascism is, you will probably hear ninety-nine inaccurate ones. I will therefore rely entirely on first- and second-hand sources, giving no credence to media narratives or what is mistakenly considered "common wisdom." I believe it is much more prudent to examine the thoughts of those who design a system than the opinions of those who only comment on it.

To begin with, I affirm the traditional Orthodox Christian perspective to be that espoused by the sources that the Church itself considers authoritative: the consensus of Saints, the Holy Scriptures, Holy Tradition as expressed in our hymns and services, and those Canons, Confessions, Catechisms and Councils which have received pan-Orthodox acceptance and subsequently, carry Ecumenical authority. Outside of these sources, no individual opinions should be considered official; the Church has never taught that a comment shared by one person - even if that person is a canonized Saint - is dogmatic in and of itself, especially when it cannot be found in the aforementioned sources. Though I have no doubt that some Protestants and Roman Catholics will read this book, those belief systems will only be mentioned where directly relevant to the Fascist leader in question. For example, we must consider the Roman Catholic view when examining the Concordat (official agreement) between the Vatican and Adolf Hitler - but even within that paradigm, the results will nonetheless be compared to the Orthodox standard. Hence the first section of this book is devoted to exploring and deciphering the traditional Orthodox Christian perspectives on the Church, the State, and the Jews.

Given the shapeshifting nature of Fascism - not only in terms of its various expressions as implemented by different leaders, but also its representation and misrepresentation in the media - approaching it simply *as Fascism* will not do justice to the study at hand. The word simply cannot be used as if it always represents the same phenomenon or universally carries the same meaning; this is true not only when comparing 20th century nationalist movements to each other, but even more so when it comes to modern usage of the term. As Paul Gottfried so accurately observed, "Fascism now stands for a host of iniquities that progressives, multiculturalists, and libertarians all oppose, even if they offer no single, coherent account of what they're condemning."[3] It is a word used primarily nowadays to excite emotion and negative associations in the mind of various audiences, regardless of whether those associations are justified by that particular use, and tends to be applied as an umbrella towards movements and paradigms of the past.

Therefore, rather than simply discuss "Fascism," I believe it makes more sense to deconstruct the various parts of each movement in order to view each piece of the puzzle through a Christian lens. Thus we will examine three particular aspects of these movements - their relationships with Christianity, the State and the Jews - in order to compare them with the traditional Orthodox view of these topics. By taking apart each Fascist machine, and studying each one of these pieces, we can then put together a "big picture" view of the ideologies and arrive at - hopefully - reasonable conclusions.

Readers well-versed in Right-wing thought will recognize this book's title as a play on Julius Evola's book <u>Fascism Viewed From The Right</u>. My concept of politics evolved greatly due to Evola's work, yet his books are tainted and tarred by his paganism. Despite Evola's clarity in certain regards, his occult leanings gave him a very different view of man than the Church teaches. His promotion of Tantra and Hermetic ideology, for example, put him far outside the boundaries of Christianity. When reading his work, there is a very real danger that one may become "initiated" by accident. Part of my motivation in

---

[3] Gottfried, P. (2016). *Fascism: The Career of a Concept.* Northern Illinois University Press. Kindle.

writing this book, therefore, was to posthumously "baptize" Julius Evola. I wanted to take the parts of his perspective that aligned with Christian thought and disabuse them of their pagan errors. I further sought to sharpen, define, clarify, and improve on his political viewpoints by placing them within the context of traditional Christianity. I suppose that only time will tell whether I have succeeded in this task.

First and foremost among Evola's perspectives, for example, was the monumental importance of order and hierarchy. As noted by E. Christian Kopff, who translated many of Evola's books into English, "A healthy state is like a healthy human. Free men are unified and coherent individuals who are not dominated by the outside, physical world, but they are also differentiated, with a proper hierarchy of spirit, soul and body within."[4] For Evola, what is within should likewise be without; the "inner man" and the world he lives in ought to exist as part of a harmonized whole. The majority of Christian history played out along these lines: an Emperor or King commanded the State, delegating tasks to help it run successfully, while a hierarchical Church served the same end in mens' souls. Church and State were separate, but typically cooperated to grant peace to both the "inner man" and society at large. Given that our world is no longer organized in such a manner, I hope that this book will help to move things back in the right direction.

Another reason I wanted to write this book is that

---

[4] Evola, J., & Morgan, J. B. (2013). *Fascism viewed from the Right*. London Arktos Media Ltd. Page 9.

many young men today - especially young Christian men - are looking at the present state of our nation with disgust. They see what's become of Western civilization and its "elected" officials, getting fat and wealthy off the backs of those who work, and who do absolutely nothing to stop its decline. The more cynical among us perceive that the decline they fail to stop may be, in fact, their intention. Feeling powerless and isolated, many men begin to look deeper into past political movements and eventually realize that *even if Fascists weren't always very nice, at least they didn't tolerate Drag Queen Story Hour*. It's an understandable journey - perhaps even an inevitable one. I believe those on that path should be treated with empathy and grace, acknowledging why they feel the way they do and not - as is almost universally common - dismissing them entirely or accusing them of holding beliefs they don't.

Since so many young men are becoming interested in Fascism, specifically due to the failure and incompetence of the officials who ought to serve and protect them, I wanted to do my best to put some boundaries on that path. It is easy to go too far in the wrong direction; I've seen it many times, both online and in person. The zeal, the anger, the bitter disappointment…though these emotions are understandable parts of the journey, it's far too easy to get sucked into the void. Thankfully, the Church has an answer that I believe will both satisfy their desire for justice and stop them from ruining their lives.

It is nearly impossible to find an objective, neutral book on either the various Fascist movements or their leaders. The available literature tends to paint men like Mussolini and Hitler as either flawless heroes, saving their nations from the evils of Judeo-Masonry, or as the physical incarnations of the principle of evil. Books that lean to one side give no credence to the other, and do not tend to provide any counter-arguments to their claims.

In addition, there is wide disagreement over what the men themselves believed. Their autobiographies say one thing; their critics, another. There are books written to prove what a good Catholic Mussolini was, and there are books written to demonstrate that his only interest in Catholicism was the leverage he had over it to aid in his political agenda. Can the men be trusted when they record their own views? Again, we find nothing but disagreement.

For these reasons and more, I have done the best I can to provide you with a book that examines the men, their motives, and their movements as neutrally and straightforwardly as possible. And since we cannot use popular opinion as a standard against which to hold these men, I've held their actions against the only standard that matters: that of Jesus Christ and His Church. By holding each man to the exact same standard, I believe I can provide a viewpoint on them which - while obviously biased in favor of.the Christian perspective - at least seeks to cut out the noise, the emotion, the anger, and the propaganda.

I am aware - and have been aware since the seed for this idea was first planted in my mind - that I would likely face two outcomes for writing this book. Firstly, I would likely be called a Fascist, both by progressives and conservatives who, in America, operate entirely within the same post-Enlightenment paradigm. Secondly it's possible, if not likely, that I'll face accusations of being a federal agent trying to inspire either violence or subversion. My Ashkenazi ethnicity does not help with accusations like these; when I encourage people to become traditional Christians instead of Fascists, I have - more than once - been met with the sentiment that I am "just another Jew trying to harm White people."

My hope is that those who know me and my work will be able to tell for themselves whether such accusations hold any water. And though I've said this many times, I'll say it again: my intention here is to help Europeans become Saints, not to hinder them from protecting their communities. I do not believe that the Church forbids ethnic communities from organizing in their own interest - to work and live among people with whom one shares a culture, a language, and a history - within certain parameters which I believe the Church has clearly outlined. If I do my job well, those European Christians currently leaning towards Fascism may pause and reflect for a moment before coming to realize there is a higher, holier, Godlier version of what they currently desire to see in America.

Though this book does contain Footnotes, it often includes long passages and direct quotes from my research material. The reason I rarely paraphrase is simple: I find that it breaks my reading immersion to think about hunting down other sources or simply having to trust that the author is being honest. I don't know how other people read, but I'm certainly not going to purchase dozens of other books and read all of them just to make sure the book I *wanted* to read is quoting them all properly. Thus I have sacrificed what may be a cleaner and more academic book format for one which is considerably longer, but quotes more source material directly. Especially in light of the propaganda surrounding the word "Fascism," and the various psychological and emotional reactions I think people will have to reading this book, I think it's very important to be as accurate as possible rather than trying to summarize just to save space. Subsequently, a large portion of <u>Fascism Viewed From The Cross</u> is quotes from the many books I read as research along the way.

But as I mentioned earlier, we have a long way to go before we address the topic of Fascism at all. We must first discern what Christianity has traditionally taught about these sensitive and controversial subjects. Discovering the answers requires a journey through history - through both halves of the historical Byzantine Empire - to separate the wheat from the chaff. May the words that follow enlighten, illuminate, protect, and guide you.

<u>Orthodoxy</u>

"This is the Faith which has established the Universe."

- The Synodikon of Orthodoxy

Orthodoxy and the Church

"He cannot have God for a Father who does not have the Church as his Mother."[5]
+ St. Cyprian of Carthage

In the second section of this book, we'll evaluate the way each of the featured Fascist leaders interacted with Christianity. For Benito Mussolini, we'll focus on the dialogue and agreements made between his political party and the Vatican. For Adolf Hitler, we will likewise study his government's relationship with the Pope - and also explore his efforts to keep Roman Catholics and Protestants from fighting in Germany. For Corneliu Codreanu, we will examine his movement's conception of the Orthodox Church and its place in the Legionary revolution. Descriptions of the major differences between the Roman Catholics, the Protestants and the Orthodox are very important…but for the sake of this book, we will not discuss them here. Instead, we will first establish the way that the ancient and Apostolic Church conceives of *itself* and its role in the world. Only once we understand the *purpose of the Church in the first place* can we then make a sound judgment on the role Christianity was given in the Fascist movements.

Let us begin with the New Testament, the earliest

---

[5] *CHURCH FATHERS: Treatise 1 (Cyprian of Carthage).* (n.d.). Www.newadvent.org. https://www.newadvent.org/fathers/050701.htm. Chapter 6.

written record of the Orthodox Church. We read in **Acts 9** of Saul's trip to Damascus, where he hoped to find and harm Christian disciples. Amidst Saul's rage and fury, *"breathing threats and murder against the disciples of the Lord,"*[6] the Uncreated Light was revealed to him and brought him to his knees. He heard a voice ask him: *"Saul, Saul, why are you persecuting Me?"*[7] and upon inquiring Who spoke, heard the response that *"I am Jesus, Whom you are persecuting."*[8] This world-shaking moment reveals a deep insight: that Christ identifies the Church with *Himself.* He did not ask Saul why he was "persecuting the Church," or "persecuting His disciples;" He asked why Saul was persecuting *Him.* In this brief but deep exchange, we learn that there is a powerful and mysterious unity not just between Christ and His Church, but also between Christ and His disciples (the victims of Saul's violence). In light of Christ's comment, they are all considered to be the singular target persecuted by the future St. Paul.

This witness, to the unity of Christ and the Church which is his Body, consistently spans millennia in the writings of the Saints. We will study two in particular who, despite composing but a small fraction of the Saints who have written about the Church over time, nonetheless provide the insight and overview that will both communicate the heart of Orthodox ecclesiology and allow our study to continue. Thus we will focus on the

---

[6]   Acts 9:1

[7]   Acts 9:4

[8]   Acts 9:5

commentary of St. Maximus the Confessor, who wrote in the 7th century, and the 20th-century writings of St. Justin Popovic.

We will begin with the grand cosmological and anthropological views of St. Maximus on the Church. As with many of his other writings, St. Maximus viewed the Church through the lens of unity and multiplicity; more specifically, how God creates unity both *in* and *between* men despite their many and varied differences. In his *Introduction* to the excellent book <u>On The Ecclesiastical Mystagogy</u>, John Armstrong summarized the view of St. Maximus by writing that the desired "unity of all things, however, is not a present reality but rather a potential that God continues to actualize as He unfolds his redemptive purposes in and through the Church. This is what Maximus means when he says that the Church is in the image of God 'because she possesses the same activity as His according to imitation and representation.' The Church is God's agent to bring about unity - unity among divided peoples in an immediate sense and unity throughout the cosmos in an ultimate sense."[9]

St. Maximus himself wrote that "the holy Church of God works the same things and in the same way as God does around us, as an image relates to its archetype. For, from among men, women, and children, nearly boundless in number, who are many in race and class and nation and language and occupation and age and persuasion and trade and manners and customs and pursuits, and

---

[9] Maximus, Confessor Saint, & Armstrong, J. J. (2019). *On the Ecclesiastical Mystagogy*. St. Vladimir's Seminary Press. Page 33.

again, those who are divided and most different from one another in expertise and worth and fortune and features and habits, those who are in the holy Church and are regenerated by her and are recreated by the Spirit - to all He gives equally and grants freely one divine form and designation, that is to be and to be called from Christ... Therefore, the holy Church is the image of God, as it has been said, because she works the same oneness around the faithful as God does. And even if they are different in their characteristics, and from different places, and have different customs, those who are present are made one according to the same oneness through faith."[10] Thus we can see that in the view of St. Maximus, the purpose of the Orthodox Church is to graft each Christian into Christ Himself - regardless of the differences between those being grafted in. The Church transcends what is worldly, what is fallen, what is artificial and what ultimately will pass away when the cosmos is transfigured into the eternal Kingdom of God.

St. Maximus even conceived of the Church itself as a representation of both man and said cosmos, of which he considered man to be a symbol and a microcosm. He wrote that "the holy Church of God is a representation and image of the entire universe, which subsists in visible and invisible realities, because the Church contains the same oneness and diversity as God. For, although the Church is one building according to its construction, she contains differences in the particularity of the physical layout. She is divided into the place designated for priests

---

[10]   Ibid. Pages 54 and 55.

and ministers alone (which we call the sanctuary), and the place accessible for all the faithful people to enter (which we call the nave). But, again, the Church is one in substance. The Church is not divided by her parts on account of the difference of the parts themselves to one another, but rather she dissolves the differences in name of the parts themselves by her reference to the unity…In the same way, the entire universe of everything that is - which was brought forth from God at the creation and is divided into the intelligible realm, which is comprised of intellectual and bodiless substance, and the realm that is sensible and bodily and which has been ingeniously interwoven from many forms and natures, and which exists somehow as another Church that is made without hands - is seen in wisdom through this Church that is made with hands. The universe possesses a sanctuary, which is the realm above and which is assigned to the powers above, and it also possesses a nave, which is the realm below and is traversed by those whose lot it is to live through sense perception. Again, the universe is one, and it is not divided by its parts; conversely, it limits the difference of these parts in their particular natures by the reference to its own undivided unity." [11]

On a more personal and immediate level, St. Maximus likened the Church to man himself: "The holy Church of God is [like] a human being, which has the sanctuary as its soul, the divine altar as its mind, and the nave as its body. And therefore the Church is as the image and likeness of a human being who was made 'according to

---

[11] Ibid. Pages 55 and 56.

the image' and 'likeness of God.' The Church sets forth
moral discipline through the nave as through the body,
and spiritually interprets natural contemplation through
the sanctuary as through the soul, and reveals mystical
theology through the divine altar as through the mind."[12]
So not only does the Church serve a very specific spiritual
purpose in the lives of men, but for St. Maximus the
building itself - to say nothing of the liturgical rites
performed within, which he elaborated on elsewhere in
his work - symbolically represents both the human being
and the universe. The vision of St. Maximus was that all
creation is a grand tapestry, each layer perfectly
interwoven with the others. The Orthodox Church, then,
is infinitely more than a man-made organization or the
materials which make up a building.

More than a thousand years later, St. Justin Popovic
made similar observations - if perhaps in language that is
more modern and thus, more immediate to the cause at
hand. Let us attend to the wisdom of this holy man: "The
mission of the Church is to make every one of her faithful,
organically and in person, one with the Person of Christ;
to turn their sense of self into a sense of Christ, and their
self-knowledge (self-awareness) into Christ-knowledge
(Christ-awareness); for their life to become the life in
Christ and for Christ; their personality to become
personality in Christ and for Christ; that within them
might live not they themselves but Christ in them **(Gal.
2:10).** The mission of the Church is still to bring about in
her members the conviction that the proper state of

---

[12] Ibid. Page 58.

human personhood is composed of immortality and eternity and not of the realm of time and mortality…and the conviction that man is a wayfarer who is wending his way in the sway of time and mortality towards immortality and all eternity…The Church is God-human, eternity incarnated within the boundaries of time and space. She is here in this world but she is not of this world *(John 18:36)*. She is in the world in order to raise it on high where she herself has her origin. The Church is ecumenical, catholic, God-human, ageless, and it is therefore a blasphemy - an unpardonable blasphemy against Christ and against the Holy Ghost - to turn the Church into a national institution, to narrow her down to petty, transient, time-bound aspirations and ways of doing things. " St. Justin further noted that "The Church is the personhood of the God-human Christ, a God-human organism and not a human organization."[13]

This is a very different conception of the Church than what is imagined by those outside of it, who may assert that the Church is a building, a collection of people, or a religious group; the Church is certainly all those things, but ultimately the Orthodox Church's roots are in Heaven and what we see here on Earth is only the visible aspect of what is fundamentally eternal and boundless. Further, St. Justin taught that its sole purpose was to unite man to Christ through the Sacraments and synergy between our

---

[13] Popovich, S. (n.d.). *"The Inward Mission of Our Church."* Retrieved January 23, 2023, from https://static1.squarespace.com/static/5e44554b0fffa302906a78f3/t/ 5ea1df5036d620033ced43c3/1587666769305/%E2%80%9CThe+Inward+Mission+of+O ur+Church%E2%80%9D+%E2%80%94+St.+Justin+Popovich.pdf

efforts and the grace of God. Any other conception of the Church - whether as a purely human institution or as a tool of the State government - is therefore alien to the Apostolic teaching.

Having established the way in which the Church defines itself, as expressed through the minds of two of its most brilliant and articulate thinkers, we can easily compare these ideas to how various Fascist leaders conceived of it. Did they view Christianity in the same way as the Saints? Did they agree that its purpose was the transfiguration of man and his becoming, by grace, what Christ is by nature? We will explore the answer to these questions in the second part of this book, but we have only just begun to build the edifice. Before we can delve into the minds of the men in question, we have two more steps to ascend: the traditional relationship between the Church and the State, and the historical dynamic between the Church and the Jews. In accordance with the order which we will follow throughout this book, let us next examine how Orthodoxy views the role and purpose of government.

Orthodoxy and the State

"Fear the LORD and the King, my son, and do not join with rebellious officials."
- **Proverbs 24:21**

As I sat down to begin work on this book, I realized that finding a traditional Orthodox understanding of relations between the Church and the State would be more difficult than I anticipated. At first I sought a dogmatic statement from anywhere in the Orthodox world clearly explaining what the Church does and does not teach on this topic. Surprisingly, I was unable to find any such statement, approaching the level of dogma, to this effect. This discovery set me down a path that has tremendously deepened my understanding of traditional Church-State relations - if only by illustrating just how nebulous they prove to be.

My research for <u>Fascism Viewed From The Cross</u> involved reading several modern books on Orthodox political theology. Without exception, they worked from the presupposition that democracy is both inevitable and permanent. One of them, Nikolas Gvosdev's <u>Emperors And Elections</u>, went so far as to suggest that the idea of autocratic monarchy has been "discredited."[14] He did not explain *how* it's been "discredited," nor who it was

<hr/>

[14] Gvosdev, N. K. (2000). *Emperors and elections : reconciling the Orthodox tradition with modern politics*. Troitsa Books. Page 9.

"discredited" by or the methods by which this supposedly occurred. His book was the only one I read that outright said as much, but the same sentiment lay just below the surface in the others: *monarchy is dead, democracy is forever*. Though this appears to be the consensus among modern political scholars (and seems to be a major point of criticism against Fascism and its leaders) we must look to what the Church itself teaches on the subject.

When considering the traditional Orthodox view of government, we must explore the Church's answers to several questions. Those questions include, but are not limited to, the following: *What is the role of government in human existence? Are nations, or states, inherently good concepts meant to help organize society? Or are they necessary evils that only exist to restrain the worst instincts and impulses of man? Should Christians love their nations and kin, or is doing so the kind of worldly "racism" and "xenophobia" we're called to reject? Is there a specific form of government the Church affirms, or are certain systems inherently anti-Christian? Further, what is the role of war? Is it ever justified for one nation to go to war against another, or does the Christian call to martyrdom extend beyond the individual all the way to an entire Empire?*

In this chapter, we'll dive into the different answers given by different Saints over time. Though these questions have not been explicitly answered by conciliar and pan-Orthodox sources - Ecumenical Councils, for example - I still believe that different perspectives are worth exploring and can add value to our search for understanding. Let us begin with the New Testament, which contains the earliest written record of Apostolic teaching on the role of government. We can find one of the answers we seek in two specific sections: **Romans 13** and **1 Peter**.

St. Paul outlined his doctrine on government in **Romans 13:1-5**, exhorting *"Let every soul be subject unto the higher powers. For there is no power but of God: the powers that be are ordained of God. Whosoever therefore resists the power, resists the ordinance of God: and they that resist shall receive to themselves judgment. For rulers are not a terror to good works, but to the evil. Will you then not be afraid of the power? Do that which is good, and you shall have praise of the same. For he is the minister of God to you for good. But if you do that which is evil, be afraid; for he bears not the sword in vain: for he is the minister of God, an avenger to execute wrath upon him that does evil. Therefore you must be subject, not only for wrath, but also for conscience's sake."* In St. Peter's first Epistle, he expressed the same sentiment: *"Submit yourselves to every ordinance of man for the Lord's sake: whether it be to the king, as supreme; or unto governors, as unto them that are sent by him for the punishment of evildoers, and for the praise of them that do well. For so is the will of God, that with well doing you may put to silence the ignorance of foolish men: As free, and not using your liberty for a cloak of maliciousness, but as the servants of God. Honor all men. Love the brotherhood. Fear God. Honor the king."*[15]

From these two passages, we can glean several important points: Firstly, that government is ordained by

---

[15]   1 Peter 2:13-17

God alone and that whoever happens to lead it does so by His permissive will. There are no government leaders who have somehow tricked God into letting them lead; their power exists, in the form that exists, because He has granted this to them for a time. Our inability to comprehend God's judgment does not negate the fact of its existence. Secondly, the Holy Bible teaches that Christians ought to submit to said government because refusal to do so is resisting the ordinance of God. Thirdly, that government has been instituted by God to reward good and punish evil. And let us not forget that Christ Himself commanded us to *"Render therefore to Caesar the things that are Caesar's, and to God the things that are God's."*[16]

St. Paul's acknowledgment that these *"higher powers"* exist, along with the fact that they are *"ordained by God,"* can lead us to safely discard the idea that anarchy is the Christian ideal. Similarly, Sts. Peter and Paul wrote in these Epistles that Christians can be sanctified by obedience to who God has placed above them; political "equality" is not only opposed to divinely-instituted hierarchy, but actually robs us of the opportunity to grow in holiness via submission. Such teachings inevitably bring us to certain questions, for example: *What about when the government is bad? What about when its leaders persecute Christianity, rewarding evil while punishing virtue? And what are the limits of our obedience?*St John Chrysostom touched on these questions in his Homily on **Romans 13**, in which the great Saint preached: "'For there is no

---

[16]   Matthew 22:21

power,' he says, 'but of God.' What say you? It may be said; is every ruler then elected by God? This I do not say, he answers. Nor am I now speaking about individual rulers, but about the thing in itself. For that there should be rulers, and some rule and others be ruled, and that all things should not just be carried on in one confusion, the people swaying like waves in this direction and that; this, I say, is the work of God's wisdom."[17] In this passage St. John taught that St. Paul meant government *itself* is good, if not every particular person who runs it, because without hierarchy the people descend into chaos. Though God Himself does not approve of every leader, those who displease Him - and even harm the people - are nonetheless only in charge because He allows it. As to why God would allow His people to be ruled by someone who hates them, St. Nikolai Velimirovic will provide the answer in the chapter *Failed Nations: The Cause and Cure*. For now, let us be satisfied with the principle that God is in charge.

Having established that government is instituted by God, let us next consider that between Church and State, there can only be four different dynamics. The Church can rule the State (Theocracy), the State can rule the Church (Sergianism), Church and State can be separate and compete (secular democracy), or Church and State can be separate and cooperate (Symphonia). This being the case, assuming that some form of government and some form of religion will always coexist wherever

---

[17] *Romans 13 Homilies of Chrysostom*. (n.d.). Biblehub.com. Retrieved January 27, 2023, from https://biblehub.com/commentaries/chrysostom/romans/13.htm

human beings can be found, the next question that we must examine is which system the Orthodox Church affirms. Once we have established the preferred relationship between Church and State, we will study specific forms of government in search of even deeper answers.

In the first case, Theocracy, the Church essentially *is* the State. Ecclesiastical leaders are also the nation's politicians, as we find in the Pope's rule of Vatican City. Though there are times in Orthodox history when a Priest or Bishop held public office, these were very much the exceptions to the rule. The Church running the State has never been the ideal and has not been very common historically; if anything, when Church-State relations became imbalanced, it was typically the State stepping on the Church's toes instead of the other way around.

The second possible dynamic between Church and State is one in which the State rules the Church: the government dictates in which activities the Church can participate, and the Church can only operate in public by obeying the dictates of the State. Should the Church disobey what the State commands, the Church becomes punished in some capacity; it can be marginalized, have its teachings and privileges altered, or even be shut down altogether. I refer to this system as "Sergianism" due to the fact that the Russian Orthodox Church was in this position under Joseph Stalin. Patriarch Sergius, the ruling primate at the time, submitted to Stalin's wishes in order to maintain the Church's public existence. Though I use the term Sergianism to refer to this dynamic, it should be noted that various Orthodox Churches have been in the same position in other times and places. The Ecumenical Patriarchate, for example, cannot be run without express permission from the Turkish government. Such has been the case ever since the Ottomans took Constantinople, and no man may become Patriarch without the State's approval.

In such situations, the primate's decision to submit is typically made because he believes that allowing the Church to exist at all - regardless of the limits and boundaries placed upon it - is a lesser evil than having no Church at all or allowing his entire flock to be Martyred. The opposing argument is essentially that letting the State run the Church insults our countless Martyrs who gave their lives for Christ; what difference exists, such an argument may go, between publicly praising a State leader who kills Christians and offering a pinch of incense to pagan idols? Though this particular subject is not the topic of our study, suffice it to say that Sergianism can have disastrous effects and - as far as I am presently aware - has no Canonical or Patristic support.

The third possible relationship is one with which all modern Americans are intimately familiar: the Church and State are separate and compete viciously with one another. The leader of one political party or another promotes sodomy, abortion, and war; Christian leaders do their best to convince their flocks not to participate, affecting public policy where they can via the formal mechanisms. There is no sense in which a moral crime necessarily becomes a civil crime, though there is some overlap in certain cases. Where that overlap occurs, the Bible or Church is not considered to be the source of said civil law in the first place; instead, appeals to "reason" or "fairness" or "human rights" are used as justifications. Thus, the coinciding of certain moral crimes with civil penalties is as divorced from God as our politicians can manage to make it. It seems they must be aware, at some level or another, that justifying civil law with moral law would lead to enormous changes in other areas that they are unwilling to adapt or address.

Thus Church and State are separate, occasionally agreeing (but for different reasons), and Christians endure the endless harassment of secular culture. Such was the state of things during the times of Roman persecution, when civil duties came into direct conflict with Christian faith. Many Christians back then were faced with the choice of either apostasy or death; thankfully, we have not yet descended into that dynamic and hopefully never will. In either case we can see the difference between the second and third relationships: in Sergianism the Church must make certain compromises just to exist in some shade of gray, whereas in open competition each individual must make a clear choice. Though one could certainly argue that the former necessarily entails the latter, we will have to save that debate for another time.

In the fourth and final system, Church and State are separate but cooperate to run society. This model, known in the Orthodox world as Symphonia, was the standard for the Christian Roman Empire. The Emperor ruled the

State, and the Bishops ruled the Church; whenever and wherever possible, they worked in harmony to serve the people. In select cases, as with the Theodosian Code that you'll learn about in the *Imperial Law* chapter, certain sections of the civil law were adopted by the Church as Canon Law.

And yet, despite all his power, the Emperor was still a layman subject to the Church. In the best cases the Emperors understood clearly the distinction between civil and ecclesiastical realms; take for example the words of Roman Emperor John II Komnenos: "In all my governing I recognize two things that exist, distinct one from the other. The first is the spiritual power, which the Great High Priest of the world, the King of the World, Christ, gave to His disciples and apostles, as an indestructible blessing…The second is secular power, controlling temporal affairs and exercising it according to the divine command only the rights of its own sphere. Both these authorities, which rule human life, are separate and distinct from one another."[18]

We find the same sentiment in the Sixth Novella of Emperor St. Justinian the Great: "There are two greatest gifts which God, in his love for man, has granted from on high: the priesthood and the imperial dignity. The first serves divine things, the second directs and administers human affairs; both, however, proceed from the same origin and adorn the life of mankind. Hence, nothing should be such a source of care to the Emperors as the dignity of the priests, since it is for the welfare [of the

---

[18] Gvosdev. Pages 40 and 41.

Empire] that they constantly implore God. For if the priesthood is in every way free from blame and possesses access to God, and if the Emperors administer equitably and judiciously the state entrusted to their care, general harmony will result, and whatever is beneficial will be bestowed on the human race."[19]

This is the ideal, the principle of Symphonia clearly described. It goes without saying that this ideal was rarely realized due to the reality of politics and the fact of man's fallen state - and yet, we cannot judge a principle by its contingents. As Codreanu wrote, and you will read about in his section of this book, the principle of Monarchy cannot be discounted due to bad Monarchs any more than we could throw out the Priesthood because of bad Priests. The Emperors quoted above spoke of God-ordained ideals, and we study them with the recognition that ideals do not always match reality. Despite that reality, there were episodes in Church history which I find beautiful and illuminating examples of the Symphonic principle; let us describe and admire one.

Sometime towards the end of the 4th century in Greece, a Roman official was killed by an urban mob. Though details of the events are described differently in different sources, it seems that a local charioteer was arrested for sexual assault (either completed or attempted) and his fans demanded his release. When said release was not granted, the mob revolted and killed the official; as

---

[19] Witte, J., & Alexander, F. S. (2007). *The Teachings of Modern Orthodox Christianity on Law, Politics, and Human Nature*. Columbia University Press. Pages 11 and 12.

backlash, Roman troops massacred a large number of civilians. The Emperor at the time, St. Theodosius the Great, is said to have either ordered or at least allowed this to occur. The Bishop of Milan and a counselor to Theodosius, St. Ambrose, caught wind of the event and wrote the Emperor a letter. In that letter, St. Ambrose gently rebuked St. Theodosius and offered him a way to regain good standing in the Church. St. Theodosius accepted St. Ambrose's suggestion and not only attended Church by standing only in the nave (entrance), but he did so wearing the clothes of a civilian. Further, he was barred from the Eucharist. Only once St. Ambrose was satisfied with this embarrassing penance did he then allow St. Theodosius to take Communion once more.[20]

Thus we see a clear example of how Church and State ideally related: the Emperor ran the nation, but when he made a mistake, he submitted to the Church to be healed[21]. This sort of humility and willingness to be corrected is an admirable trait in any leader, and a trait of which we are all - including our leaders - in dire need. Through the grace and mercy of God, may He inspire them to know their place and remember that they, too, have a Ruler.

Now that we know the Church's preference on government - namely, that it exist in the first place and work in harmony with the Church - let us move on to the question of what *form* that government should take. There

---

[20] *Massacre of Thessalonica*. (2020, July 31). Wikipedia. https://en.wikipedia.org/wiki/Massacre_of_Thessalonica

[21] *CHURCH FATHERS: Letter 51 (Ambrose)*. (n.d.). Www.newadvent.org. https://www.newadvent.org/fathers/340951.htm

are those who argue, as mentioned above, that Monarchy is antithetical to Christianity; others argue that not only is Monarchy good, but that it's actually the *only* acceptable form of government for an Orthodox Christian to support. Historically, we find a range of opinions. For example, in 1990, Patriarch Alexei II of Moscow wrote that "there is no political system, there is no state, there is no nation, which would have been created for eternity."[22] This is very much in line with St. Augustine's view on politics as outlined in his book City of God. On the other hand, in 1393, Patriarch Anthony of Constantinople argued that "The Holy Emperor occupies a high place in the Church; he is not the same as other local princes and lords. The Emperors in the beginning established and maintained piety throughout the universe; they summoned the Ecumenical Councils; by their laws they established the observance of what the divine and sacred laws say of right dogmas and the proper ordering of Christian life…It is impossible for Christians to have the Church but not to have the Emperor. For Empire and Church are in close union, and it is impossible to divide them from each other."[23]

As opposed to the Augustinian view, this latter notion much more closely resembles the political theology outlined by Eusebius of Caesarea in his *Oration in Praise of Constantine*. Thus we typically find two views in the Church: the Augustinian, in which Christians ought to have very little to do with the "City of Man," and the

---

[22] Gvosdev. Page 39.

[23] Ibid. Page 47.

Eusebian, in which the State or *polis* can be a way for God to sanctify society through a divinely-appointed Monarch. I have never read a quote, from even a single Saint, defending the concept of democracy; the closest that I've seen could be extrapolated from St. Augustine's work only in the sense that *if* the masses of people were pious and holy Christians, they would not require a government due to being governed internally by the Holy Spirit. I agree with St. Augustine that if people governed their own conduct by the laws and commandments of God, no external leadership or compulsion would be necessary.

Since Orthodox rulers can be found on both sides of this equation, we must - as always - look for a conciliar, pan-Orthodox, authoritative answer to determine if one exists. But as I mentioned earlier, there does not appear to be any official dogma on what form the government should take. It's true that Monarchy has certain inherent benefits, such as swiftness of action and uniformity of praxis among the people. It's also true that a bad Monarch can destroy an entire nation, with almost no opposition, much more quickly and completely than a more conciliar form of government. It's true that a "democracy" like what we have in modern America leads to mass public support of evil; it's also true that a democracy of Christians would lead to a better State than an atheist King.

Despite my disappointment at not finding a clear answer - and the willingness to grapple with uncertainty that we must engage with as a result - we are left with the simple truth that all nations will eventually pass away. Only once this world has been transfigured into the eternal Kingdom of God will we have the peace, the stability, the joy, and the love that we all misguidedly look for in worldly institutions. And there is no question that, when that dreadful day comes, we will all learn who the true Monarch is. All our thirst for justice and order, all our seeking for the righteous to be rewarded and the wicked punished, will be fulfilled in glorious fashion by He Who is the true Judge.

Perhaps most importantly, for the purpose of this book, I do not need to make an argument either for or against Monarchy. Since Fascism is often criticized for being inherently autocratic, all I must do is demonstrate that the Church supports the concept. Whether that support is dogmatic or not is beside the point; if we can find evidence that the Church takes no issue with the concept, then we can later disregard that particular aspect of Fascism as being worthy of criticism from an Orthodox perspective.

To that end - just as I cannot find a Saint who preferred democracy - I likewise cannot find a Saint who spoke ill of Monarchy. Even if a reader is aware of a quote in either of these directions, it would not change the overall trend we find in our Church's hagiography on these topics and we must remember, as indicated in an earlier chapter, that an individual opinion from a Saint does not mean that the Church as a whole shares or teaches that particular opinion.

Those Saints who weighed in on this topic appear to

universally affirm the value of Monarchy. Back in the 4th century, St. Gregory the Theologian wrote that "The three most ancient opinions about God are atheism (or anarchy), polytheism (or polyarchy), and monotheism (or monarchy). The children of Greece played with the first two; let us leave them to their games. For anarchy is disorder: and polyarchy implies factious division, and therefore anarchy and disorder. Both these lead in the same direction - to disorder; and disorder leads to disintegration; for disorder is the prelude to disintegration. What we honor is monarchy."[24]

Though St. Gregory was making a point about theology and not politics, we can easily extrapolate his sentiment to realize its political application: having no leader leads to chaos, and having multiple leaders leads to division and conflict. Therefore, the best preventative measure against anarchy or conflict is to have one ruler in charge.

The Patriarch of Georgia, Ilia II, even commented in 2013 that "The Bagrationi Dynasty was terminated in 1801, and since then Georgian people have nurtured a dream to restore the ancient, divinely blessed dynasty."[25] St. John of Kronstadt, a 19th-century Russian Orthodox Priest, taught that "Hell is a democracy but Heaven is a Kingdom.[26] Thus we can see that not only in the ancient

---

[24] June 20, D. W. A., & Comments, 2016 36. (2016, June 20). *On Christian Monarchy*. The Soul of the East. https://souloftheeast.org/2016/06/20/is-it-time-for-kings-to-replace-democracy-four-arguments-from-a-christian-viewpoint/

[25] Ibid.

[26] frlynch. (2020, November 9). *The Democracy of Hell*. The Inkless Pen. https://inklesspen.blog/2020/11/09/the-democracy-of-hell/

world but also in modern times, Orthodox leaders appear to prefer Monarchy. A Monarch can be criticized, and many times he deserves to be. But we cannot judge a system by the sins of the men who adopt it; we may only judge a system by the Scriptures and the Saints.

All the above leads us to the final questions for this chapter: *Does a Christian owe loyalty to the nation in which he lives? Should he die in its wars and defend it from enemies, or turn a blind eye and focus on salvation? And if he loves his nation and the neighbors with whom he shares it, how should he view other groups?* Though these are complex topics - some of the most pressing of our time - the Church has provided one answer through the mouth of Metropolitan Philaret of New York. With permission from Orthodox Ethos,[27] the Metropolitan's wisdom is here reprinted:

"Naturally, one will love one's own family and the relatives he grew up with, most of all, and secondly, the whole country, the people to which one belongs. One is tied to this people both by state and civil obligations and by culture and customs. One is bound to one's people, to one's own homeland, and one loves them. This love for homeland is that Christian patriotism which cosmopolitanists so strongly struggle against. Christian patriotism is, of course, alien to those extremes and errors into which 'super-patriots' fall. A Christian patriot, while loving his nation, does not close his eyes to its inadequacies, but soberly looks at its properties and characteristics. He will never agree with those 'patriots'

---

[27] *Home.* (n.d.). Orthodox Ethos. Retrieved January 27, 2023, from http://www.orthodoxethos.com

who are inclined to elevate and justify everything native (even national vices and inadequacies). Such 'patriots' do not realize that this is not patriotism at all, but puffed up national pride - that very sin against which Christianity struggles so strongly. No, a true patriot does not close his eyes to the sins and ills of his people; he sees them, grieves over them, struggles with them and repents before God and other peoples for himself and his nation. In addition, Christian patriotism is completely alien to the hatred of other peoples. If I love my own people, then surely I must also love the Chinese, the Turks or any other people. Not to love them would be non-Christian. No, God grant them well-being and every success, for we are all people, children of one God.

The most important information which we find concerning patriotism is in the Holy Scripture. In the Old Testament, all the history of the Jewish people is filled with testimony of how the Jews loved their Sion, their Jerusalem, their temple. This was a model of true patriotism, of love for one's people and its sacred things. Significantly, our Christian Church has adopted this glorification of holy things by the Jews for our services (although with a slightly different, Christian understanding) and chants, 'Blessed is the Lord of Sion, Who dwelleth in Jerusalem. Alleluia' **(Ps. 134:21)**. The prophet Moses showed an especially striking example of love for his people. On one occasion, immediately after having received the testament from God, the Israelite people betrayed their God and worshipped a golden calf. Then, the justice of God's Truth became strongly

41

inflamed. Moses began to pray for his people who had sinned. He remained on the mountain for forty days and forty nights in prayer. The Lord told him, *'Now let Me alone, and I will be very angry with them and consume them'* **(Ex. 32:10)**. In these words of God, there is a remarkable testimony about the power of the prayer of a righteous person, by which he, in the bold words of St. John Chrysostom, in some way binds God. The great prophet began to pray even more fervently and finally exclaimed, *'And now if Thou wilt forgive their sin, forgive it; and if not, blot me out of Thy book, which Thou hast written'* **(Ex. 32:32)**. And the Lord harkened to Moses. Is this not the highest struggle of self-denying patriotism?

We see a similar example in the New Testament in the life of the great Apostle Paul. No one hindered his work of preaching more wrathfully and stubbornly than did his fellow countrymen. They hated Paul and considered him to be a betrayer of the faith of their fathers. Nevertheless, the Apostle says, *'For I could wish that myself were accursed from Christ for my brethren, my kinsmen according to the flesh'* **(Rom. 9:3)**. From these words, we see his love for his native people. This love was so great that, like Moses, he was prepared to sacrifice even his personal, eternal salvation for the salvation of his people.

We have an example in the life of the Saviour Himself. In the Gospel we read that He came only to His own people and spoke to them first of all. On another occasion, He said, turning to Jerusalem, *'O Jerusalem, Jerusalem, which killest the prophets, and stonest them that are sent unto thee; how often would I have gathered thy children together, as*

a hen doth gather her brood under her wings…' **(Luke 13:34)**.
When He rode into Jerusalem to the cries of 'Hosannah,'
when all the people rejoiced, the Saviour wept. He did not
weep for Himself, but for this, His city, and because of the
ruin of those who were now crying to Him, 'Hosannah!'
but in a few days would cry, 'Crucify Him.' Thus did He
love His own people with a profound and moving love.

The feeling of patriotism, therefore, is not rejected and
condemned by Christianity. It does not condemn, despite
the false views of cosmopolitanists, the righteousness of
the preeminent love for one's neighbors. We already
know the words of the Apostle, *'If any provide not for his
own, and specially for those of his own house, he hath denied
the faith, and is worse than an infidel'* **(1 Tim. 5:8)**. Once
more we emphasize that such love and care must not be
an egoistic, self-enclosing love. While caring for those
with whom one comes into a direct contact, a Christian
must never forget other people in his Christian love - his
neighbors, and brothers in Christ. In conclusion, let us cite
these words of Apostle Paul (from the Epistle to the
Galatians): *'As we have therefore opportunity, let us do good
unto all men, especially unto them who are of the household of
faith'* **(Gal. 6:10)**.

Naturally, this Christian patriotism we have spoken of
requires from each of us as great a service as possible to
the nation. This service is fulfilled most of all in service to
the government or society. The value of such service is
even more significant if it is rendered unselfishly - free of
any material calculations and considerations. A person
serves the country in one way or another when he

participates in its life, for example, by expressing himself in the press or in civil elections, etc. In this, one must strive to bring benefit to the whole country, the whole people, and not merely to one's own personal or party interests. Then one's conscience will be at peace. It may be that one will not attain great external success, but let him, nevertheless, fulfill the duty of a patriot and a faithful child of the nation in an honorable and Christian manner.

There is a saying, 'A friend in need is a friend indeed.' Love for the nation is most clearly manifested in times of national trials and troubles. We all know how it feels when someone close to us is ill. We do not want diversions or comforts. In our sorrow and concern, we sometimes cannot even eat or drink or sleep. One who truly loves his nation will manifest similar feelings during times of national troubles. If our heart is filled with nothing but our own personal experiences and interests, if we moan and sigh while our deeds remain far from our words, then our love for the nation is poor indeed.

One of the clearest and most self-denying struggles of service to one's homeland is to die for the nation. A Christian soldier is a defender of the homeland, and clearly fulfills Christ's precept, *'Greater love hath no man than this, that a man lay down his life for his friends'* **(John 15:13)**. War in itself is absolutely evil, an extremely sad phenomenon and deeply contrary to the very essence of Christianity. Words cannot express how joyous it would be if people ceased to war with one another and peace reigned on earth. Sad reality speaks quite otherwise, however. Only some dreamers far removed from reality and some narrowly one-sided sectarians can pretend that war can be omitted from real life.

It is quite correct to point out that war is a violation of the commandment, *'Thou shalt not kill.'* **(Ex. 20:15)**. No one will argue against that. Still, we see from Holy Scriptures that in that very same Old Testament time when this commandment was given, the Israelite people fought on command from God, and defeated its enemies with God's help. Consequently, the meaning of the commandment *'Thou shalt not kill,'* does not refer unconditionally to every act of removing a person's life. This commandment forbids killing for revenge, in anger, by personal decision or act of will. When our Saviour explained the deep meaning of this commandment, He pointed out that it forbids not only actual killing, but also unchristian, vain anger. Nevertheless, in a conversation with the apostles about the last days, the Lord told them, *'Ye shall hear of wars and rumours of wars: see that ye be not troubled: for all these things must come to pass'* **(Mathew 24:6)**. With these words, the Lord refutes all statements that war is avoidable.

True, we have already examined the fact that war is a negative phenomenon. Yet, it will exist, sometimes as the sole defense of truth and human rights, or against seizure, brutal invasion and violence. Only such wars of defense are recognized in Christian teaching. In fact, we hear of the following event in the life of St. Athanasius of the Holy Mountain. Prince Tornikian of Georgia, an eminent commander of the Byzantine armies, was received into monasticism at St. Athanasius' monastery. During the time of the Persian invasion, Empress Zoe recalled Tornikian to command the armies. Tornikian flatly refused on the grounds that he was a monk. But St. Athanasius said to him, 'We are all children of our homeland and we are obligated to defend it. Our obligation is to guard the homeland from enemies by prayers. Nevertheless, if God deems it expedient to use both our hands and our heart for the commonwealth, we must submit completely…If you do not obey the ruler, you will have to answer for the blood of your compatriots whom you did not wish to save, and for the destruction of the Churches of God.' Tornikian submitted, defeated the enemy and rescued the homeland from danger.

In a conversation with Mohammedans, about war, St. Cyril, the Enlightener of the Slavs, said, 'We meekly endure personal offenses; but as a society, we defend each other, laying down our lives for our neighbors, so that you having taken them captive, do not force them to deny their faith or perform acts against God.' Finally, what Russian does not know the example of St. Sergius of Radonezh, who blessed Prince Dimitry Donskoy to go to war, prayed for the success of the Russian army, and commemorated those soldiers who died on the field of battle? One can, of course, sin and sin greatly while participating in war. This happens when one participates in war with a feeling of personal hatred, vengeance, or vainglory and with proud personal aims. On the contrary, the less he thinks about himself, and the more he is ready to lay down his life for others, the closer the Christian soldier approaches the martyr's crown."[28]

Though Roman Catholicism has published Papal encyclicals and other official documents related to the State and governance, Eastern Orthodoxy has published almost nothing of the sort. The only one that I'm aware of - certainly the only one translated into English that I've seen - is called *The Basis Of The Social Concept*. Adopted by the Council of Russian Orthodox Bishops in the year 2000, it can subsequently be considered the Russian Church's formal expression of beliefs. On the following pages you will find select passages from that declaration. I encourage you to use the next section as a reference guide while you read the *Fascism* section of this book, as it will provide you with a side-by-side comparison of various Fascist policies with how the Church has encouraged us to live.

---

[28] Team, T. O. E. (2022, March 29). *Patriotism & War - Metropolitan Philaret of New York Excerpt from "On the Law of God."* Orthodox Ethos. https://www.orthodoxethos.com/post/patriotism-war-metropolitan-philaret-of-new-york-excerpt-from-on-the-law-of-god

The Basis Of The Social Concept

As described in the final paragraph of the document, the *Bas[e]s of the Social Concept of the Russian Orthodox Church* "are called to serve as a guide for the Synodal institutions, dioceses, monasteries, parishes and other canonical church institutions in their relations with various secular bodies and organizations and the non-church mass media. This document shall be used by the church authorities to make decisions on various issues relevant within particular states or a narrow period of time, as well as very particular subject matters. The document shall be included in the curriculum of the theological schools of Moscow Patriarchate. As changes take place in public and social life and new problems significant for the Church emerge in this area, the bases of the Church's social concept may be developed and improved. The results of this process shall be adopted by the Holy Synod, the Local or Bishops' Councils."[29]

This section of <u>Fascism Viewed From The Cross</u> will not be an in-depth examination of each and every one of the document's points; not only are most of them beyond the scope of this book, dealing with issues ranging from marriage to euthanasia, but I also do not feel comfortable analyzing the document in detail without the guidance of

---

[29] *XVI. International relation. Problems of the globalisation and secularism* | *The Russian Orthodox Church.* (2021). Mospat.ru. https://old.mospat.ru/en/documents/social-concepts/xvi/

Russian Orthodox clergy. Instead, this chapter will only cite sections of the document which are relevant for our study. I encourage you to read the entire thing for yourself, which you can find by entering "Basis Of The Social Concept" in a search engine or typing this URL into your browser:

https://old.mospat.ru/en/documents/social-concepts/

Furthermore, I have changed the spelling of certain words from an Anglicized to an American form. This has no bearing on the content of the document, and the meanings have not been changed at all. I have also not added or subtracted any words, but simply entered an ellipsis ("…") to highlight where I have skipped sections and paragraphs that were not immediately relevant. I have also italicized verses from the Holy Bible, while using Bold format on the names of the verses. The document contains 16 major sections, each containing subsections on various topics. The ones most useful for a study of Fascism, specifically in the context of the movements and events you'll be reading about soon, are as follows. I encourage you to use this chapter not only for your own edification and knowledge, but as a reference for the rest of this book which you can look back to for comparisons between what you'll soon read and what the Russian Orthodox Church has declared via Synod.

I. 3. "It is inadmissible to shun the surrounding world in a Manichean way. Christian participation in it should be based on the awareness that the world, socium and state are objects of God's love, for they are to be transformed and purified on the principles of God-commanded love. The Christian should view the world and society in the light of his ultimate destiny, in the eschatological light of the Kingdom of God."[30]

I. 4. "Fulfilling the mission of the salvation of the human race, the Church performs it not only through direct preaching, but also through good works aimed to improve the spiritual-moral and material condition of the world around her. To this end, she enters into co-operation with the state, even if it is not Christian, as well as with various public associations and individuals, even if they do not identify themselves with the Christian faith. Without setting herself the direct task to have all converted to Orthodoxy as a condition for co-operation, the Church hopes that joint charity will lead its workers and people around them to the knowledge of the Truth, help them to preserve or restore faithfulness to the God-given moral norms and inspire them to seek peace, harmony and well-being — the conditions in which the Church can best fulfill her salvific work."[31]

II. 1. "In the contemporary world, the notion of 'nation' is used in two meanings, as an ethnic community and the aggregate citizens of a particular state. Relationships between church and nation should be

---

[30]   *I. Basic theological provisions | The Russian Orthodox Church.* (n.d.). https://old.mospat.ru/en/documents/social-concepts/i/
[31]   Ibid.

viewed in the context of both meanings of this word…
Being universal by nature, the Church is at the same time
one organism, one body (**1 Cor. 12:12**). She is the
community of the children of God, '*a chosen generation, a
royal priesthood, an holy nation, a peculiar people… which in
time past were not a people, but are now the people of God*' (**1
Pet. 2:9-10**). The unity of these new people is secured not
by its ethnic, cultural or linguistic community, but by
their common faith in Christ and Baptism. The new
people of God '*have no continuing city here, but seek one to
come*' (**Heb. 13:14**). The spiritual homeland of all
Christians is not earthly Jerusalem but Jerusalem '*which is
above*' (**Gal. 4:26**). The gospel of Christ is preached not in
the sacred language understandable to one people, but in
all tongues (**Acts 2:3-11**). The gospel is not preached for
one chosen people to preserve the true faith, but so that
'at the name of Jesus every knee should bow, of things in
heaven, and things in earth, and things under the earth;
and that every tongue should confess that Jesus Christ is
Lord, to the glory of God the Father' (**Phil. 2:10-11**)."[32]

II. 2. "The universal nature of the Church, however,
does not mean that Christians should have no right to
national identity and national self-expressions. On the
contrary, the Church unites in herself the universal with
the national…Among saints venerated by the Orthodox
Church, many became famous for the love of their earthly
homeland and faithfulness to it. Russian hagiographic

---

[32] *II. Church and nation* | *The Russian Orthodox Church.* (n.d.).
https://old.mospat.ru/en/documents/social-concepts/ii/

sources praise the holy Prince Michael of Tver who 'gave his life for his fatherland,' comparing his feat to the martyrdom of the holy protomartyr Dimitrius of Thessaloniki: 'The good lover of his fatherland said about his native city of Thessaloniki, 'O Lord, if you ruin this city, I will perish together with it, but if you save it, I will also be saved.''

In all times the Church has called upon her children to love their homeland on earth and not to spare their lives to protect it if it was threatened. The Russian Church on many occasions gave her blessing to the people for them to take part in liberation wars. Thus, in 1380, the venerable Sergius the abbot and miracle-maker of Radonezh blessed the Russian troops headed by the holy Prince Dimitry Donskoy before their battle with the Tartar-Mongol invaders. In 1612, St. Hermogen, Patriarch of Moscow and All Russia, gave blessing upon the irregulars in their struggle with the Polish invaders. In 1813, during the war with the French aggressors, St. Philaret of Moscow said to his flock: 'If you avoid dying for the honor and freedom of the Fatherland, you will die a criminal or a slave; die for the faith and the Fatherland and you will be granted life and a crown in heaven.'

The holy righteous John of Kronstadt wrote this about love of one's earthly homeland: 'Love the earthly homeland… it has raised, distinguished, honored and equipped you with everything; but have special love for the heavenly homeland… that homeland is incomparably more precious that this one, because it is holy, righteous and incorruptible. The priceless blood of the Son of God has earned that homeland for you. But in order to be members of that homeland, you should respect and love its laws, just as you are obliged to respect...the laws of the earthly homeland.'"[33]

II. 3. "Christian patriotism may be expressed at the same time with regard to a nation as an ethnic community and as a community of its citizens. The Orthodox Christian is called to love his fatherland, which has a territorial dimension, and his brothers by blood who live everywhere in the world. This love is one of the ways of fulfilling God's commandment of love to one's neighbor which includes love to one's family, fellow-tribesmen and fellow-citizens.

The patriotism of the Orthodox Christian should be active. It is manifested when he defends his fatherland against an enemy, works for the good of the motherland, cares for the good order of people's life through, among other things, participation in the affairs of government. The Christian is called to preserve and develop national culture and people's self-awareness."[34]

II. 4. "At the same time, national sentiments can cause such sinful phenomena as aggressive nationalism, xenophobia, national exclusiveness and inter-ethnic enmity. At their extremes, these phenomena often lead to the restriction of the rights of individuals and nations, wars and other manifestations of violence. It is contrary to

---

[33] Ibid.

[34] Ibid.

Orthodox ethics to divide nations into the best and the worst and to belittle any ethnic or civic nation. Even more contrary to Orthodoxy are the teachings which put the nation in the place of God or reduce faith to one of the aspects of national self-awareness. Opposing these sinful phenomena, the Orthodox Church carries out the mission of reconciliation between hostile nations and their representatives. Thus, in inter-ethnic conflicts, she does not identify herself with any side, except for cases when one of the sides commit evident aggression or injustice."[35]

III. 1. "The emergence of the temporal state should not be understood as a reality originally established by God. It was rather God's granting human being an opportunity to order their social life by their own free will, so that this order as a response to the earthly reality distorted by sin, could help avoid a greater sin through opposing it by means of temporal power.

Explaining the teaching of Christ on the right attitude to state power, St. Paul wrote: '*Let every soul be subject unto the higher powers. For there is no power but of God: the powers that be are ordained of God. Whosoever therefore resisteth the power, resisteth the ordinance of God; and they that resist shall receive to themselves damnation. For rulers are not a terror to good works, but to the evil. Wilt thou them not be afraid of the power? do that which is good, and thou shalt have praise of the same: for he is the minister of God to thee for good. But if thou do that which is evil, be afraid; for he beareth not the sword in vain: for he is the minister of God, a revenger*

---

[35] Ibid.

to execute wrath upon him that doeth evil. Wherefore ye must needs be subject, not only for wrath, but also for conscience sake. For this cause pay ye tribute also: for they are God's ministers, attending continually upon this very thing. Render therefore to all their dues: tribute to whom tribute is due; custom to whom custom; fear to whom fear; honour to whom honour' (**Rom. 13:1-7**). The same idea was expressed by St. Peter: *'Submit yourselves to every ordinance of man for the Lord's sake: whether it be to the king, as supreme; or unto governors, as unto them that are sent for the praise of them that do well. For so is the will of God, that with well doing ye may put to silence the ignorance of foolish men: as free, and not using your liberty for a cloak of maliciousness, but as he servants of God'* (**1 Pet. 2:13-16**). The apostles taught Christians to obey the authorities regardless of their attitude to the Church. In the apostolic era, the Church of Christ was persecuted both by the Jewish and Roman State authorities. This did not prevent the martyrs and other Christians of that time from praying for prosecutors and recognizing their power."[36]

III. 2. "The fall of Adam brought to the world sins and vices which needed public opposition. The first of them was the murder of Cain by Abel (**Gen. 4:1-16**). Aware of this, people in all known societies began to establish laws restricting evil and supporting good. For the Old Testament people, God Himself was the Lawmaker Who gave rules to regulate not only religious life proper but

---

[36] *III. Church and state* | *The Russian Orthodox Church*. (2021). Mospat.ru. https://old.mospat.ru/en/documents/social-concepts/iii/

also public life (**Ex. 20-23**).

God blesses the state as an essential element of life in the world distorted by sin, in which both the individual and society need to be protected from the dangerous manifestations of sin. At the same time, the need for the state arose not because God willed it for the primitive Adam, but because of the fall and because the actions to restrict the dominion of sin over the world conformed to His will. Holy Scriptures calls upon powers that be to use the power of state for restricting evil and supporting good, in which it sees the moral meaning of the existence of state (**Rom. 13:3-4**). It follows from the above that anarchy is the absence of proper order in a state and society, while calls to it and attempts to introduce it run contrary to the Christian outlook (**Rom. 13:2**)…At the same time, Christians should avoid attempts to make it absolute and failure to recognize the limits of its purely earthly, temporal and transient value conditioned by the presence of sin in the world and the need to restrain it. According to the teaching of the Church, power itself has no right to make itself absolute by extending its limits up to complete autonomy from God and from the order of things established by Him. This can lead to the abuse of power and even to the deification of rulers."[37]

III. 3. "In the contemporary world, state is normally secular and not bound by any religious commitments. Its co-operation with the Church is limited to several areas and based on mutual non-interference into each other's

---

[37] Ibid.

affairs...The Church should not assume the prerogatives of the state, such as resistance to sin by force, use of temporal authoritative powers and assumption of the governmental functions which presuppose coercion or restriction. At the same time, the Church may request or urge the government to exercise power in particular cases, yet the decision rests with the state. "[38]

III. 4. The classical Byzantine formula of relationships between state and church power is contained in the Epanagoge (later 9th century): 'The temporal power and the priesthood relate to each other as body and soul; they are necessary for state order just as body and soul are necessary in a living man. It is in their linkage and harmony that the well-being of a state lies.'

This symphony, however, did not exist in Byzantium in an absolutely pure form. In practice it was often violated and distorted. The Church was repeatedly subjected to caesarean-papist claims from the state authorities, which were essentially the demands that the head of the state, the emperor, should have the decisive say in ordering church affairs. Along with the sinful human love of power, these claims had also a historical reason. The Christian emperors of Byzantium were direct successors of the Roman pagan rulers who, among their numerous titles, had that of pontifex maximus, chief priest. The caesarean-papist tendency manifested itself most bluntly and dangerously for the Church in the policy of heretical emperors, especially in the iconoclastic

---

[38] Ibid.

era.

Unlike Byzantine basileuses, Russian tsars had a different legacy. For this and other historical reasons, relationship between the church and the state authorities was more harmonious in Russian antiquity. However, there were also deviations from the canonical norms (under Ivan the Terrible and in the confrontation between Tsar Alexis Mikhailovich and Patriarch Nikon)."[39]

III. 5. "…the persecuted Church is also called to endure the persecution with patience, without refusing to be loyal to the state persecuting her…Legal sovereignty in the territory of a state belongs to its authorities. Therefore, it is they who determine the legal status of a Local Church or her part, either giving her an opportunity for the unhampered fulfillment of church mission or restricting this opportunity. Thus, state power makes judgment on itself and eventually foretells its fate. The Church remains loyal to the state, but God's commandment to fulfill the task of salvation in any situation and under any circumstances is above this loyalty…If the authority forces Orthodox believers to apostatize from Christ and His Church and to commit sinful and spiritually harmful actions, the Church should refuse to obey the state."[40]

III. 7. "…the Church should give more attention not to the system of the outer organization of state, but to the inner condition of her members' hearts. Therefore, the

---

[39] Ibid.

[40] Ibid.

Church does not believe it possible for her to become an initiator of any change in the form of government. Along the same line, the 1994 Bishops' Council of the Russian Orthodox Church stressed the soundness of the attitude whereby 'the Church does not give preference to any social system or any of the existing political doctrines.'"[41]

III. 8. "...there are areas in which the clergy and canonical church structures cannot support the state or cooperate with it. They are as follows:
- a) political struggle, election agitation, campaigns in support of particular political parties and public and political leaders;
- b) waging civil war or aggressive external war;
- c) direct participation in intelligence and any other activity that demands secrecy by law even in making one's confession or reporting to the church authorities."[42]

III. 11. "To avoid any confusion of church and state affairs and to prevent the church authority from acquiring temporal nature, the canons prohibit the clergy from participating in the affairs of state government. Apostolic Canon 81 reads: 'It does not befit a bishop or a presbyter to go into the affairs of the people's government, but to be always engaged in the affairs of the Church.' Apostolic Canon 6 and Canon 10 of the Seventh Ecumenical Council

---

[41] Ibid.
[42] Ibid.

speak of the same."[43]

IV. 2. "The secular law has as its task not to turn the world lying in evil into the Kingdom of God, but to prevent it from turning into hell."[44]

IV. 9. "The Church of Christ, preserving her own autonomous law based on the holy canons and keeping within the church life proper, can exist in the framework of very diverse legal systems which she treats with respect. The Church invariably calls upon her flock to be law-abiding citizens of their earthly homeland. At the same time, she has always underlined the unshakable limits to which her faithful should obey the law. In everything that concerns the exclusively earthly order of things, the Orthodox Christian is obligated to obey the law, regardless of how far it is imperfect and unfortunate. However, when compliance with legal requirements threatens his eternal salvation and involves an apostasy or commitment of another doubtless sin before God and his neighbor, the Christian is called to perform the feat of confession for the sake of God's truth and the salvation of his soul for eternal life. He must speak out lawfully against an indisputable violation committed by society or state against the statutes and commandments of God. If this lawful action is impossible or ineffective, he must take up the position of civil disobedience."[45]

---

[43] Ibid.

[44] *IV. Christian ethics and secular law | The Russian Orthodox Church.* (2021). Mospat.ru. https://old.mospat.ru/en/documents/social-concepts/iv/

[45] Ibid.

V. 4. "The existence of Christian (Orthodox) political organizations and Christian (Orthodox) units in larger political associations is perceived by the Church as positive as it helps lay people to engage in common political and public work based on Christian spiritual and moral principles. These organizations, while being free in their activity, are called to consult the church authorities and to co-ordinate their actions in implementing the Church's position on public issues."[46]

VII. 3. "The Church cannot approve the alienation and re-distribution of property with violations of the rights of its legitimate owners."[47]

VIII. 1. "War is a physical manifestation of the latent illness of humanity, which is fratricidal hatred (**Gen. 4:3-12**). Wars have accompanied human history since the fall and, according to the Gospel, will continue to accompany it: *'And when ye hear of wars and rumors of wars, be ye not troubled: for such things must needs be'* (**Mk. 13:7**). This is also testified by the Apocalypse in its story of the last battle between good and evil at Mount Armageddon (**Rev. 16:16**). Generated by pride and resistance to the will of God, earthly wars reflect in fact the heavenly battle. Corrupted by sin, man found himself involved in the turmoil of this battle. War is evil. Just as the evil in man in

---

[46] *V. Church and politics | The Russian Orthodox Church.* (n.d.). https://old.mospat.ru/en/documents/social-concepts/v/
[47] *VII. Property | The Russian Orthodox Church.* (2021). Mospat.ru. https://old.mospat.ru/en/documents/social-concepts/vii/

general, war is caused by the sinful abuse of the God-given freedom; *'for out of the heart proceed evil thoughts, murder, adulteries, fornications, thefts, false witness, blasphemies'* (**Mt. 15:19**)."[48]

VIII. 2. "While recognizing war as evil, the Church does not prohibit her children from participating in hostilities if at stake is the security of their neighbors and the restoration of trampled justice. Then war is considered to be necessary though undesirable but means. In all times, Orthodoxy has had profound respect for soldiers who gave their lives to protect the life and security of their neighbors. The Holy Church has canonized many soldiers, taking into account their Christian virtues and applying to them Christ's world: *'Greater love hath no man but this, that a man lay down his life for his friends'* (**Jn. 15:13**)."[49]

VIII. 3. "*'They that take the sword shall perish with the sword'* (**Mt. 26:52**). These words of the Savior justify the idea of just war. From the Christian perspective, the conception of moral justice in international relations should be based on the following basic principles: love of one's neighbors, people and Fatherland; understanding of the needs of other nations; conviction that it is impossible to serve one's country by immoral means. These three principles defined the ethical limits of war established by

---

[48] *VIII. War and peace | The Russian Orthodox Church.* (2021). Mospat.ru. https://old.mospat.ru/en/documents/social-concepts/viii/

[49] Ibid.

Christendom in the Middle Ages when, adjusting to reality, people tried to curb the elements of military violence. Already at that time, people believed that war should be waged according to certain rules and that a fighting man should not lose his morality, forgetting that his enemy is a human being too...In defining just war, the Western Christian tradition, which goes back to St. Augustine, usually puts forward a number of conditions on which war in one's own or others' territory is admissible. They are as follows:

* war is declared for the restoration of justice;

* war is declared only by the legitimate authority;

* force is used not by individuals or groups but by representatives of the civil authorities established from above;

* war is declared only after all peaceful means have been used to negotiate with the opposite party and to restore the prior situation;

* war is declared only if there are well-grounded expectations that the established goals will be achieved;

* the planned military losses and destruction will correspond to the situation and the purposes of war (the principal of proportionate means);

* during war civilians will be protected against direct hostilities;

* war may be justified only by the desire to restore law and order.

In the present system of international relations, it is sometimes difficult to distinguish an aggressive war from a defensive war. The distinction between the two is

especially subtle where one or two states or the world community initiate hostilities on the ground that it is necessary to protect the people who fell victim to an aggression (see XV. 1). In this regard,
the question whether the Church should support or deplore the hostilities needs to be given a special consideration every time they are initiated or threaten to begin.

Among obvious signs pointing to the equity or inequity of a warring party are its war methods and attitude towards its war prisoners and the civilians of the opposite side, especially children, women and elderly. Even in the defense from an aggression, every kind of evil can be done, making one's spiritual and moral stand not superior to that of the aggressor. War should be waged with righteous indignation, not maliciousness, greed and last (**1 Jn. 2:16**) and other fruits of hell. A war can be correctly assessed as a feat or a robbery only after an analysis is made of the moral state of the warring parties. *'Rejoice not over thy greatest enemy being dead, but remember that we die all,'* Holy Scriptures says (**Sirach 8:8**). Christian humane attitude to the wounded and war prisoners is based on the words of St. Paul: *'If thine enemy hunger, feed him; if he thirst, give him drink; for so doing thou shalt heap coals of fire on his head. Be not overcome of evil, but overcome evil with good'* (**Rom. 12:21-22**)."[50]

VIII. 4. "In the icons of St. George the Victor, the black dragon is trampled by the hoofs of a horse always painted

---

[50] Ibid.

brightly white. This vividly shows that evil and the struggle with it should be completely separated, for in struggling with sin it is important to avoid sharing in it. In all the vital situations where force needs to be used, the human heart should not be caught by bad feelings akin to evil spirits and their like. It is only the victory over evil in one's heart that enables one to use force in justice. This view asserting love in human relations resolutely rejects the idea of non-resistance to evil by force. The Christian moral law deplores not the struggle with sin, not the use of force towards its bearer and not even taking another's life in the last resort, but rather malice in the human heart and the desire to humiliate or destroy whosoever it may be."[51]

IX. 2. "The prevention of crime is possible first of all through education and enlightenment aimed to assert in society the authentic spiritual and moral values. In this task the Orthodox Church is called to intensive co-operation with school, mass media and law-enforcement bodies. If the people lack a positive moral ideal, no measures of coercion, deterrence or punishment will be able to stop the evil will...the Church insists on the need of humane attitude towards suspects, persons under investigation and those caught in criminal intent. The crude and improper treatment of these people can either fortify them on the wrong track or push them on it. For this reason, those awaiting a verdict should not be disfranchised even in custody. They should be

---

[51] Ibid.

guaranteed advocacy and impartial justice.

…The priest is called to show special pastoral sensitivity in case of a confession revealing a criminal intent. While keeping sacred the secrecy of confession without any exceptions and in any circumstances, the pastor is obliged to make all possible efforts to prevent a criminal intent from being realized. First of all it concerns threats of homicide, especially the massacre possible in the acts of terrorism or execution of a criminal order during war. Remembering that the souls of a potential criminal and his intended victim have equal value, the priest should call the penitent to make authentic repentance, that is, to abandon his evil intent. If this call is not effective, the pastor, keeping secret the penitent's name and other circumstances which can help identify him, may give a warning to those whose life is threatened. In difficult cases, the priest should apply to the diocesan bishop."[52]

IX. 3. "Any crime committed and condemned by law presupposes a fair punishment. Its meaning is to reform an infringer, to protect society from a criminal and to stop his illegal activity. The Church, without taking upon herself to judge an infringer, is called to take care of his soul. That is why she understands punishment not as revenge, but a means of the inner purification of a sinner.

Establishing punishment for culprits, the Creator says to Israel: *'Thou shalt put evil away from among you'* (**Deut.**

[52] *IX. Crime, punishment, reformation | The Russian Orthodox Church.* (2021). Mospat.ru. https://old.mospat.ru/en/documents/social-concepts/ix/

21:21). Punishment for crime serves to teach people. Thus, establishing punishment for false prophesy, God says to Moses: *'All Israel shall hear, and fear, and shall do no more any such wickedness as this is among you'* (**Deut. 13:11**). We read in the Proverbs of Solomon: *'Smite a scorner, and the simple will beware: and reprove one that hath understanding, and he will understand knowledge'* (**Prov. 19:25**). The Old Testament tradition knows of several forms of punishment including the death penalty, banishment, restriction of freedom, corporal punishment and fine or order to make a donation for religious purposes.

Confinement, banishment (exile), reformatory labor and fines continue as punishments in the contemporary world. All these penalties are relevant not only in protecting society from the evil will of a criminal, but are also called to help in reforming him. Thus, confinement or restriction of freedom gives a person who outlawed himself an opportunity to reflect on his life in order to come back to liberty internally purified…It is important at the same time to ensure that inmates are not subjected to inhumane treatment, that the conditions of confinement do not threaten their life and health and that their moral condition is not influenced by the pernicious example of other inmates.

…The death penalty as a special punishment was recognized in the Old Testament. There are no indications to the need to abolish it in the New Testament or in the Tradition or in the historical legacy of the Orthodox Church either. At the same time, the Church has often assumed the duty of interceding before the secular

authority for those condemned to death, asking it show
mercy for them and commute their punishment.
Moreover, under Christian moral influence, the negative
attitude to the death penalty has been cultivated in
people's consciousness. Thus, in the period from the mid-
18th century to the 1905 Revolution in Russia, it was
applied on very rare occasions. For the Orthodox church
consciousness, the life of a person does not end with his
bodily death, therefore the Church continues her care for
those condemned to capital punishment.

The abolition of death penalty would give more
opportunities for pastoral work with those who have
stumbled and for the latter to repent. It is also evident that
punishment by death cannot be reformatory; it also
makes misjudgment irreparable and provokes ambiguous
feelings among people. Today many states have either
abolished the death penalty by law or stopped practicing
it. Keeping in mind that mercy toward a fallen man is
always more preferable than revenge, the Church
welcomes these steps by state authorities. At the same
time, she believes that the decision to abolish or not to
apply death penalty should be made by society freely,
considering the rate of crime and the state of law-
enforcement and judiciary, and even more so, the need to
protect the life of its well-intentioned members."[53]

X. 6. "The virtue of chastity preached by the Church is
the basis of the inner unity of the human personality,
which should always be in the state of harmony between

---

[53] Ibid.

its mental and bodily powers. Fornication inevitably ruins the harmony and integrity of one's life, damaging heavily one's spiritual health. Libertinism dulls the spiritual vision and hardens the heart, making it incapable of true love. The happiness of full-blooded family life becomes unattainable for the fornicator. Sins against chastity also lead to negative social consequences. In the situation of a spiritual crisis of the human society, the mass media and the products of the so-called mass culture sometimes become instruments of moral corruption by praising sexual laxity, all kinds of sexual perversion and other sinful passions. Pornography, which is the exploitation of the sexual drive for commercial, political or ideological purposes, contributes to the suppression of the spiritual and moral principles, thus reducing man to an animal motivated by instinct alone.

The propaganda of vice is especially harmful for the still infirm souls of children and youth. Through books, films and other video products, as well as the mass media and some educational curricula, teenagers are often taught an idea of sexual relations extremely humiliating for the human dignity, since it gives no room to such notions as chastity, marital faithfulness and selfless love. Intimate relations between man and woman are not only exposed for show, offending the natural feeling of prudence, but also presented as an act of purely corporal gratification without any association with inner communion or any moral obligations. The Church urges the faithful to struggle, in co-operation with all morally healthy forces, against the propagation of this diabolical temptation, which, by destroying the family, undermines the foundations of society."[54]

XIV. 3. "From the Orthodox perspective, it is desirable that the entire educational system should be built on religious principles and based on Christian values. Nevertheless, the Church, following the age-old tradition, respects the secular school and is willing to build relations with it on the basis of human freedom. At the same time, the Church considers it inadmissible to impose on students anti-religious and anti-Christian ideas and to assert the monopoly of the materialistic worldview (see XIV. 1). The situation typical of many countries in the 20th century when state-run schools were made instruments of militant atheistic education should not be repeated. The Church calls to remove the consequences of atheistic control over the system of public education. Unfortunately, the role of religion as forming the spiritual self-awareness of peoples is underestimated in many curricula on history to this day. The Church keeps reminding people of the contribution Christianity has made to the treasury of the world and national cultures. The Orthodox believers regret the attempts to borrow uncritically the educational standards, principles and curricula of the organizations known for their negative attitude to Christianity in general and to Orthodoxy in particular. The danger of occult and neo-heathen influences and destructive sects penetrating into

---

[54] *X. Personal, family and public morality* | *The Russian Orthodox Church*. (n.d.). https://old.mospat.ru/en/documents/social-concepts/kh/

the secular school should not be ignored either, as under their impact a child can be lost for himself, for his family and for society."[55]

XV. 1. "The propaganda of violence, enmity and hatred and ethnic, social and religious discord and the sinful exploitation of human instincts, including for commercial purposes, are inadmissible."[56]

XVI. 1. "The use of military force is believed by the Church to be the last resort in defense against armed aggression from other states. This defense can also be carried out on the basis of assistance by a state which is not an immediate object of attack at the one attacked. States base their relations with the outside world on the principles of sovereignty and territorial integrity. These principles are viewed by the Church as basic for the defense by a people of their legitimate interests and as the corner stone of international treaties and, therefore, of entire international law. At the same time, it is evident to the Christian consciousness that any human ordinance, including the sovereign power of a state, is relative before Almighty God."[57]

[55] *XIV. Secular science, culture and education* | *The Russian Orthodox Church.* (n.d.). https://old.mospat.ru/en/documents/social-concepts/xiv/
[56] *XV. Church and mass media* | *The Russian Orthodox Church.* (2021). Mospat.ru. https://old.mospat.ru/en/documents/social-concepts/xv/
[57] *XVI. International relation. Problems of the globalisation and secularism* | *The Russian Orthodox Church.* (2021). Mospat.ru. https://old.mospat.ru/en/documents/social-concepts/xvi/

XVI. 3. "While recognizing the globalization as inevitable and natural and in many ways facilitating people's communication, dissemination of information and more effective production and enterprise, the Church points to the internal contradictions of these process and to their threats. Firstly, the globalization begins to change, along with the conventional ways of organizing production, the conventional ways of organize society and exercising power. Secondly, many positive fruits of the globalization are available only to nations comprising a smaller part of humanity, but having a similar economic and political system. Other nations to whom five sixths of the global population belong have found themselves on the margins of the world civilization. They have been caught in debt dependence on financiers in a few industrial countries and cannot create dignified living conditions for themselves. Discontent and disillusionment are growing among them.

The Church raises the question concerning the need to establish comprehensive control over transnational corporations and the processes taking place in the financial sector of economy. This control, aimed to subject any entrepreneurial and financial activity to the interests of man and people, should be exercised through all mechanisms available in society and state...The followers of Christ therefore are called to promote the interconnectedness of the faith and the cultural heritage of nations, opposing resolutely any manifestations of anti-culture and commercialization of the space allocated to information and arts."[58]

XVI. 4. "The contemporary international legal system is based on the priority given to the interests of the earthly life of man and human communities over religious values (especially in those cases when the former and the latter come into conflict). This priority is sealed in the national legislation of many countries. It is often built in the principles regulating various activities of the governmental bodies, public educational system, etc. Many influential public mechanisms use the same principle in their open confrontation with faith and the Church, aimed to oust them from public life. These manifestations create a general picture of the secularization of public and social life.

While respecting the worldview of non-religious people and their right to influence social processes, the Church cannot favor a world order that puts in the center of everything the human personality darkened by sin. This is why, invariably open to co-operation with people of non-religious convictions, the Church seeks to assert Christian values in the process of decision-making on the most important public issues both on national and international levels. She strives for the recognition of the legality of religious worldview as a basis for socially significant action (including those taken by state) and as an essential factor which should influence the development (amendment) of international law and the

---

[58] Ibid.

work of international organizations."[59]

As you can see, the Russian Orthodox Church appears to have adopted elements from both Eusebius and St. Augustine. From Eusebius, while not formally championing Monarchy, the Church nonetheless views the State as positive force and commands its faithful to participate in society. From St. Augustine, the Church accepts the notion that government was not a prelapsarian concept but was rather given by God, post-fall, to restrain sin. Though many of the Russian Orthodox Christians that I've spoken with are fervent defenders of Monarchy, the Church's official stance seems to refrain from making a formal proclamation.

Having studied all the information presented thus far, we may reasonably conclude that there is no particular Orthodox dogma in regard to the ideal - or even *only legitimate* - form of government. *The Basis of the Social Concept* seems to explicitly proclaim the exact opposite: that we do *not* uphold any one specific form of government as being inherently superior to all others. Different times and places have emphasized different systems, though it is interesting that when the Saints speak on the topic they almost universally seem to prefer Monarchy. In that light, we may not criticize Fascism based purely on its autocratic character. We may certainly take issue with various actions undertaken by its leaders in the times and places wherein they deviated from *how* a Christian Monarch ought to run the State, but we can

[59]   Ibid.

neither attack them for being Monarchs nor condemn other Christians for being Monarchists. Those who boldly proclaim that Orthodox Christians cannot support Monarchical governments are, to be charitable, unfamiliar with the history of the topic. Regardless of whether a particular government is autocratic or democratic, the Church tries to cooperate insofar as it can do so without violating its own canons and morality.

Though not a canonized Saint, Ivan Ilyn outlined beliefs in his essay *On Forms of Sovereignty* which appear to provide a balanced and practical perspective. In that essay, Ilyn wrote that "every people and every land are a living individuality with their special characteristics, their own unrepeatable history, soul, and nature. To every people is therefore due its own special individual form of sovereignty and a constitution corresponding to that people only. There are no identical peoples, and there should not be identical forms of sovereignty and constitutions. Blind borrowing and imitation is absurd, dangerous, and can become ruinous...What political myopia would be necessary in order to impose upon all peoples a form of monarchy, even upon those who have not a shadow of the monarchical mentality? (For example: the United States, Switzerland, or rebellious Mexico, where Emperor Maximillian was killed by the mutinous republicans three years after his enthronement). However, is it not just as irresponsible to force a republican form of government upon the life of a people that developed over long centuries a monarchical sense of the state? (For example: England, Germany, Spain, Serbia,

Russia…) What kind of doctrinal fanaticism was needed in 1917 to assemble a certain super-democratic, super-republican, super-federative constitution in Russia and plunge the land, with its most individual history, soul, and nature, into the chaos of meaningless and directionless disintegration that could only end in the tyranny of unconscionable internationalists!…What can we expect from the enactment of such programs apart from national disasters?"[60] You will hear more from Ilyn in his essay *On Fascism*, included at the end of this book.

Now that we've studied the concept of the State through the lens of the Orthodox Church, let us analyze the final piece of the puzzle before moving on to the Fascist movements: the traditional Christian view of Jews as a people and Judaism as the religion they practice.

---

[60] April 24, M. H., & Comments, 2015 8. (2015, April 24). *Ivan Ilyin: On Forms of Sovereignty*. The Soul of the East. https://souloftheeast.org/2015/04/24/ivan-ilyin-on-forms-of-sovereignty/comment-page-1/

Orthodoxy and the Jews

Biblical and Patristic Rhetoric

Before we can compare the Fascist treatment of Jews with the traditional Christian view, we must first establish precisely how the Orthodox Church has historically engaged with Judaism and the people who practice it. To do this we must look - as always - to the Saints. And when we look to the Saints we cannot impose modern understandings of race, racism, anti-Semitism, multiculturalism, tolerance, or diversity upon them; we must take our cues from what God revealed both *to* and *through* the Saints, in the way He did and in the time and manner in which He did, without regard for 21st century ideology. Only in this manner may we discover the pure teachings of God through the Orthodox Church without the stain and blemish of worldliness..

As such, we will study three particular spheres of engagement between Orthodox Christian Saints and Judaism: *Rhetoric*, *Church Canons*, and *Imperial Law*. By *Rhetoric* I refer to what is written in both the Scriptures and the work of men like St. John Chrysostom, with a special focus on what such sources have traditionally taught about both Judaism as a religion and about Jews as a community. We will delve not only into the words they used but the reasons and context behind said words; only in this manner may we understand them as they meant to be understood without cherry-picking their thoughts and warping them into what was not intended. By *Church Canons* I refer to the specific ecclesiastical and pastoral Canons, as handed down by various Orthodox Saints and Councils through the millennia, regulating how Orthodox Christians ought to interact with Jews in various capacities and situations. Finally by *Imperial Laws* I refer to the specific Roman laws regarding Jews - including how Christians should or should not treat Jews - enacted and imposed by the Orthodox Emperor Saints Constantine, Theodosius, Theodosius II and Justinian. By examining Jewish life in the Christian Roman Empire, we can develop a bird's-eye view of how the Jewish and Christian communities interacted in that environment.

There are two primary reasons for why we must always stick to the Saints, and the teachings of Orthodox Councils and Canons, when discussing interactions with the Jewish community. Firstly, Orthodox Christians recognize that God has glorified certain individuals as Saints to be upheld as examples of the Orthodox worldview. If the Saints are unanimous or near-unanimous on a certain subject, we take that as God's authoritative view of said subject. The Canon of St. Vincent declares that the true Orthodox Faith is that which was held "everywhere, always, by all;" this means that ideologies, perspectives, and opinions mean nothing unless they can be found in the consensus of the Saints. This dynamic safeguards the Holy Orthodox Church from innovation and modernism - when it's followed as it should be - and reminds us that our God, Jesus Christ, is *"the same yesterday, today, and forever."* [61] The second reason we must always form our worldview with regard to the Orthodox mind or phronema, as communicated through the consensus of the Saints, is that it protects our approach to difficult questions from the meddling and subversion of those who claim to be Orthodox but who, in reality, seek to undermine the Church in order to enthrone ideology instead. When modernists who seek to alter the Orthodox Faith criticize the ideas and opinions of the Saints, what they are really criticizing is the Church and - by proxy - God Himself. They are fundamentally angry at God, Eric Voegelin might suggest, for creating a world which does not adapt itself to their own passions and preferences. Subsequently, they seek to overthrow God and the Church which He planted.

It's no secret that Orthodox history is rife with anti-Jewish rhetoric, and we must approach the topic with honesty and courage if we are to make sense of what we observe. And in order to build our case for an Orthodox standard against which to later compare Fascism, we must not pretend that history is other than it is. We must not make excuses for what we find, and neither must we groan, grovel or apologize for what the Saints and Christ Himself have said. Let us take the ancient Saints at their word and, rather than read them with 21st century eyes, try instead to understand their point of view. With that said, let us embark on our journey to discover what the Church has traditionally taught about Jews and the tension between Jewish and Christian communities.

---

[61] Hebrews 13:8

Our earliest account of conflict between Jews and Christians comes from the New Testament; a typical interaction between a Christian and a Jew shows the Christian attempting to share wisdom and grace, while the hard-hearted and obstinate Jew misses the message - and may even attack the Christian in response. Jews are often depicted conniving, conspiring, falsely accusing, and even killing the Christians who proclaim the incarnation of the Messiah. We read of such incidents all throughout the New Testament, but find them particularly concentrated in the **Books of Acts**.

As we read in St. Luke's testimony recorded in that book, many Jews converted and received Holy Baptism both on Pentecost and on the days which followed. Some converted after witnessing miracles, such as when the disabled man outside the Temple gained his health through the intercessions of St. Peter[62], and others joined the Church after hearing that same Saint persuasively convict them of deicide.[63] Other Jews, such as the Sadducees in **Acts 4**, were outraged by the Apostles' preaching and had Sts. Peter and John thrown in prison. Thus we see the only two reactions Jews demonstrated toward Christianity as recorded in the New Testament: either a wholehearted embrace or a vitriolic rejection.

In an especially fascinating section of **Acts 4**, we see the Sanhedrin and the elders of Israel acknowledge that miracles were done in the name of Jesus while conspiring

---

[62] Acts 3:6-8

[63] Acts 3:13 - Acts 4:4

to stop His name from being spread.[64] This goes beyond the killing of Christ, in ignorance of Who He Is, and becomes something else entirely; the dynamic shifts from spiritual blindness to a deliberate, calculated effort to stop people from receiving miracles and healing in His name. Thankfully, the Apostles ignored Jewish threats and continued to preach the Gospel boldly.

When God-rejecting Jews in the **Book of Acts** were unable to refute Apostolic wisdom, they often resorted to lying and violence instead. We see this demonstrated clearly in **Acts 6:10-12**, following a dispute between St. Stephen and the Jews: "*And they were not able to resist the wisdom and the Spirit by which he spoke. Then they secretly induced men to say, 'We have heard him speak blasphemous words against Moses and God.' And they stirred up the people, the elders, and the scribes; and they came upon him, seized him, and brought him to the council.*" On trial in **Acts 7:53**, St. Stephen fearlessly confronted them: "*'You stiff-necked and uncircumcised in heart and ears! You always resist the Holy Spirit; as your fathers did, so do you. Which of the prophets did your fathers not persecute? And they killed those who foretold the coming of the Just One, of whom you now have become the betrayers and murderers, who have received the law by the direction of angels and have not kept it.'*"

This accusation, spoken by the Holy Spirit[65] through the first Christian martyr, would get you fired from any job and banned from most social media platforms were you to repeat it. It unambiguously declares that the Jews

---

[64]   Acts 4:16-17

[65]   Matthew 10:19-20

received a special revelation - which they rejected - from Almighty God, Who they killed. God tells us through the Scriptures, both the Old and New Testaments, that Jews have always persecuted the fragment of their own faithful who tried to tell them the Truth. The Bible unambiguously refers to those first-century Jews as *"betrayers and murderers"* of Christ, a claim that even many Christians in the modern world have attempted to dispute.

After executing St. Stephen based on false accusations, Jews attempted to kill St. Paul in **Acts 9:22-23**: *"But Saul increased all the more in strength, and confounded the Jews who dwelt in Damascus, proving that this Jesus is the Christ. Now after many days were past, the Jews plotted to kill him."* Once again we see the pattern established with the ministry and death of St. Stephen; Jews heard the Gospel and those who didn't convert became possessed with bloodlust and hate. It should be noted that pagans in **Acts 9:29** attempted to kill St. Paul as well, but this was a relatively rare occurrence compared to the predictability and frequency of Jewish violence. It thus comes as no surprise when we read that King Herod's murder of the Apostle James *"pleased the Jews."*[66] Perhaps it's this very malice which, as you'll read about in the *Imperial Laws* chapter of this book, inspired Emperor St. Constantine to protect Jewish converts the way he did.

Often we read, as in the aforementioned passage from **Acts 6**, that Jews inspired others to angry action when they wanted a specific outcome. Sometimes they did the

---

[66] Acts 12:2-3

dirty work themselves, while other times they spread lies and riled up crowds in order to achieve their goals instead. We see another example of this in **Acts 13:50**, when Sts. Paul and Barnabas were preaching in Antioch. Many Jews there were converted by the Apostles' grace and wisdom, but those who did not convert went to the other extreme: *"But the Jews stirred up the devout and prominent women and the chief men of the city, raised up persecution against Paul and Barnabas, and expelled them from their region."* The same phenomenon is seen at Iconium in the following chapter: *"But the unbelieving Jews stirred up the Gentiles and poisoned their minds against the brethren."*[67] A few verses later, in **Acts 14:19**, the Jews actually followed the Saints from other cities to Lystra: *"and having persuaded the multitudes, they stoned Paul and dragged him out of the city, supposing him to be dead."* Rarely did a Jew hear the Gospel and stay neutral; they either became Christians or went mad. In this case, they followed the Apostles from city to city trying to convince other people to kill them.

We see this dichotomy exemplified yet again in **Acts 17:5.** After learning that St. Paul successfully converted some Jews in Thessalonica, we read that *"the Jews who were not persuaded, becoming envious, took some of the evil men from the marketplace, and gathering a mob, set all the city in an uproar and attacked the house of Jason, and sought to bring them out to the people."* The Jews who rejected the Gospel in Thessalonica, just like the Jews who followed St. Paul from Iconium to Lystra, then went to Berea to

---

[67] Acts 14:2

cause trouble: *"But when the Jews from Thessalonica learned that the word of God was preached by Paul at Berea, they came there also and stirred up the crowds."*[68] Over and over, God draws our attention to the dynamic between Jews and Christians by including stories of such conflicts in His Word. In a speech to the Elders of Ephesus, St. Paul himself identified the culprits: *"'You know, from the first day that I came to Asia, in what manner I always lived among you, serving the Lord with all humility, with many tears and trials which happened to me by the plotting of the Jews.'"*[69] After the speech, there are further accounts of Jews conspiring to hurt St. Paul in **Acts 23** and **Acts 25**. Page after page of Holy Scripture describes the same situations in different times and places.

Given that Christians consider the Holy Scriptures to be God-breathed and infallible, a Christian who takes issue with criticism of Jews - either as individuals or a group - is not left with many choices. Should he choose to believe that said criticism is inherently evil, he necessarily concludes that God has spoken wickedly, unfairly, or immorally; in so choosing, the person who takes this path has separated himself from Christianity. One cannot maintain a Christian view of God or the Scriptures while simultaneously believing that the Bible contains evil sentiments that have to whitewashed, explained away, or otherwise denied.

I say this without judgment, as I empathize with the degree of psychological and emotional manipulation that

---

[68] Acts 17:13

[69] Acts 20:18-19

has led so many Christians to believe Jews are a uniquely innocent and special class which must be protected at all costs. Having grown up Jewish myself, I have seen this from both sides of the fence. However, Christians ultimately have to decide between the programming they've received on this topic from the world and the teachings they've received on it from God. That leads me to the second - and in my opinion far superior - option: a Christian struggling with these concepts can humble himself before the authority of Almighty God and His revelation to humanity, putting his own will and opinions to the side in obedient submission to Christ.

Beyond the Bible, we find sharp distinctions drawn between Christianity and Judaism, often with a great deal of venom toward the latter, in every Christian writing which addressed the topic over the following centuries. Sts. Ignatius of Antioch, Hilary of Poitiers, Gregory of Nyssa, Cyril of Alexandria, Jerome, Ambrose, Augustine and more all contributed to the emerging genre known as "Adversus Judaeos:" *Against the Jews*. Most famously, St. John Chrysostom devoted 8 entire homilies to the subject - and we will analyze these homilies soon. Anti-Jewish writings and rhetoric attacked two primary targets: the falsity of Judaism as a religion and the immorality of the Jewish people. Both routes were taken - sometimes in the same breath - because both served the Christian apologist's primary goal with the topic: to prevent Christians from converting to Judaism. As you'll learn in the chapters on *Church Canons* and *Imperial Laws*, this sentiment went beyond the words of individual Saints and became a major focus of both ecclesiastical and civil power.

By highlighting the many ways in which God has demonstrated that Judaism is obsolete, the skilled Christian orator could persuade the more educated members of his flock to remain in the Church instead of wander toward the synagogue. By attacking the character of immoral Jews, the same orator could frighten more simple and sensitive Christians away from associating with the group at all. Sometimes, anti-Jewish rhetoric simply expressed the speaker's displeasure with the Jewish people after a personal interaction gone sour. We find all of the above in the most elaborate discourses the Church has produced on the topic. Though as mentioned such literature was relatively common in the Patristic period, we will focus on the work of St. John Chrysostom and St. Cyril of Alexandria due to the force of their speech and their special relevance to the topic at hand.

We will begin with St. John Chrysostom. Though his homilies were primarily intended to bring Judaizing Christians away from the synagogue and back into the fold of Orthodox praxis, Judaism as a religion and Jews as people were frequent targets of St. John's invective. In order to understand the great Saint's critiques, we must address the topic honestly and boldly; most importantly, we must contextualize his comments both in the time period in which they were made and within the genre of rhetoric which he was practicing. Let's begin with an examination of the Judaizing phenomenon, and then move onto Judaism as a religion and finally, Jews as a people.

Judaizing was the practice of a Baptized Orthodox Christian going to the synagogues to celebrate Jewish holidays, fasts, and feasts. It was such a popular distraction from Orthodoxy in 4th-century Antioch that it was addressed by several Saints who observed it. Each of the 8 homilies collected in St. John's <u>Adversus Judaeos</u> was delivered just before major Jewish celebrations began - when St. John knew the danger of Judaizing was greatest. In the first homily he explained that his primary motivation for keeping Christians out of the synagogue was that, due to the weak faith of those attending the ceremonies of both religions, there was a very real danger of apostasy.[70] Further, he wrote that Christians attending synagogue was a sure way to convince the Jews that their religion was the higher and holier one: "I exhort you to flee and shun their gatherings. The harm they bring to our weaker brothers is not slight; they offer no slight excuse to sustain to the folly of the Jews. For when they see that you, who worship the Christ Whom they crucified, are reverently following their rituals, how can they fail to think that the rites they have performed are the best and that our ceremonies are worthless? For after you worship and adore at our mysteries, you run to the very men who destroy our rites."[71]

It seems that some Christians were under the false impression that, due to the presence of the Old Testament

---

[70] *Adversus Judaeos: Chrysostom, John, Translator, Anonymous: 9798715867506: Amazon.com: Books.* (2023). Page 18.
[71] Ibid.

in the synagogues, the gatherings themselves must be holy; St. John corrected this error by adding "let no man venerate the synagogue because of the holy books; let him hate and avoid it because the Jews outrage and maltreat the holy ones, because they refuse to believe their words, because they accuse them of the ultimate impiety."[72]

St. John emphasized his message by consistently using powerful rhetoric: "Let me get the start on you by saying this now, so that each of you may win over his brother. Even if you must impose restraint, even if you must use force, even if you must treat him ill and obstinately, do everything to save him from the devil's snare and to free him from fellowship with those who slew Christ."[73] St. John repeated this explanation at the beginning of Homily 4, writing that "I took no part in polemics [in the past] because there was no one causing me concern. But today the Jews, who are more dangerous than any wolves, are bent on surrounding my sheep; so I must spar with them and fight with them so that no sheep of mine may fall victim to those wolves."[74] In his second homily on the topic, St. John observed that most of the Judaizing Christians were women; he not only scolded them for the weakness of their faith, but also their husbands for allowing them near the synagogue.[75] St. John even considered Judaizing to be such a threat to the Christian soul that, in Homily 6, he taught his flock that it was

---

[72] Ibid. Page 19.
[73] Ibid. Page 13.
[74] Ibid. Page 84.
[75] Ibid. Pages 54 and 55.

better to bring a Judaizing Christian back to sanity than to give alms to the poor and hungry.[76]

Each homily on the topic had a dual purpose: to prevent Christians from Judaizing and to bring back those who already were. The homilies, especially the fifth, were full of Biblical analysis to demonstrate that post-Christ Judaism was no longer the religion of God. This appeal seems to have been aimed at the members of his flock who were more educated on religion and theology; as mentioned above, for the common man, he vilified Jews as people and highlighted their constant immorality. Of course, these are not mutually exclusive sentiments and the synergy between them is an eternal testament to what happens to a people - and their method of worship - when they reject the Living God and He leaves them to their darkness.

For example, St. John wrote in Homily 1 that "Nothing is more miserable than those people who never failed to attack their own salvation. When there was need to observe the Law, they trampled it under foot. Now that the Law has ceased to bind, they obstinately strive to observe it. What could be more pitiable than those who provoke God not only by transgressing the Law but also by keeping it? On this account Stephen said: '*You stiff-necked and uncircumcised in heart, you always resist the Holy Spirit,*' not only by transgressing the Law but also by wishing to observe it at the wrong time."[77] He repeated this charge several more times, later clarifying that "By

---

[76] Ibid. Page 184.

[77] Ibid. Page 6, citing Acts 7:51.

fasting now, the Jews dishonor the law and trample underfoot God's commands because they are always doing everything contrary to his decrees. When God wished them to fast, they got fat and flabby. When God does not wish them to fast, they get obstinate and do fast; when He wished them to offer sacrifices, they rushed off to idols; when He does not wish them to celebrate the feast days, they are all eager to observe them."[78]

In short, St. John believed in Hieromartyr St. Stephen's observation that whatever God asked of the Jews, they did the opposite. When they had the Temple in Jerusalem, where God confined several of the Jewish rites, they worshiped demons instead; when the Temple was gone and they could not celebrate their rituals, the Jews suddenly wanted nothing more. It seems that St. John kept bringing attention to this problem in the hopes that his flock would not want to imitate such people or consider them role models of holiness.

He further accused the Jews of being "shameless and obstinate, ready to fight at all times against obvious facts"[79] and expressed that they "live for their bellies, they gape for the things of this world, their condition is not better than that of pigs or goats because of their wanton ways and excessive gluttony. They know but one thing: to fill their bellies and be drunk, to get all cut and bruised, to be hurt and wounded while fighting for their favorited charioteers."[80] Jews in <u>Adversus Judaeos</u> were frequently

---

[78] Ibid. Page 93.

[79] Ibid. Page 151.

[80] Ibid. Page 12.

compared to dangerous wild animals, criminals, drunkards, and worse; in his 2nd homily St. John even called the Jews "abominable and lawless and murderous and enemies of God."[81] Such phrases, metaphors, and accusations are often pointed to on the internet by those who wish to justify violence or harassment against Jews. I do not judge said people for being angry, nor for wishing to adopt the worldview of our Saints. What I propose, and will demonstrate throughout this book, is that St. John's homilies and the rhetoric they contain should be understood for what they were and ought never to serve as a justification for violence.

Like the Holy Hierarchs of Cappadocia, St. John excelled at the art of rhetoric which he'd studied and mastered in his youth. As such, we can look for and discover certain techniques these learned orators used which can add context and nuance to their choice of words. For example, two of the most popular rhetorical methods in antiquity were the *encomium* and the *psogos.* The former was meant to praise and flatter, often used to describe an Emperor or someone else with whom one trained in rhetoric wished to gain favor. The latter, by way of contrast, was meant to vilify and defame. As noted by Robert Wilken in his book <u>John Chrysostom and the Jews: Rhetoric and Reality in the Late 4th Century,</u> "Each employed the same list of topics - birth, environment, personal life, bodily characteristics, virtues (or vices), and actions - and both used exaggeration."[82]

---

[81]   Ibid. Page 42.

[82]   Robert Louis Wilken. (2004). *John Chrysostom and the Jews : rhetoric and reality in*

Having chosen which method to employ, the speaker would list everything they could think of to either glorify or attack the speech's subject.

Christian orators can be found employing both, and this context is important because it helps us understand the genre of literature that we're dealing with - which is otherwise very easy to take out of context. If one simply reads <u>Adversus Judaeos</u> and nothing else, it's easy to conclude that St. John had a special vendetta against Jews and that such language was otherwise never used. In reality, such language was relatively common for Christian Saints going after religious foes. For example, in one of his *Orations*, St. Gregory the Theologian said the following about the Arian bishop George of Cappadocia: "There was a monster from Cappadocia, born on our farthest confines, of low birth, and lower mind, whose blood was not perfectly free, but mongrel, as we know that of mules to be; at first he was a servant at the table of others for the price of a barley cake, having learned to say and do everything with an eye to his stomach, but in the end he sneaked into public life, filling its lowest offices, such as that of contractor for swine's flesh, the soldiers' rations. Then betraying this trust and proving himself a scoundrel for the sake of his stomach, he fled without any of his belongings, and after passing, as exiles do, from country to country and city to city, finally, in an evil hour for the Christian community, like one of the plagues of Egypt, he reached Alexandria. There, he ceased his wanderings, and he began his villainy. Good for nothing

the late 4th century. Wipf & Stock. Page 112.

92

in all other respects, without culture, without fluency in conversation, without even the form and pretense of reverence, his skill in working villainy and confusion was unequalled."[83]

To the modern eye or ear - and much like the words of St. John Chrysostom - such language can seem extreme, vicious, and merciless. In a sense, it is; but when we understand that we are reading a *psogos*, we realize that the speaker was not frothing at the mouth with anger but rather dispassionately using a specific kind of speech that was widespread and easy to recognize at the time. Metaphors for evil, comparisons with animals, and accusations of intoxication or stupidity were all common. They were employed with a specific purpose in mind and is akin to "persuasion by performance." Let us not mistake such things for being other than they are, or feed our own lower passions with what we don't understand.

It may surprise you to learn that despite everything St. John had to say about the Jews, he considered Judaizing Christians to be even worse than Jews themselves. This alone demonstrates that what may sound like "hateful" or "racist" language to modern ears was not spoken from any sort of racial animus. He made the point more than once in his 4th homily, in which he stated that Judaizing Christians "deserve a stronger condemnation than any Jew."[84] He later elaborated: "I blame the Jews for violating the Law. But I blame you much more for going along with the lawbreakers, not only those of you who run to the

---

[83] Ibid. Page 115.

[84] *Adversus Judaeos*. Page 90.

synagogues but also those of you who have the power to stop the Judaizers but are unwilling to do so. Do not say to me: 'What do I have in common with him? He is a stranger, and I do not know him.' I say to you that as long as he is a believer, as long as he shares with you in the same mysteries, as long as he comes to the same Church, he is more closely related to you than your own kinsmen and friends. Remember, it is not only those who commit robbery who pay the penalty for their crime; those, too, who could have stopped them but did not, pay the same penalty. Those guilty of impiety are punished, and so, too, are those who could have led them from godless ways but did not, because they were too timid or lazy to be willing to do so."[85] That St. John directed his angst and anger toward errant members of his flock, more so than even to the Jews themselves, should indicate that he was concerned with spiritual and not genetic problems.

It must also be noted that despite his vicious invective, at no point in St. John's most infamous homilies did he encourage violence against the Jews - nor are there any reports that after hearing the sermons delivered live, the Christians of 4th-century Antioch picked up their torches and stormed the local synagogue. It seems his flock understood his performance for what it was: a combination of Biblical exegesis, apologetics, and *psogos* meant to dazzle, entertain, horrify, amuse, and keep them in the Church with every verbal tool at the Saint's disposal. His intention was not to harm Jewish bodies, but rather to save Christian souls.

---

[85] Ibid. Page 106.

In the century following St. John Chrysostom's work on the topic, St. Cyril was elevated to the Patriarchal throne of Alexandria. St. Cyril debated with Jews, wrote apologetics against Judaism, and after a particular incident even exiled the Jewish community from his city. We will cover that incident shortly, but first we must examine the context of Jewish-Christian relations in that region at the time of St. Cyril's episcopacy.

Once Christianity came to power in the Roman Empire, relations between Christians and Jews began to deteriorate. After all, a new religion claiming to have a superior interpretation of Judaism's traditional Scriptures was bound to engender resentment. If the Jewish understanding of the Old Testament was true, then Christianity's could not be; the opposite was true as well. The Messiah had either arrived or He had not. The prophecies were either fulfilled or they were not. It was one or the other, without room for both theological systems to co-exist. Thus it should not come as a surprise that, as you'll learn more about in the chapter on *Imperial Laws*, Jews in the Christian Roman Empire often teamed up with other groups against the Church. As quoted from Victor Tcherikover in Wilken's book <u>Judaism and the Early Christian Mind</u>, "Jews became openly hostile to the new rulers…and proffered assistance to any group of persons or to any social or religious movement in opposition to the official Church. Thus they certainly supported the Arians, and the Fathers of the Church classed Jews and Arians together as the fiercest enemies of orthodoxy. The Jewry of the Roman Empire, though dispersed and lacking a national center in a state of its own, was nevertheless a considerable force, not to be overlooked by the Christian Church."[86]

In Alexandria, this conflict often manifested as Jewish support for Arian bishops over Orthodox ones: "The Arian bishop Gregory was appointed to take Athanasius' place. When the time came for his entrance into Alexandria, Catholics tried to prevent him from being consecrated, but Philagrius, the prefect of Alexandria, was an Arian supporter. According to Athanasius this prefect gathered together a large mob of heathens and Jews and set them against the Catholics with swords and clubs. They broke into the churches and desecrated holy objects, seized the virgins and monks, and burned the Scriptures."[87] By the time of St. Cyril's episcopal reign, animosity between the local Jews and Christians had already boiled to a fever pitch. Upon his ascension to the bishopric, St. Cyril quickly began using the power of his office to stamp out the influence of other religions; one of his first major actions was to shut down the churches, and confiscate all religious property, from those belonging to the Novatian schism.[88] A few years later, according to the historian Socrates, St. Cyril attempted to drive the Jews out of Alexandria on account of a violent disturbance.

As Socrates recorded, the conflict began with the fact that Jews often spent their Sundays dancing in public rather than studying their faith as they should have been.

[86] *Judaism and the Early Christian Mind: A Study of Cyril of Alexandria's Exegesis and Theology: Wilken, Robert L.: 9781592449125: Amazon.com: Books.* (2023). Page 46.

[87] Ibid. Pages 46 and 47.

[88] Ibid. Page 54.

This dancing often caused a great disturbance due to the size of the crowds that tended to form around the dancers, and Jews opposed all measures to keep said dancing under control. When the Alexandrian prefect Orestes published a new set of rules against the dancing, a follower of Cyril's by the name of Hierax apparently applauded the rules a little too forcefully. When the Jews noticed what Hierax was doing, they went into an uproar and Orestes - who had long disliked the growing power of the bishops in Alexandria - decided to make an example of Hierax by having him tortured. When St. Cyril caught wind of this, he threatened the Jews and told them to stop causing problems at once. According to Socrates, the Jews "determined to make a nightly attack on the Christians. They therefore sent persons into the streets to raise an outcry that the church named after Alexander was on fire. Thus many Christians on hearing this ran out, some from one direction and some from another, in great anxiety to save their church. The Jews immediately fell upon them and slew them…At daybreak the authors of this atrocity could not be concealed: and Cyril, accompanied by an immense crowd of people, going to their synagogues - for so they call their house of prayer - took them away from them, and drove the Jews out of the city, permitting the multitude to plunder their goods. Thus the Jews who had inhabited the city from the time of Alexander the Macedonian were expelled from it, stripped of all they possessed, and dispersed some in one direction and some in another."[89] Though some suspect

---

[89] Ibid. Pages 55-57.

that Socrates' account of the expulsion was exaggerated, due to the number of Jews in Alexandria and the degree to which the shipping industry there relied upon them, the story nonetheless demonstrates just how bad conflict between the two groups was during St. Cyril's episcopacy. Jews and Christians went after each other and the aggression was far from one-sided.

St. Cyril's opinion on Jews did not only rely on the incident described above nor on the regular debates between Jews and Christians in the area. He was intimately familiar with the Old Testament as well as Josephus and Jewish oral tradition. Thus when he spoke or wrote about Jews and Judaism, like St. John Chrysostom before him, he did so from a place of both religious literacy and personal encounter. As noted by Wilken, St. Cyril's "exegetical works are studded with hundreds of references to Jews and Judaism; Jews provide the occasion for discussion of theological, historical, and exegetical questions. Unwavering and intractable in his attack, Cyril never gets the Jews off his mind."[90]

St. Cyril's polemic against the Jews was often indistinguishable from what we find in other Fathers; his writings refer to them as the "most deranged of all men," "senseless," "blind," "uncomprehending," "demented," "foolish God haters," "unbelievers," "unrighteous" and "killers of the Lord."[91] To the dismay of would-be reformers of our faith, similar language can be found in the Lenten Triodion. All of this reflects theological

---

[90] Ibid. Pages 59 and 60.

[91] Ibid. Page 61.

dispute, the fear of Christians turning to Judaism or Jewish converts reverting to their old ways, or physical altercations that required the intervention of both communities' leadership to try and resolve. At the end of the day, the Saints were far more concerned with standing up for their faith than with being polite. They used invective to vilify their opponents - just as was done to them - and always remained primarily concerned with the well-being of their flocks. As I hope to demonstrate throughout this book, their approach to these difficult and nuanced topics was worlds away from how their words were later interpreted and what was justified by appealing to certain sentiments. But regardless of later distortions of their perspective, the fact remains that the Bible and Fathers did not seem to possess the notion that Judaism or Jews were above criticism or reproach.

Given the weight of Biblical and Patristic invective against Judaism and those who practice it, we are left to ask ourselves which is more likely: that God has revealed His thoughts on the topic through the Church and the Scriptures it produced, or that the Apostles and Saints were not just wrong - but consistently wrong, across time and space, all in exactly the same way. If we're being honest and humble, I think it's unlikely we'll conclude that we have deeper insight into this topic than the Church does. Do you submit to the voice of the Holy Spirit, as spoken through our Prophets and Saints?

Now that we've examined Christian rhetoric against Jews and Judaism, we will progress our study from that of *words* to that of *action* instead. Beyond the homilies, what concrete actions did Christians take on these topics when - and where - they had the power to do so? In order to discover the answers to these questions, which will form a necessary and rock-solid foundation for our comparison between Orthodoxy and Fascism, we must look to both the ecclesiastical and the civil realms of power. We will begin with an overview of Orthodox *Church Canons* which sought to regulate the interactions between the Christian and Jewish communities. Once we've completed that leg of the journey, we will conclude with a deep dive into *Imperial Laws*.

Orthodoxy And The Jews

Church Canons

As was demonstrated by our study of Sts. John Chrysostom and Cyril of Alexandria, the Church's primary contention with Jews was the danger they posed to Christians when both groups lived in close proximity. The Church's fear of Judaizing and other forms of apostasy were not limited to the laity, either; over and over, we find holy Canons regulating the conduct of clergy in regard to concelebration with both schismatic cults and non-Christians altogether. Before we examine these Canons and the official Interpretations that help explain them, I'd like to remind you that the Orthodox Church does not consider Canons to be *prescriptive*. They are not laws or blueprints upon which the Church is built that must be followed to the letter at all times; they are rather considered to be medicinal in nature and were written in response to particular issues.

Like medicine, which can become a poison when given to the wrong person or in the wrong dose, the application of Canons is up to the Bishops - and through them, the Priests under their obedience - to either follow strictly (*akrivia*) or flexibly (*ekonomia*). There are limits to the power exercised by Bishops in regard to Canons, but that discussion is outside the scope of our present study. Instead, I mention this only to communicate that discovering an ancient Canon does not mean that it is still followed, or even necessarily *should* be followed, today. We cannot look to said Canons as rules or fixed instructions given that many of them are not applied due to the weakness of the modern flock; in addition, "Each autocephalous Orthodox Church follows its own statute which applies the principles found in the ancient canons to the concrete requirements of Church life in specific parts of the world."[92]

According to St. John the Faster's 8th Canon, for example, the sin of masturbation is to be penanced with 40 days of excommunication; during those 40 days, the penitent may eat and drink nothing but bread and water, and must perform 100 prostrations each day.[93] Though strictness of this degree may be found in certain monasteries, such penances are not typically imposed by parish Priests. It seems most modern Bishops have determined that such harsh medicine would not be as spiritually fruitful for the flock as exercising this Canon with flexibility. There are many such examples I could use to highlight the point in question and which ought to help us pause and reflect if we hear someone insist that all Canons - regardless of context or the decisions of our Bishops - must be followed to the letter at all times.

That said, none of the above detracts from the power or purpose of our Canons; when and where we find the same topic addressed in a similar way over and over again, and especially if no more recent Canons have

[92] *Canons of the Holy Fathers.* (n.d.). Www.holytrinitymission.org. http://www.holytrinitymission.org/books/english/canons_fathers_rudder.htm#_Toc78634065
[93] Ibid.

addressed the topic in a different way, then I believe we can consider that theme to be the voice of the Holy Spirit in the Church.

Let us now examine how the Church has canonically dealt with Jews, Judaism, and Judaizing. Later, we can look back on this chapter and compare it to how these topics were treated in select 20th-century nationalist movements. We find the relevant and authoritative Canons in the Apostolic Canons, the Ecumenical Councils, and the Council of Laodicaea. They are listed in this chapter, along with their Interpretations where helpful, as recorded in <u>The Rudder</u>[94] compiled by St. Nikodemos of the Holy Mountain. We will begin with the relevant Apostolic Canons.

"Canon VII: If any Bishop, or Presbyter, or Deacon celebrate the holy day of Easter before the vernal equinox with the Jews, let him be deposed."[95]

"Canon LXV: If any Clergyman, or Layman, enter a synagogue of Jews, or of heretics, to pray, let him be both deposed and excommunicated." **Interpretation**: "The present Canon reckons it a great sin for a Christian to enter a synagogue of Jews or of heretics in order to pray. 'For what portion hath a believer with an infidel?' (II Cor. 6:15), according to the divine Apostle. For if the Jews themselves are violating the Law by going into their synagogues and offering sacrifices, in view of the fact that the offering of sacrifices anywhere outside of Jerusalem is

---

[94] *RUDDER OF THE ORTHODOX CATHOLIC CHURCH THE COMPILATION OF THE HOLY CANONS by SAINTS NICODEMUS and AGAPIUS.* (n.d.). http://saintjonah.org/articles/rudder.pdf
[95] Ibid. Page 73.

forbidden, according to the Law (as is attested by divine
St. Justin in his dialogue with Tryphon, and by
Sozomenus in his Ecclesiastical History, Book 5, ch. 21,
and by St. Chrysostom in his second discourse against the
Jews), how much more is not that Christian violating the
law who prays along with the crucifiers of Christ?
Moreover, it is also to be emphasized that any church of
heretics, or any religious meeting of theirs, ought not to
be honored or attended, but rather ought to be despised
and rejected, on the ground that they believe things
contrary to the beliefs of Orthodox Christians. Hence it is
that the present Canon ordains that if any clergyman or
layman enters the synagogue of the Jews or that of
heretics for the sake of prayer, the clergyman shall be
deposed from office and at the same time be
excommunicated on the ground that he has committed a
great sin, but as for the layman he is to be
excommunicated only, since, inasmuch as he is a layman,
he has sinned to a less degree than has the clergyman, in
so doing, and because as a layman he is not liable to
deposition and cannot therefore be deposed. Or, to speak
more correctly, as others interpret the matter, the
clergyman that enters a synagogue of Jews or heretics to
pray shall be deposed from office, while any layman that
does the same thing shall be excommunicated. Read also
the interpretation of Ap. C. VII and that of Ap. C. XLV."[96]

"Canon LXX: If any Bishop, or Presbyter, or Deacon, or
anyone at all who is on the list of clergymen, fasts
together with Jews, or celebrates a holiday together with

[96] Ibid. Page 177.

them, or accepts from them holiday gifts or favors, such as unleavened wafers, or anything of the like, let him be deposed from office. If a layman do likewise, however, let him be excommunicated." **Interpretation**: "In case anyone prays in company with excommunicated persons only, he is excommunicated; or if it be that he does so with persons that have been deposed only, he is deposed from office: how much more, then, is it not proper that any clergyman fasts in company with the Christ-killing Jews or celebrates any festival with them ought to be deposed from office, or if any layman do the same, he should be excommunicated? Hence it is that the present Apostolical Canon ordains that if any bishop or presbyter o[r] deacon, or anyone else at all that is on the list of clergymen, fasts along with the Jews or celebrates Easter (i.e., Passover) along with them, or any other festivals or holidays, or accepts any festival gifts from them, such as unleavened wafers (which they eat during the days of their Passover; and on every feast day of theirs and on the occasion of every sacrifice they offer unleavened wafers or something similar thereto), let him be deposed from office. If, on the other hand, any layman does likewise, let him be excommunicated. For even though the ones who accept such things and join in fasting or celebrating are not of the same mind as the Jews and do not entertain the same religious beliefs and views as the latter (for if they did, they ought not only to be deposed or excommunicated, as the case might be, but also to be consigned to anathema, according to c. XXIX of Laodicea), yet, as a matter of fact, they do afford occasion for scandal and give rise to a suspicion that they are actually honoring the ceremonies of the Jews, a thing which is alien to Orthodoxy. I omit mention of the fact that such persons are also polluting themselves by associating with Christ-killers. To them God says 'My soul hates your fasting and your cessation from work and your festivals.' See also the Interpretation of Ap. C. VII."[97]

"Canon LXXI: If any Christian conveys oil to a temple of heathen, or to a synagogue of Jews, in their festivals, or lights lamps for them, let him be excommunicated." **Interpretation**: "This Canon too, like the one above, excommunicates any Christian that should offer oil to a temple of heathen or of idolaters, or to a synagogue of Jews, when they are having their festivals, or should light their lamps. For in doing this he appears to believe that their false ceremonies and rites are true, and that their tainted mysteries are genuine. Read also the Interpretation of Ap. C. VII."[98]

We also find the following Canons on this topic from the 4th, 6th, and 7th Ecumenical Councils.

"Canon XIV [4th EC]: Inasmuch as Anagnosts and Psalts in some provinces have been permitted to marry, the holy Council has made it a rule that none of them shall be allowed to take a wife that is of a different faith. As for those who have already had children as a result of such a marriage, if they have already had their offspring baptized by heretics, let them bring them into the communion of the catholic Church. But if they have not

---

[97] Ibid. Pages 191 and 192.
[98] Ibid. Page 192.

baptized them, let them no longer have any right to baptize them with heretics, nor, indeed, even to contract a marriage with a heretic, or a Jew, or a Greek, unless they first promise and undertake to convert the person joined to the Orthodox Christian to the Orthodox faith. If, on the other hand, anyone transgresses this rule of the holy Council, let him be liable to a Canonical penalty."[99] The Interpretation and Concord reiterate that Orthodox Christians should not marry those outside the Faith, nor allow their children to do so.

"Canon XI [6th EC]: Let no one enrolled in the sacerdotal list, or any layman, eat the unleavened wafers manufactured by the Jews, or in any way become familiar with the Jews or call them in case of sickness, or take any medicines from them, or even bathe with them in public bathing beaches or bathhouses. If anyone should attempt to do this, in case he is a clergyman, let him be deposed from office; or in case he is a layman, let him be excommunicated."[100] **Interpretation**: "The present Canon commands that no person in holy orders and no layman may eat any unleavened wafers sent him by Jews, nor indeed be in any way friendly with Jews, nor when he finds himself ill may he call them and take their remedies, or even bathe with them in baths and bathing places. In case anyone should do this, or any of these things, if he is a clergyman, let him be deposed from office; but if he is a layman, let him be excommunicated. Read also Ap. Cc.

---

[99] Ibid. Page 324.

[100] Ibid. Page 366.

VII and LXX."[101]

"Canon VIII [7th EC]: Inasmuch as some persons who have been misled by their inferences from the religion of the Jews have seen fit to sneer at Christ our God, while pretending to be Christians, but secretly and clandestinely keeping the Sabbath and doing other Jewish acts, we decree that these persons shall not be admitted to communion, nor to prayer; nor to church, but shall be Jews openly in accordance with their religion; and that neither shall their children be baptized, nor shall they buy or acquire a slave. But if any one of them should be converted as a matter of sincere faith, and confess with all his heart, triumphantly repudiating their customs and affairs, with a view to censure and correction of others, we decree that he shall be accepted and his children shall be baptized, and that the latter shall be persuaded to hold themselves aloof from Jewish peculiarities. If, on the other hand, the case is not thus, they are not to be accepted under any other circumstances whatsoever."[102]

Interpretation: "The present Canon decrees that no one is to join in communion or prayer with, or even admit into church, those Jews who only hypocritically have become Christians and have joined the Orthodox faith, but secretly deny and mock Christ our God, while keeping the Sabbath and other Jewish customs (or, more explicitly, circumcising their sons, deeming anyone unclean that takes hold of a corpse or leper, and other similar vagaries); but, on the contrary, such persons are to

[101] Ibid. Page 502.
[102] Ibid. Page 502.

be Jews as they were before, and no one shall baptize their children nor let them buy a slave or acquire one by exchange or gift or in any other fashion. But if any Jew should be actually converted in good and guileless faith and with all his heart confess the orthodoxy of Christians, openly disparaging the religion of the Jews, in order that other Jews may be reproved and corrected, we ought to accept such a person, and baptize his children, ordering them persuasively to abstain from Jewish superstitions. But as for those who do not become converted in such a manner, we must not admit them on any account whatever."[103]

Concord: "In agreement with the present Canon ch. 44 of Title I of Book I of the Basilica decrees that if any Jew accused of any crime or owing a debt should on account thereof pretend that he has become willing to be a Christian, he is not to be accepted thus until he has paid his debt or has been acquitted of the crimes of which he has been accused. Likewise ch. 47 of the same Title and Book decrees that no Jew shall have a slave who is a Christian, nor circumcise anyone who is being catechized; neither shall any other heretic have a slave who is a Christian, but the moment he acquires him, the slave shall become free. Read also the Footnote to c. II of the 1st."[104] The footnote to this Canon relates the story of a Jewish man who "had himself baptized many times as a trade" and that "in this way he made a lot of money."[105] But

---

[103] Ibid. Pages 502 and 503.

[104] Ibid. Page 503.

[105] Ibid.

when he got to Constantinople and presented himself for
another Baptism, the font dried up completely. It was
refilled and dried up once again, miraculously declaring
to all present that he was presenting himself for Baptism
falsely.

Finally, we find the following Canon from the Council
of Laodicea.

"Canon XXIX: That Christians must not Judaize and
rest on Saturday but must work on this day preferring to
rest as Christians on Sunday if able to do so. If they be
found to be Judaists, let them be anathema with Christ."
Interpretation: "Saturday, as is denoted by the word itself,
was a holiday of the old Law which was devoted to rest
and on which the Jews cease from all labor, whereas
Sunday is a holiday devoted to rest by virtue of the new
grace of the Gospel. So Christians, being children of grace,
ought not to celebrate Saturday as a holiday and rest on
that day, and in this respect Judaize, as the present Canon
enjoins, but, on the contrary, they ought to work on
Saturday, and honoring Sunday on account of the Lord's
resurrection, they ought to take their rest on this day, if
they can do so. But if they appear to be Judaizing by such
idleness on Saturday, let them be anathema, or, in other
words, let them be separated from Christ both in the
present age and in the future. As concerning anathema,
see the preface to the Council of Gangra. Even St.
Augustine attests the fact that Christians ought to work
on Saturday, and not remain idle."[106]

The sentiments expressed in these Canons are

---

[106] Ibid. Page 628.

commonly repeated in others, but the latter are not included here due to the redundancy of listing them. Over and over the Church teaches not to accept unleavened bread from Jews or partake in their festivals. In many places the Canons related to Jews, Judaism and Judaizing are nearly identical to the Canons regulating Orthodox behavior in regard to other faiths in general. Jews, heretics, and pagans are often grouped together and dismissed in the same breath; <u>The Rudder</u> clearly states that it is a sin to concelebrate religious services with them, attend their religious buildings for the purpose of prayer, or aid them in celebrating their own services in any way.

In other ways, the question of Jews is handled differently than it is for other groups. For example, <u>The Rudder</u>'s rhetoric against Jews is often harsher than that against pagans on account of the Jews having killed Christ, whereas the heretics or Greek pagans did not commit this act along with them. Beyond that, Orthodox Christians are forbidden by Canon XI of the 6th Ecumenical Council from visiting Jewish doctors or receiving medicine from them. As we read in Canon VIII of the 7th Ecumenical Council, there was also an issue with false converts from Judaism who (despite pretending to confess Christ) secretly maintained their Jewish practices or had material motives for "converting." The Canon makes clear that only genuine converts - as indicated by a willingness to repudiate Jewish errors - are to receive Baptism and Communion. As you'll learn in the following chapter, several of these Canons overlap with *Imperial Laws* decreed by various Royal Saints.

As you can plainly discern, the Church's concern was primarily one of peaceful disengagement rather than open hostility; She commands the flock to separate from Jews as a people as well as from Judaism and its practices. This is the consistent witness of the Orthodox Church and is declared, with authority, by our Holy Canons. To accuse the Canons of discrimination, racism, anti-Semitism or other modern terms is to impose a paradigm upon the Church from which it does not operate and with which it has no concern. Rather than adapting itself to the zeitgeist of a particular age, the Church speaks with eternal wisdom as guided by God in order to protect, grow, and maintain the flock of Christ. May God grant that we allow our minds and our lives to be guided by the Church's teachings.

Having examined the authoritative Canons which address these topics, let us do the same for the *Imperial Laws* decreed by Royal Saints.

Orthodoxy and the Jews

Imperial Laws

Having studied the role of *Rhetoric* and *Church Canons* in regard to the traditional Christian view of Judaism, let us complete our analysis with an overview of Christian *Imperial Laws*. More specifically, we will examine laws implemented by Royal Saints on the topic of Judaism from the rise of Emperor St. Constantine in the early 4th century to the 6th-century reign of Emperor St. Justinian. A brief introduction to the topic is necessary, as it's not quite as simple as an Emperor's decree taking immediate effect throughout the Roman Empire.

To begin with, the vast majority of the relevant laws are contained within the Theodosian Code and the Justinian Corpus. At the time of their compilation, both of these legal codices were considered authoritative sources of Roman law. As the Justinian Corpus was put together centuries after the Theodosian Code, a fair amount of it reiterates, edits, or updates what was compiled by Emperor St. Theodosius II. One complicating factor in properly understanding these laws is that when they were brought together into these official compilations, the editors deleted the preambles which originally explained the context, circumstances, and situations which brought about the need for each law to be drafted. For example, we often read in these legal codes that the Emperors addressed particular individuals in response to a petition…but we do not know exactly what brought about said petitions in the first place. It is also not always clear whether the laws were meant to be published throughout the Empire or only implemented in the specific regions named by the Emperors in their responses.[107] As a general rule, a law decreed by an Emperor was considered to be permanent in the Empire unless specifically redacted by a future one. Hence we often find, when reading through the laws, references to the rulings of "the ancient emperors" and "the former laws."[108]

Further nuance is required because Emperors rarely ruled over both halves of the Empire at once, and after the First Novel of St. Theodosius II laws passed in the East were typically not promulgated in the West (or vice-versa). In that document, he ruled that laws enforced in one half of the Empire were not to be enforced in the other unless that second half also explicitly made the same decree. Thus we are presented with a situation in which the Eastern Roman Emperor, for example, may not even have been aware of laws passed by the Western Emperor.[109] The Theodosian Code itself was promulgated in both halves of the Empire within a year of its publication, however, and its most religious section (Book 16) was even accepted by the Church as an authoritative source of Canon Law.[110] The Justinian Corpus likewise

[107] Linder, A. (1987). *The Jews in Roman Imperial Legislation*. Wayne State University Press; Jerusalem. Pages 18-20.

[108] Ibid. Page 25.

[109] Ibid. Page 26.

[110] Ibid. Page 33.

became law for both halves of the Empire when it was published.

Roman Imperial Law used two terms to describe various religions, "religio" and "superstitio." Generally speaking, Emperors used "religio" when describing a religious group in a positive context and "superstitio" when speaking or writing with condescension. In the pagan Roman Empire "religio" typically (but not always) meant the Roman state religion, while "superstitio" meant anything foreign or hostile to it; once the Empire became Christian, "religio" meant Christianity and "superstitio" meant everything else. This distinction took awhile to emerge and set completely, as before 416 both terms were applied to Judaism whereas afterward Judaism was strictly "superstitio."[111] As noted by Amnon Linder in his book The Jews in Roman Imperial Legislation, "The laws relating to the Jews fall into three main groupings: (1) those concerning relations between the Jews and the government; (2) those concerning relations between Jews and non-Jews; (3) those concerning relations between Jews and other Jews."[112] We will focus on the first and second types, as the internal relations of the Jewish community are not relevant to our purpose.

Some of the relevant laws refer strictly to Jews or Judaism, but these categories were very often grouped with others such as Samaritans, pagans, and heretics. This distinction is important because it underlines a constant

---

[111] Ibid. Pages 56 and 57.
[112] Ibid. Page 67.

theme that the Saints were more concerned with religion than with race; were biology their priority instead of faith, Jews would always appear by themselves in the legal codes. Instead, the majority of all laws that mentioned Jews between 408 and 545 grouped them together with pagans and heretics; Linder explained that this "indicates a fundamental change in the Jewish policy of the Imperial government towards the beginning of the fifth century, and was bound to affect the legal status of the Jews during that period. Throughout the greater part of the fourth century the Jews still benefitted from the legal status Tertullian defined as 'religio licita,' a religion recognized and protected by the State. By the end of that century, however, the State tended to assimilate them into other religions and sects prohibited, or severely restricted, by law, and to apply to the Jews interdictions and restrictions formerly applied against pagans and heretics only."[113]

Furthermore, Jews who converted to Christianity were not referred to, in Imperial Law, with the term "Jew;" the word only, and specifically, referred to non-Christians and never to a Christian of Jewish ethnicity. For this and other reasons, false conversions from Judaism to Christianity appear to have been relatively common and as much a cause of concern for the Roman Empire as it was for the Orthodox Church as expressed via the Canons. More on that shortly.

As I sat down to examine the role of Jews and Judaism in Christian Imperial Law, I hoped to find a consistent

---

[113] Ibid. Pages 62 and 63.

thread of legal decrees which demonstrated - in an unbroken chain, passed down from generation to generation - the mind of the Church expressed clearly and firmly. If that turned out to be the case, so I thought, then the information I discovered could provide an eternal witness to the Holy Spirit's guidance on this topic. As you'll learn in just a moment, there is some element of accuracy to this notion; despite occasional deviations and exceptions, certain aspects of the Christian Roman legal codes tended to communicate similar views over the centuries.

In other ways, different Royal Saints had different views at different times. Often they agreed with each other and accepted the rulings of their predecessors. Other times they did not, and changed course in light of a new context. Sometimes the same Saint would change his mind on a given topic; for example, Emperor St. Theodosius II ruled in 417 that Jews could inherit Christian slaves on the condition that said Jews did not circumcise or otherwise try to convert them. A few years later, in 423, he updated his previous ruling and forbade Jews from owning Christian slaves altogether. And despite such laws, there is also evidence that the Empire often had trouble enforcing them. This phenomenon is demonstrated simply by the number of times that laws regarding Jews and Christian slaves had to be passed by different Emperors, including a law issued by Emperor St. Justinian in 534 which implied that Jews in Africa still owned Christian slaves despite its having already been illegal for a century.[114]

The lack of Imperial persecution toward Jews came as a major surprise to me. I dove into the legal codes expecting to find harsh and unfair treatment of Jews based on rumors I've heard throughout my life…and yet, when I actually read what the Saints said, the truth was almost always the opposite. It's true that our Royal Saints spoke ill of Judaism and the people who practiced it, regularly referring to Jews with terms like "nefarious," "impious" or "sacrilegious" and to Judaism itself as a "disease," "contagion," "perversity," "superstition,""insanity," "madness" and "plague."[115] But when it came to practical action, Christian Roman Emperors universally forbade violence against law-abiding Jews and the synagogues in which they gathered. Based on comments from the Emperors themselves, it appears that Christian fanatics often took justice into their own hands and attacked people of other faiths along with their houses of worship.

Thus we find laws protecting synagogues beginning with Emperor St. Theodosius I, through Emperors Honorius and Arcadius, and down to Emperor St. Theodosius II and beyond.[116] Again we see the phenomenon of Emperors having to issue the same law many times due to its not being properly enforced, as when St. Theodosius II warned Christians in 423 not to injure "peaceful Jews and pagans who are not attempting

---

[114] Ibid. Page 83.

[115] Ibid. Page 60.

[116] Ibid. Page 74.

anything seditious or unlawful."[117] It should be noted that despite the Royal Saints' protection of existing synagogues, they also forbade Jews from building new ones.[118]

We find the only exception to the general protection of synagogues in a law from St. Justinian, issued in 535, which placed severe limitations on the activities of Jews, heretics and pagans in Africa. The law was a response from the Emperor to a request from that year's Council of Carthage asking the government for "a more militant policy against the Arians."[119] In a severe and sweeping measure, St. Justinian ordered that all Churches and Church vessels be immediately confiscated from heretics and returned to the Orthodox Church. He further reiterated the warning against Jewish ownership of Christian slaves, ordered that all synagogues be converted into Churches, and forbade all non-Orthodox in the region from either holding public office or practicing their religions at all - "for it is perfectly absurd to permit impious men to deal with sacred matters." As to heretics in government, St. Justinian explained that they "shall not be allowed to administer any public office neither shall they serve in any public administration out of any ambition, lest the heretics be seen to have been placed over the Orthodox to rule them, when it is enough for them that they stay alive, certainly they shall not demand any authority for themselves and afflict through

---

[117] Ibid. Page 65.
[118] Ibid. Page 74.
[119] Ibid. Page 381.

it suffering on Orthodox people and on the most righteous worshippers of God Almighty."[120]

It appears that some of the harsher rulings in this law may have contributed to local riots in the following year - and they may have even been repealed as a result, as they were not included in future summaries of Roman law. It is worth mentioning that this was not the first time Jews had been banned from all but the most basic government jobs; St. Theodosius II, along with Emperor Valentinian III, had already banned Jews, Samaritans, pagans, and heretics from such roles just under a century earlier.[121]

While Jews were universally protected from harassment or violence conducted by those falsely claiming to act "under the cover of venerable Christianity,"[122] Royal Saints also insisted that Jews could not mock or harm the Orthodox Faith. For example, a law issued by Emperor St. Theodosius II in 408 dealt with a Jewish tradition at the time in which an effigy of Haman was crucified and burned during the celebration of Purim. This was taken to be a mockery of Christ's execution, and led to at least one violent riot. Thus, St. Theodosius II outlawed the practice: "The governors of the provinces shall prohibit the Jews from setting fire to Aman in memory of his past punishment, in a certain ceremony of their festival, and from burning with sacrilegious intent a form made to resemble the saint cross in contempt of the Christian faith, lest they mingle

---

[120] Ibid. Page 386.
[121] Ibid. Page 325.
[122] Ibid. Page 86.

the sign of our faith with their jests, and they shall restrain their rites from ridiculing the Christian Law, for they are bound to lose what had been permitted them till now unless they abstain from those matters which are forbidden."[123]

Such bans on non-Orthodox vitriol against Christians was not, however, limited to Jews; a few months after the Purim ruling, St. Theodosius II issued another law (this time with Honorius) cracking down on anti-Christian violence in Africa. More specifically, riots and harassment by Jews and Donatists had reached such intensity that clergy across the region were being assaulted. That, together with constant interruption of Orthodox services, led the Emperors to order that "a just and retributive chastisement be inflicted upon those who shall attempt to do anything that is contrary and adverse to the Catholic sect."[124] A similar law, passed the following year, confirms the cooperation of Jews with schismatics and heretics in trying to cause harm to the Orthodox Church.[125]

One of the reasons that our Royal Saints forbade Jews from owning Christian slaves or building new synagogues was to prevent Jews from converting Christians to Judaism. We find this particularly explicit statement in 409, in a law issued by Emperors Honorius and St. Theodosius the II: "For it is certain, that whatever differs from the faith of the Christians is contrary to

---

[123] Ibid. Pages 236 and 237.
[124] Ibid. Page 240.
[125] Ibid. Page 244.

Christian Law. Some people, moreover, oblivious of their life and their position, dare to transgress the Law to such an extent, that they force some to cease being Christian and adopt the abominable and vile name of the Jews. Although those that have committed this crime shall be legally condemned under the laws of the ancient emperors, still it does not bother us to admonish repeatedly, that those imbued in the Christian mysteries shall not be forced to adopt the Jewish perversity, which is alien to the Roman Empire, and abjure Christianity."[126] Though Arian and not a Saint, Emperor Constantius II was so concerned about Christians leaving the faith for Judaism that he even ordered the confiscation of all a proselyte's property.[127]

Thus we see that as with the Canons of the Holy Orthodox Church, the religious laws of the Christian Roman Empire were mainly concerned with the danger of Christian apostasy. These laws, like the Canons, were designed to help keep Christians within the bounds of the Christian faith. The limitations placed on other religions - and the rhetoric that went along with them - seem to have existed largely in service of that goal.

A 383 law issued by Emperors Gratian, Valentinian II and St. Theodosius laid heavy penalties on the heads of converts from Christianity to other religions. Under this law, Christians who converted away from the true Faith lost the right to bequeath their property to their families in a will. Converts to Judaism and Manichaeanism were

[126] Ibid. Page 258.
[127] Ibid. Page 153.

to be given harsh (but unspecified) penalties along with whoever was responsible for persuading the Christian to join those faiths instead of remaining with the Church. This law appears to have been aimed at both those who actually converted away from Christianity and those who remained formally Christian but participated in the services of other faiths.[128] Another Imperial measure, issued in 388 and with a clear parallel to the Church's Canons, forbade marriage between Christians and Jews on pain of the same civil penalties typically imposed for adultery. By promulgating this law, intended to maintain the purity of the Christian Faith, Emperors added State punishment to what was already, by then, an excommunicable offense to the Church.

The harshest law from an Emperor Saint in this regard is also the first ever issued on the topic. Not only was it an Imperial priority to protect Christians from being led astray, but Jewish converts to Christianity must have been particularly vulnerable; in 329 Emperor St. Constantine issued the following decree: "We want the Jews, their principals and their patriarchs informed, that if anyone - once this law has been given - dare attack by stoning or other kind of fury one escaping from their deadly sect and raising his eyes to God's cult, which as we have learned is being done now, he shall be delivered immediately to the flames and burnt with all his associates. But if one of the people shall approach their nefarious sect and join himself to their conventicles, he

---

[128] Ibid. Page 169.

shall suffer with them the deserved punishments."[129] He reiterated this law in 335: "If one of the Jews shall unlock for himself the door of eternal life, shall bind himself to the holy cults and choose to be Christian, he shall not suffer ought of harassment or molestation in the hands of the Jews."[130]

From these laws, and the Saint's commentary, we can discern some very illuminating information. Firstly, we learn that Jews harassed their own converts to Christianity with such malice and regularity that the Emperor himself was forced to intervene. Secondly, we can see a plain example of the aforementioned phenomenon that the Saint's view of Jews was more religious than biological; by embracing Christianity, a Jew was no longer considered to be a part of "the Jews" but rather of Christianity ("God's cult"). None of the Royal Saints I've studied deviated from this perspective.

We find another drastic ruling issued by Emperors Valentinian III and St. Theodosius II in 425. In order to reaffirm the power of Christians in the Empire while minimizing the influence of the non-Orthodox, a number of laws were promulgated which undid anti-Christian laws passed by the false emperor Johannes while also kicking the non-Orthodox out of major cities. In addition, Jews and pagans were banned from practicing law or serving in the Imperial administration on the grounds that they were likely to misuse their power over

---

[129] Ibid. Pages 126 and 127.
[130] Ibid. Page 146.

Christians.[131] As with similar cases, the justification for these laws was the well-being of Christians and to prevent them from being exposed to noxious spiritual influence: "We order that the Manichaeans, all the heretics or schismatics and astrologers, and every sect hostile to the Catholics must be expelled from the very sight of the various cities, so that they shall not be defiled even by the contagious presence of the criminous. We also deny to the Jews, and to the pagans, the right to practice law and to serve in the State service; we do not wish people of the Christian Law to serve them, lest they substitute, because of this mastery, the venerable religion by a sect."[132]

The following section of the law grants schismatics in particular a short period of time to repent from their errors and rejoin the Church: "We grant them a delay of twenty days, beginning with the day they are warned. Unless they return to the communion's unity within this period, they shall be expelled to the hundredth milestone, and waste away in the wilderness they have chosen."[133]

Of all the Emperor Saints in our study, St. Justinian seems to have been most familiar with Jewish teaching and, subsequently, we find the outlawing of several Jewish traditions in his final ruling on the topic. In that ruling, issued in 553, the Saint forbade the teachings of the Sadducees who, unlike the Pharisees, denied the resurrection of the dead and other ancient Jewish

---

[131] Ibid. Page 306.

[132] Ibid. Page 308.

[133] Ibid. Page 309.

teachings fulfilled in Christianity. Further, he demanded that Jews use the Septuagint or a similar translation whenever conducting their services in Greek due to the fact that many post-Apostolic translations of the Old Testament intentionally edited the wording of prophecies so that Christ appeared not to have fulfilled them. Finally, he completely banned the use of the Mishnah - the collection of Pharisaic oral traditions which would later be codified into the Talmud - "which he condemned, in accord with the well-known patristic usage, as an entirely human tradition, devoid of any Divine inspiration, origin or authority, and contrary to Christian faith."[134] Breaking these laws brought down penalties including the confiscation of property, exile, or corporal punishment. Earlier, in 531, St. Justinian forbade Jews and pagans from testifying against Orthodox Christians in court.[135]

The preeminence of Orthodox Christianity - especially given its emphasis on mercy and forgiveness - naturally led to false conversions in order to escape from material punishments and find cover under the Church's loving wings. This seems to have been a relatively constant theme for Jews, toward whom several related laws were promulgated. For example, a 397 law issued by Emperors Arcadius and Honorius insisted that Jews could not join the Church to avoid either paying debts or being punished by the courts in criminal proceedings. Thus, Jewish converts were to be refused reception in the Church until all their debts were paid off and/or the

---

[134] Ibid. Page 404.
[135] Ibid. Page 371.

individuals in question were cleared by the State of criminal charges. In his commentary on this law, Linder added: "It seems that the Church cooperated with the State in the application of the present law, for the ninth century text of the obligatory oath taken by Jewish converts to Christianity still included the declaration that the convert's acts were motivated by love for Christianity and not by fear from criminal charges preferred against him or for similar reasons."[136]

A few decades later, in 416, a related law was passed by Emperors Honorius and St. Theodosius II to follow up on the first ruling: whereas converting from Christianity to Judaism was typically punished (and prevented whenever possible), Jews who had converted under false pretenses were allowed to return to Judaism unharmed. The Emperors justified this decision with the belief that letting false converts return to their original faith was "of greater benefit to Christianity" than allowing them to stay.[137] Thus we can see the spiritual tightrope walked by these ancient Saints; the Emperors promoted the superiority of the Orthodox Church, while their laws and the Church's Canons made sure to clamp down on the false conversions that followed from the benefits of being Orthodox. This balance seems to have required constant upkeep and maintenance as evidenced by the regular reissuing of previous Laws and Canons.

In conclusion, Orthodox Royal Saints extended legal protection to law-abiding Jews while using the power of

---

[136] Ibid. Page 199.

[137] Ibid. Page 276.

the Empire to prevent Jews from harming Christians, converting Christians to Judaism, or spreading Judaism throughout the Empire in general. This sentiment is perhaps best exemplified in the following ruling from Emperors Honorius and St. Theodosius II in 420: "No one shall be destroyed for being a Jew, though innocent of crime, nor shall any religion whatsoever execute him while he is exposed to contumely. Their synagogues and habitations shall not be burnt up indiscriminately, nor wrongfully damaged without any reason. For even if someone is entangled by his crimes, the vigour of the courts and the protection of public law appear to have been instituted in our midst for this very reason, that no one shall have the power to permit himself to take vengeance. But, just as we wish to provide in this law for all the Jews, we order that this warning too should be given, lest the Jews grow perchance insolent, and elated by their security commit something rash against the rever[e]nce of the Christian cult."[138]

The Royal Saints' main spiritual priority was the growth and maintenance of Christianity; their main concern was losing members of the flock. Even if the laws were not always entirely consistent, the perspective and reasoning behind them fit under the same umbrella beneath which we find the Canons. And hence we see exemplified the Orthodox Symphonic model: Church and State working hand-in-hand to shepherd souls toward Christ. May God grant all who hold power in this world the wisdom and discernment to do likewise.

---

[138] Ibid. Page 285.

Fascism

"All nationalism is either redemptive or destructive, according to whether or not it is animated by Christian faith."
- Fr. Dumitru Staniloae

Italy

"It was necessary to destroy forever all the nerve centers of disorder."[139] *- Benito Mussolini*

Julius Evola wrote in Fascism Viewed From The Right that "The fundamental significance that Fascism gradually assumed as it defined itself and triumphed is, from our point of view, that of a reaction, stemming from the forces of the returning veterans and nationalists, in response to a crisis that was essentially a crisis of of the very idea of the state, of authority and of centralized power in Italy. In the period that immediately followed the First World War, Italy presented itself as a secular state, in which the influence of Freemasonry was considerable, with a weak and mediocre liberal democratic government and a monarchy without real power; in other words, constitutional and parliamentary, a state that on the whole lacked a 'myth' in the positive sense, that is, a superior animating and formative idea that could have made of it something more than a mere structure of public administration."[140]

Alexander Stille, in his book Benevolence And Betrayal, described post-War Italy in even more dire terms: "At war's end the country fell into a deep

---

[139] Mussolini, B. (2012). *My Autobiography*. Courier Corporation. Page 123.

[140] Evola, J., & Morgan, J. B. (2013). *Fascism viewed from the Right*. London Arktos Media Ltd. Page 30.

economic crisis, marked by inflation and devaluation of the lira. As the cost of living rose in 1919, riots broke out and people looted food shops. When the government failed to deliver the land reforms it had promised after Caporetto [Italy's worst defeat in the War], peasants occupied the fields. Workers and trade unions, which had never supported the war effort, began an aggressive campaign of strikes. They looked with excitement to the Bolshevik Revolution that had taken place in Russia and talked about duplicating it in Italy…Not only did the left terrify the middle classes, it went out of its way to alienate the millions of soldiers returning from the front. Along with excoriating the war effort, the socialists actually prevented war veterans from joining their party. Members of the radical left insulted and jeered at returning soldiers. Unionized streetcar drivers in some instances stopped their vehicles if a man in uniform came on board."[141]

Evola added to his previous observation that "It became increasingly obvious that a nation in these conditions was in no position to confront the serious problems imposed by the forces set in motion by the war and the post-war period, nor to combat the revolutionary social lures diffused in the masses and the proletariat by Leftist activists. Thus, the merit of Fascism was, above all, to have revived in Italy the idea of the state and to have created the basis for an active government, by affirming

---

[141] Stille, A. (2003). *Benevolence and betrayal : five Italian Jewish families under fascism.* Picador. Page 35.

the pure principle of authority and political sovereignty."[142] As we begin our study of Mussolini's Italy, including an examination of those pre- and post-war forces against which the Fascists fought, I believe it will become clear that Evola's perception of the situation was both accurate and lucidly expressed.

Mussolini began the fifth chapter of his autobiography with his own description of post-WWI Italy: "The flame of war flickered and went out. But the years 1919 and 1920 that immediately followed the end of the war seemed to me the darkest and most painful periods of Italian life. Dark thunderclouds hung above our unity. The progress of Italy's unification was threatened. I watched the gathering storm…Already in January, 1919, the Socialists, slightly checked during the war, began, the moment the ink was drying on the armistice, their work of rebellion and blackmail."[143]

He placed the blame for this scenario on "Politicians and philosophers, profiteers and losers - for at least many had lost their illusions - sharks trying to save themselves; promoters of the war trying to be pardoned; demagogues seeking popularity; spies and instigators of trouble waiting for the price of their treason; agents paid by foreign money, in a few months, threw the nation into an awful spiritual crisis. I saw before me with awe the gathering dusk of our end as a nation and a people."[144]

---

[142] Evola. Page 30.

[143] Mussolini. Pages 46 and 47.

[144] Ibid. Page 48.

The Fascist movement began in earnest early in 1919. As Mussolini told the story: "On the twenty-third of March, 1919, I laid down the fundamental basis, at Milan, of the Italian *fasci di combattimento* - the fighting Fascist program...The meeting was of a purely political character. I had advertised in the *Popolo d'Italia* that it would have for its object the foundation of a new movement and the establishment of a program and of methods of action for the success of the battle I was intending to fight against the forces dissolving victory and the nation."[145] He further clarified that this meeting "was of anti-socialist character, and as a political aspiration, it was hoped a new Italy would be created that would know how to give value to the victory and to fight with all its strength against treason and corruption, against decay within and intrigue and avarice from without."[146]

Fascist violence did not begin until Socialists and their agents had taken over significant portions of Italy. Mussolini wrote that in 1920, "there was adopted among the railway employees the systematic practice of preventing the movement of trains carrying soldiers, carabinieri or policemen. Sometimes a similar policy extended also to the clergy. Against this inconceivable abuse of power, I alone protested. The Italian people were suffering passively from a stupid conception of their opportunities and from blindness which closed their eyes to their own power and pride. Those who dared to resist

---

[145] Ibid. Page 52.
[146] Ibid. Page 54.

and were critical or the bureaucracy or of government policy were persecuted by the government itself…The growing exaltation of the bewitched masses and the incredible weakness of the government culminated at the beginning of September with the occupation of the factories on the part of the metal workers. The occupation of the factories was to be an example of Bolshevism in action. The doctrine to be illustrated was the taking possession of the means of production. The workmen, with their childish understanding, and much more the chiefs who were betraying them - and well aware of their treachery as they did so - pretended that they were able to administer directly, without an order from any one planned beforehand, all the workshops, all the processes, and even the sales of the output. In truth, though it is not commonly realized, they did nothing but make some side arms, such as daggers and swords. They lost not less than twenty-one days in forced leisure and childish manifestations of hatred and impotence.

The occupation once begun, the managers, the owners, and the employees of the establishments were sequestered by the workmen. The trade-marks and factory signs were taken away, while upon the roofs and the doors of the factories the red banners with the sickle and hammer, symbol of the soviets, are hoisted with cheers. In every establishment a committee was formed subject to a socialist-communist set of by-laws. Telephones were used to threaten all who were keeping out of the movement and who, like us of the *Popolo D'Italia*, were setting out to war against this grotesque soviet society. The seizure of the factories was accompanied by the most ferocious acts…there were dead at Monfalcone, there were dead in Milan and there were dead in other towns on the peninsula."[147]

Everywhere the Bolsheviks gained power over towns and factories, they set up pseudo-courts and sentenced political enemies to death. They took over factory after factory, city after city, with no meaningful opposition from the Italian government. It is against that backdrop that Mussolini and the Fascists, having exhausted peaceful means of solving the problem, began to take up arms in defense of Italy. Communists and Fascists began to battle on the streets, often leading to fatalities on both sides. Mussolini was under no illusion about what he and his movement were doing: "The only straight road was to beat the violent forces of evil on the very ground they had chosen…it was necessary to establish the order and discipline wanted by the masses, but impossible to obtain them through milk-and-water propaganda and through words, words and more words - parliamentary and journalistic sham battles."[148] He ordered his fighting units to respond with force wherever left-wing chaos or violence reared its head.

As time went on, more and more Italians began to support Fascism both ideologically and even electorally: "In November, 1919, I had not succeeded in gaining more than 4,000 votes. In 1921 I was at the head of the list with

---

[147] Ibid. Pages 83, 86 and 87.
[148] Ibid. Page 91.

178,000 votes."[149] With his new parliamentary powers and increasing ability to organize the Fascists, Mussolini turned his movement into the Fascist National Party. His goal was to provide Italy with a meaningful government despite the strikes and opposition he faced.

After 3 years of struggle against both leftist revolutionaries and anti-Fascist conservatives, Mussolini and his black-shirted fighting squads marched on Rome. Surveying the situation, King Victor Emmanuel III sent for Mussolini to join him in the royal palace so they could discuss the future government of Italy. In late October of 1922, the King formally tasked Mussolini with the organization of government - and proclaimed him the new Head of State.

---

[149]   Ibid. Page 104.

Mussolini And The Church

"We are a Catholic nation, not only because the vast majority of our people is Catholic, but because Catholicism is inseparable from our history."[150] *- Benito Mussolini*

For each of the nationalists analyzed in our study, we will examine their approach to Christianity along two lines. Firstly, we will do our best to determine their personal beliefs; their theology, Christology, ecclesiology, etc., will be evaluated according to the best available data along with what interpretation of said data appears to make the most sense. Then, we will dissect their movements' interactions and engagement with the predominant forms of Christianity in their countries. For example, Codreanu will be investigated in terms of his local Orthodox Church; Hitler, with Protestants and Catholics; Mussolini, with Roman Catholicism and the Vatican that played such a prominent role in the history of Italy. Accordingly, we will begin with Mussolini's private beliefs.

Early in his autobiography, Mussolini described himself as "deeply a Catholic;"[151] the remainder of the book, however, seems to indicate that his Catholicism ended where his Fascism began. One of the Italian political parties during his youth, the Popular Party

---

[150] Coppa, F. J. (1999). *Controversial concordats : the Vatican's relation with Napoleon, Mussolini, and Hitler.* Catholic University Of America Press. Page 89.
[151] Mussolini, B. (2012). *My Autobiography.* Courier Corporation. Page 25.

(which he stated was "led by the priests"[152]), opposed
Mussolini and his movement. As a result of their trying to
control and censor his influence, he declared that "Two
religions are today contending with each other for the
sway over the world - the black and the red. From two
vaticans to-day depart encyclical letters - from that of
Rome and from that of Moscow. We declare ourselves the
heretics of these two expressions."[153] It must be noted that
by "Moscow" he was referring to Bolshevism and not to
Orthodox Christianity. Regardless, one is left to wonder
what precisely Roman Catholicism meant to Mussolini if
he considered himself a heretic. Later in his book, he
wrote that "Absolute monarchy has been and can never
return, any more than blind acceptance of ecclesiastical
authority."[154] It appears from several such comments in
his autobiography that Mussolini's main issue with
Catholicism was his perception that the institution sought
control over himself and others.

At the same time, he clearly recognized the importance
of Catholicism in terms of Italian identity and unity: "The
Fascist State is not indifferent to the fact of religion in
general, or to that particular and positive faith which is
Italian Catholicism. The State professes no theology, but a
morality, and in the Fascist State religion is considered as
one of the deepest manifestations of the spirit of man;
thus it is not only respected but defended and protected.
The Fascist State has never tried to create its own God, as

---

[152] Ibid. Page 73.
[153] Ibid. Page 74.
[154] Ibid. Page 235.

at one moment Robespierre and the wildest extremists of the Convention tried to do; nor does it vainly seek to obliterate religion from the hearts of men as does Bolshevism. Fascism respects the God of the ascetics, the saints and heroes, and equally, God as He is perceived and worshipped by simple people."[155]

He claimed to live a relatively ascetic life and described himself as being uninterested in money, gambling, smoking, drinking, or luxurious meals.[156] However, Mussolini never once mentioned going to Mass or confessing to a priest in his autobiography. It's possible that he simply never did these things, giving lip service to Christianity because he knew it was important to most Italians. It's also possible that doing them was such a normal and routine part of Italian life that he engaged in them constantly but didn't think they were worth mentioning. In either case, nowhere in his life story do we find reflections on Christ, theology, or repentance. Mussolini's love life, it should also be noted, did not reflect Christian teachings on chastity.

Further, he described himself as a free thinker who rebelled against ideas that came from outside of his own mind and experience: "I do not believe in the influence which comes from perusing the books about the lives and characters of men. For myself, I have used only one big book. For myself, I have had only one great teacher. The book is life - lived. The teacher is day-by-day experience. The reality of experience is far more eloquent than all the

---

[155] Ibid. Page 239.
[156] Ibid. Page 152.

theories and philosophies on all the tongues and on all the shelves."[157] Further, his point of view appears to necessitate a rejection of Divine Revelation and its expression through the Ecumenical Councils. Though his epistemology did not extend beyond his experience, it's unclear whether he felt cognitive dissonance between that reality and his professed religious sentiment.

Thus it seems that while Catholicism was something important to him, at least in theory or as a part of his Italian identity, Mussolini nonetheless did not appear to consider himself subject to its ideas when it came to perceived limitations on his own beliefs or behavior. That said - and this will be a constant theme throughout Fascism Viewed From The Cross - the ultimate litmus test for a nationalist's faith boils down to choices made when religion and ideology come into conflict. When and where you must choose between them, which side tends to win out? In that vein, we will now examine the conflicts between the Fascist State and Roman Catholicism.

For the sake of context, a brief introduction is necessary. At the time of Mussolini's ascent to power, the Vatican was in a precarious position: from 754 to 1870 it had ruled the region - split up into the Papal States - but during the *Risorgimento*, the Kingdom of Italy was united under the King of Piedmont-Sardinia instead. The House of Savoy, which produced that royal line, overthrew the Papal States and declared itself the rightful ruler of Italy. The Vatican refused to recognize this shift in power, and for 60 years the Popes had declared themselves "prisoners

---

[157] Ibid. Pages 18 and 19.

in the Vatican"[158] rather than acknowledge their loss of Rome to the Piedmont royalty. "The Roman Question," as this dilemma was called, had no end in sight when the Fascist party formed. Mussolini's reign provided the Vatican with a new opportunity, and the Lateran Accords (which you will read about shortly) put an end to the question once and for all.

Despite the issues Mussolini had with Roman Catholicism, he spent an enormous amount of time and energy learning to work with its leadership. For example, he always supported those clergy who he believed were doing their duty: "I made a provision favoring the clergy also; it was the question of a just and necessary disposition. This would have been inconceivable in the days of Masonic demagogy and social democracy, which was dominated by a superficial and wrathful anti-clericalism. Our clergy number about 60,000 in Italy. They are extraneous to the controversy, which I may call historical, between the State and Church."[159]

The Vatican's working together with Fascists is often criticized by those unfamiliar with the history of Church-State relations in general, and more specifically with how the Vatican has traditionally dealt with secular leaders. Opponents of such cooperation may look at various agreements as being indicative of Vatican approval towards that particular State's government, leader and moral code. Such people suggest, for example, that the

[158] *Prisoner in the Vatican.* (2023, February 28). Wikipedia. https://en.wikipedia.org/wiki/Prisoner_in_the_Vatican
[159] Mussolini. Page 214.

agreement (called a Concordat in the Roman Catholic world) between Pope Pius XI and Benito Mussolini is proof that the Vatican supported the Fascist movement. In order to arrive at a more accurate understanding, we must untangle the truth of such Concordats by examining their purpose and historical usage. With that context in place, we will move on to specific policies outlined in this particular Concordat.

Frank Coppa wrote in his book <u>Controversial Concordats</u> that Pius XI, who was Pope from 1922 to 1939, "appreciated the advantages of adjusting the Church's relations with the civil authorities by means of concordats in which the Church surrendered incidentals to preserve essentials. Approval of such agreements represented a compromise on the part of the Church with governments that did not fully recognize its claims to independence. Pius VII (1800-1823), in concluding a concordat with Napoleon, followed Rome's policy of dealing with *de facto* governments without presuming to judge their moral worth. From the fall of Napoleon's empire to the proclamation of Italian unity in 1861, the Church signed some thirty such accords. While Leo XIII (1878-1903) and Pius X (1903-1914) initiated only a few, Pius XI concluded ten from 1922 to 1939, in addition to entering working arrangements with Portugal and Czechoslovakia. Convinced that such agreements helped the Church," Coppa added, "Pius XI negotiated them with fascist, socialist, and democratic regimes."[160]

Thus we can see, given the diversity of civil authorities

---

[160] Coppa. Pages 81 and 82.

with whom Popes signed such Concordats, that it would be absurd to assume each one had some kind of special blessing by the Vatican to be the arbiter of civic morality or a God-inspired administration. If any one of those systems was considered an ideal and Godly form of government, then it would not make sense for the Vatican to have signed agreements with any of the others. After all, one cannot claim that Fascism, socialism, and democracy are all the true and correct form of government because these systems are largely in conflict with each other. Rather than the Pope giving an explicit blessing or mark of approval, Coppa noted that through such Concordats "Rome sought to guarantee the life of ecclesiastical organizations in various countries by making concessions that did not undermine the spiritual functions of the Church."[161]

It must also be noted that the Vatican did not watch Mussolini's actions - either as the socialist editor of the *Avanti*, or the future Fascist editor of the *Il Popolo D'Italia* newspapers - and immediately begin to bless him as a leader. In the wake of World War I, with so many factions all fighting for dominance in Italy, the Vatican spent most of its political capital calling for peace between said factions. It wasn't until after Mussolini's "March On Rome" in 1922, when he was blessed by Italian King Victor Emmanuel III to become Italy's Head of State, that the Pope considered the Fascist State to be the legitimate government of Italy. Once Mussolini received his charge from the King, he became Italy's legal and rightful ruler.

---

[161] Ibid. Page 82.

That being the case, the Vatican did what it always did: try to make peace with the sovereign of the State in order to continue its own existence without being suppressed. It should also be noted that the Vatican often attained its ends far more easily with authoritarian figures than liberal democratic states, as one man in charge can make decisions more quickly than a plurality of parties (which typically included intense anti-clericalism anyway).[162]

Once in power, Mussolini began to help the Vatican almost immediately. He ended his first speech in Parliament by invoking the aid of God and, as noted by Coppa on Page 88 of <u>Controversial Concordats,</u> "restored Catholic instruction in the public schools, while rooting anti-clericalism out of the universities and freemasonry out of the Party." Despite being viciously anti-Christian in his youth, particularly during his time as a socialist agitator, Mussolini changed his tune in either the face of genuine conversion or - and this may just as likely be the case - political expediency. Regardless of Mussolini's motivation, Italian Catholics began warming up to his leadership as he opposed their traditional enemies of "liberalism, freemasonry and socialism."[163]

Furthermore, Mussolini promoted Christianity in the nation and worked with the Vatican to find compromises wherever possible - including a restoration of the Pope's former power in the Lateran Agreement of 1929. As agreed between King and Pope, Roman Catholicism was granted a wide range of privileges and influence in

---

[162] Ibid.

[163] Ibid. Page 89.

exchange for, essentially, agreeing not to agitate against the Fascist government.

Coppa summarized that "The Lateran Agreement included three accords: a conciliation treaty that terminated the Roman Question and declared Vatican City to be a neutral and inviolable territory; a concordat, which regulated Church-State relations in Italy, and a financial convention, intended to provide some compensation for Papal territory annexed during the unification. It was a bilateral agreement having the status of a treaty under international law rather than simply an Italian bill, as was the Law of Guarantees, which it superseded."[164]

The Articles of the Concordat also included the recognition of Catholicism as the sole religion of Italy, the sovereignty of the Vatican in international affairs, and - at long last - Papal recognition of the Kingdom of Italy. Amongst other privileges, the Concordat granted the Vatican the right to communicate with the Catholic world free of government interference, the exemption of clergy from military service and jury duty, guarantees that Vatican property would not be demolished without ecclesiastical approval, the right to design the religious curriculum for all Italian state schools, and the State's recognition of Roman Catholic holidays. The Roman Question having been solved, and the Vatican having been granted sovereignty, Pope Pius XI declared that "The concordat is thus the instrument which perfects the

---

[164] Ibid. Page 95.

spiritual union of Italy with the Church."[165]

Coppa added that Mussolini "reaped benefits from the Accords. Among other things he was able to reduce if not eliminate the opposition against him in part of the hierarchy and the clergy, while removing doubts and reservations that the broader Catholic population still preserved toward his government. The Accords thus enabled Mussolini to broaden the consensus for Fascism."[166] The Fascist State could now run Italy unopposed while proclaiming itself the defender of Italian Christianity. Having achieved in a few short years what the liberal government was unable to achieve in nearly 70, Mussolini thus instituted a Catholic version of Orthodox Church-State Symphonia and, by doing so, won an enormous amount of respect from both the secular and religious worlds. Many looked upon the Lateran Agreements as the single greatest achievement of his Fascist government.

But as with all compromises, many were also left unhappy on both sides. Several Roman Catholic factions felt that the Pope had conceded too much to Mussolini, while many Fascists were as angry as the liberals regarding how much power the Vatican now had within the State. Relations between the two remained tense and, increasingly as Mussolini's reign tended more and more toward the totalitarian, the Pope often chastised Mussolini's behavior and rebuked parts of his speeches to Parliament.

---

[165] Ibid. Page 102.
[166] Ibid. Page 105.

Though the Vatican saw great stability in Mussolini's heavy-handed leadership, it also rebuked him when the Pope felt that Mussolini was overstepping his proper boundaries as the secular head of State. For example, when Mussolini's organization for Fascist youth came into being, he banned all other youth organizations - including Catholic ones. In 1927, Pope Pius XI wrote a scathing letter to Mussolini's Secretary of State, accusing Mussolini of interfering with the Vatican's prerogatives; in this case, the right to raise and educate children according to Roman Catholic teaching. Though the Lateran Agreement was concluded in 1929, this concern from the Pope never truly went away. He often complained, in letters and even encyclicals, about the encroaching on Catholic youth groups by the Fascist government.

Coppa wrote that "the Pope deplored the oath which required the young to execute orders without discussion while complaining that schoolchildren were deliberately diverted from Church services to military and athletic events."[167] Mussolini argued that some of the Catholic youth groups were getting too political to be in accordance with the Agreement, and the Pope responded that such groups were above and beyond any of the Agreement's political concerns. The Pope was careful, however, not to criticize Fascism *per se*; he wrote in an encyclical that his purpose was to "condemn all those things in the [Fascist] program and in the activities of the party which have been found to be contrary to Catholic

---

[167]   Ibid. Page 110.

doctrine and Catholic practice, and therefore incompatible with the Catholic name and profession."[168]

Mussolini responded to this encyclical by accusing the Church of trying to create a state-within-a-state, giving credence to the arguments some Fascist intellectuals had made as the Lateran Agreement was being drawn up in the first place. He claimed that the Pope was using the Catholic Action lay organizations to attack his regime - in its parts if not its totality - and subsequently, was engaging in the kind of political action which violated their treaty. Less than a year after the Agreement was signed, Fascists began to attack the offices of the Jesuit journal *Civiltà Cattolica*, and Mussolini disbanded Catholic youth groups entirely. It seems that Mussolini wanted the Vatican's total approval, free of any criticism whatsoever, and could not stomach the Pope's disagreements with some of the Party's activities. The Vatican and the State, working together on paper, quickly became rather like two opposing totalitarian regimes doing their best to check the power of the other. Thus we see the other side of the Symphonic ideal: that it rarely seems to last for long.

In 1931, Mussolini and the Pope worked on the Accord For Catholic Action - yet another agreement by which each sought to maintain its power and prerogatives. Once again the result was controversial, with various parties claiming capitulation by its preferred side of the treaty. The youth groups were allowed to continue their existence, but could not be led by anyone who had

---

[168] Ibid.

previously fought against the Fascists. Their activities were also restricted to the purely religious sphere. Coppa noted that "the Vatican rather than the Fascists triumphed. Mussolini failed to eliminate this widespread organization, which remained covertly anti-Fascist and challenged his totalitarian claims."[169] This pattern seems to have continued throughout Mussolini's reign: that no matter how hard he tried to fight against the Vatican, the Vatican usually got the upper hand. Coppa observed that "Even in the later 1930s, as repression increased, various Catholic Action groups conducted an ideological campaign against Fascism utilizing clandestine publications and discussion groups to condemn the totalitarian, racist, and anti-Christian doctrines of the Regime."[170]

As Fascist Italy began to look more like National Socialist Germany, particularly via its issuance of the 1938 Aryan Manifesto and the racial laws that came with it, Pope Pius XI became more and more disenchanted with Fascism. He called the Aryan Manifesto "a true form of apostasy" and urged Catholic Action groups to combat what Coppa called Mussolini's "hypernationalism and pagan idolatry of the state."[171] A few months after the passing of the Aryan Manifesto, the Pope called it a "gross and grave error," adding that its tenets were "contrary to Catholic doctrine."[172] One of the racial laws

---

[169] Ibid. Page 113.
[170] Ibid. Pages 114 and 115.
[171] Ibid. Page 116.
[172] Ibid. Pages 116 and 117.

even violated the Concordat of 1929, Article 34, which required the State to recognize the sacrament of marriage under the Vatican's jurisdiction. When Mussolini declared that Italian "Aryans" could no longer marry members of other races, the Pope rightly called this out as a reneging on their agreement.

Coppa concluded that "As a result of the Pope's efforts, the Church in its structure, activities, and corporate life remained outside the net of the totalitarian state...The Church was one of the few institutions that Fascism failed to infiltrate or control, and Mussolini proved unable to make it an instrument of his regime."[173] Near the end of World War 2, Mussolini - by then a mere puppet of the Nazis in the Salò Republic - claimed that he had given the Vatican too much leeway in the Lateran Agreement. He expressed regret at having made so many concessions, and wished that he'd had more unilateral control. In the grand game of politics, the Pope outplayed the Duce.

---

[173] Ibid. Pages 118-110.

Mussolini And The State

"Let Parties die and the Country be saved."[174]
- Benito Mussolini

As you've just learned, Mussolini's initial conception of Church-State relations was about as good as a Catholic could hope for: a State that not only refused to meddle directly in Roman Catholic affairs, or to turn said institution into just another instrument of the State, but rather a State that respected, defended, and protected the Vatican as a vital and necessary part of a healthy nation's existence. However, he disliked some of the Vatican's political stances and often found himself and his people in conflict with it. When and where those conflicts came to a head, each side tried to dominate the other. Beyond Mussolini's views of how the Fascist Party ought to engage with Roman Catholicism, we will now examine his conception of the State *itself:* its form, purposes, and intended ultimate outcome.

To begin with - like most other historical nationalists and traditionalists - Mussolini strongly opposed the concept of universal-suffrage democracy: "Fascism denies that the majority, by the simple fact that it is a majority, can direct human society; it denies that numbers alone can govern by means of a periodical consultation, and it affirms the immutable, beneficial and fruitful inequality

---

[174] Mussolini, B. (2012). *My Autobiography*. Courier Corporation. Page 160.

of mankind, which can never be permanently leveled through the mere operation of a mechanical process such as universal suffrage. The democratic regime may be defined as from time to time giving the people the illusion of sovereignty, while the real effective sovereignty lies in the hands of other concealed and irresponsible forces. Democracy is a regime nominally without a king, but it is ruled by many kings - more absolute, tyrannical and ruinous than one sole king, even though a tyrant."[175] Like many other people who consider the topic deeply, Mussolini concluded that universal-suffrage democracy was inadequate on the following two levels: Firstly, that the concept itself was insufficient for the successful governance of society, and secondly, that regardless of the claims it makes about the rights and privileges of the average citizen, the truth is that democracy is just oligarchy behind a mask. In other words, it isn't real - and even if it were, it wouldn't be a good thing anyway.

In his autobiography, Mussolini explained at length how he envisioned the Fascist State. He described it as "an embodied will to power and government: the Roman tradition is here an ideal of force in action. According to Fascism, government is not so much a thing to be expressed in territorial or military terms as in terms of morality and the spirit. It must be thought of as an Empire - that is to say, a nation which directly or indirectly rules other nations, without the need for conquering a single square yard of territory."[176] He

---

[175] Ibid. Page 232.
[176] Ibid. Page 239.

further declared that "the Fascist State is unique and an original creation. It is not reactionary, but revolutionary, in that it anticipates the solution of the universal political problems which elsewhere have to be settled in the political field by the rivalry of parties, the excessive power of the Parliamentary regime and the irresponsibility of political assemblies; while it meets the problems of the economic field by a system of syndicalism which is continually increasing in importance, as much in the sphere of labor as of industry; and in the moral field enforces order, discipline, and obedience to that which is the determined moral code of the country…the Fascist State organizes the nation, but leaves a sufficient margin of liberty to the individual; the latter is deprived of all useless and possibly harmful freedom, but retains what is essential; the deciding power in this question cannot be the individual, but the State alone."[177]

Thus we may deduce that he envisioned Fascist Italy as both a revival of the Roman Empire and a new formulation of its style - one that could solve not only its own problems, but also the problems of every nation that adopted its ideals - and which prevented its citizens from doing things that were deemed harmful to themselves and society. According to Mussolini's outline and definition, Fascism proper could be considered a sort of secular authoritarianism which nonetheless promoted, despite its love of war and fighting, religion as a major unifying force. We'll consider more about violence in a

---

[177] Ibid. Pages 238 and 239.

moment, but above all let us keep in mind Mussolini's goal in all this: "I want to make Italy great, respected, and feared; I want to render my nation worthy of her noble and ancient traditions."[178]

In regard to the specific form of government which he believed would lead to that outcome, Mussolini promoted a flexible view that took a number of factors into account. Rather than insist on one concrete manifestation, he believed that the government ought to take whatever expression best served its interests in a particular time and place. As described in *The Political and Social Doctrine of Fascism*, "Fascism uses in its construction whatever elements in the Liberal, Social or Democratic doctrines still have a living value; it maintains what may be called the certainties which we owe to history, but it rejects all the rest - that is to say, the conception that there can be any doctrine of unquestioned efficacy for all times and all peoples...The State is the guarantor of security both internal and external, but it is also the custodian and transmitter of the spirit of the people, as it has grown up through the centuries in language, in customs and in faith. And the State is not only a living reality of the present, it is also linked with the past and above all the future, and thus transcending the brief limits of individual life, it represents the immanent spirit of the nation. The forms in which States express themselves may change, but the necessity for such forms is eternal."[179]

This sentiment is remarkably similar to that expressed

---

[178] Ibid. Page 224.
[179] Ibid. Pages 235-237.

by Orthodox philosopher Ivan Ilyn in his essay *On Forms Of Sovereignty*. The theme of the article, and Mussolini's perspective, was that different forms of government work best for different people, at different times, in different contexts. Each of these layers is further affected by history, culture, geography, the availability or lack of agricultural potential in the region, and more.

Thus we may conclude that Mussolini's view of the State was that it ought to primarily serve the people and their interests, taking whatever official form was most likely to do so at any given time, without leaving it up to the masses to determine the direction of society. He supported the King not because of some deep-seated respect for the principle of Monarchy, but rather because it seemed to work - and far more importantly, the King allowed the Fascists their March On Rome, ending with his request that Mussolini form a new government. The King was useful, and therefore good. Had he ceased to be useful, he would have ceased to be good. Mussolini's view of government was thus entirely pragmatic, without regard to abstractions or philosophy.

Though Mussolini didn't take issue with the principle of Monarchy in and of itself, he and many others felt that King Victor Emmanuel III was not taking sufficient measures to protect Italy. Evola wrote in <u>Fascism Viewed From The Right</u> that "if there had been a true monarchy in Italy, a monarchy as a power committed to intervene energetically in every situation of crisis and collapse in the state, and not as a simple symbol of sovereignty, Fascism never would have arisen; there would have been no 'revolution.' The critical situation in which the nation found itself before the March on Rome would have been overcome exclusively and rapidly through a 'revolution from above' (with a possible suspension of constitutional encumbrances), which is the only admissible revolution in a traditional regime, and through a successive reorganization of structures that had proven ineffective. Since that was not the situation in Italy, other paths had to be followed."[180]

Once Mussolini's government was given the royal stamp of approval, it set to work creating a particular mode of organization. In his introduction to <u>Fascism Viewed From The Right</u>, E. Christian Kopff stated that "Evola explains the principles of a true Right. A strong central state creates a nation and its people, not *vice versa*. At the moral and political center of the best states is a king (*rex*), who may, however - and under Fascism did - choose a leader (*dux*) to administer the state. Strong central leadership does not subvert and, in fact, encourages subsidiarity or federalism, where most decisions and political activity occur at appropriate lower levels. Subsidiarity does not imply democracy, the kingdom or realm of quantity (René Guénon's *Règne de la Quantity*). On the contrary, Fascism established a Chamber of Corporations where the estates, professions, and vocations of the land were represented on the basis of importance and achievement, not of pure number."[181]

---

[180] Evola, J., & Morgan, J. B. (2013). *Fascism viewed from the Right*. London Arktos Media Ltd. Pages 51 and 52.
[181] Ibid. Page 9.

Mussolini asserted that he did not believe in absolute Monarchy and, to his future chagrin, never attempted to overthrow the King of Italy. He settled on what he called a "dual rule:" the governance of Italy being shared by the King and by Fascism. Practically, this took the form of the Militia and the Grand Fascist Council, with many factions of each being devoted to either the King or the Duce. It was a constant balancing act for Mussolini throughout his reign, as he sought to advance the Fascist cause while diminishing the King's power by comparison. Once the Grand Fascist Council gave itself the right to choose the King's successor - putting an end to the Monarchical paradigm's usual path of handing the Crown from father to son - the King began to hate Mussolini and his movement. It's likely this move was one of many which contributed to Mussolini's later betrayal by King Victor. Towards the end of his life, Mussolini regretted his submission to the King during the March On Rome; in retrospect, similarly to what he expressed regarding the Church, he considered his attempt at compromise to be a fatal mistake to his regime.

Like the other nationalists you'll read about in <u>Fascism Viewed From The Cross,</u> Mussolini hated politicians and the party system: "I speak of movement and not of party, because my conception always was that Fascism must assume the characteristics of being anti-party...all the conceptions of the so-called historical parties seemed to be dresses out of measure, shape, style, usefulness. They had grown tawdry and insufficient - unable to keep pace with the rising tide of unexpected political exigencies, unable to adjust to the formation of new history and new conditions of modern life...I had a perfect and sure consciousness of the end I was driving at. This was my problem - to find the way, to find the moment, to find the form."[182]

In other words, he felt that the old political system was obsolete and lacked the vision necessary to revive Italy from its state of disrepair. There is surely no doubt that a politician or party which lacks a coherent goal will be incapable of rising above its contemporary circumstances, regardless of the historical time and place. If the goal is simply to attain power at another party's expense, it may well achieve its prize - but to what end? What will have changed beyond the fact that one party has now taken the ball from the other, invariably to return it just a few years later, while the nation continues its decline at full speed?

Further, he recognized that when a certain degree of chaos had been achieved by those who sought to undermine social harmony, democratic pluralism and the factionalism it necessarily entails became incapable of solving the problem: "I knew very well that a strong government would quickly put in order the Socialists and the anarchists, the decadents and wreckers and the instigators of disorder."[183]

Speaking of force, let us consider Mussolini's perspective on violence and war. Much like Adolf Hitler, who you'll read about shortly, Mussolini loved fighting and conflict. Commenting on his own time as a shock

---

[182] Mussolini. Page 53.

[183] Ibid. Page 49.

trooper in World War 1, he wrote: "What we suffered the first months - cold, rain, mud, hunger! They did not succeed in dampening in the slightest degree my enthusiasm and my conviction as to the necessity and the inevitableness of war."[184] From the trenches, he ordered his newspaper *Popolo d'Italia* to "continue always to call for war to the end"[185] and "demanded on the part of the central government severe action against slackers and whosoever undermined the spirit of war."[186]

Mussolini's pro-war stance was partly borne of his belief that it brought out the best in men: "War alone brings up to its highest tension all human energy and puts the stamp of nobility upon the peoples who have the courage to meet it. All other trials are substitutes, which never really put men into the position where they have to make the great decision - the alternative of life or death."[187]

On a certain level, I believe the Orthodox could agree that having to choose between living in cowardice or dying for your beliefs is not fundamentally wrong; after all, the Church has canonized as Saints innumerable Martyrs who chose to give their lives for God rather than deny Him to save themselves. There is no question that being faced with death is the ultimate trial that reveals who we are, and one I pray that my loved ones and I will never have to face in this life. After all, it is easy to say

---

[184]   Ibid. Page 34.
[185]   Ibid. Page 35.
[186]   Ibid. Page 41.
[187]   Ibid. Page 230.

that we believe in God when all that's required is that we fast from meat, say our prayers, or go to Church on Sundays. Facing torture and death demands an entirely different level of self-sacrifice, and the best we can do to prepare for that possibility is to die to ourselves daily in whatever way God has ordained for us. We can put our egos aside to act selflessly for others, ask forgiveness even when we were not in the wrong, do good to those who harm us or keep careful watch over the sensory input which we allow into our *nous*. May God grant us the strength to do even these little feats, which are impossible for our fallen selves to achieve without the grace of Him Who heals us.

Mussolini's view that conflict refines and purifies a man is not necessarily wrong if seen in a Baptized sense: those who engage in spiritual warfare are the only ones who truly make progress. The more we fight, and get back up again when we lose, the farther we will end up going. But St. Paul exhorted us that *"we do not wrestle against flesh and blood, but against principalities, against powers, against the rulers of the darkness of this age, against spiritual hosts of wickedness in the heavenly places."*[188] The warfare we're called to - even for those enrolled in military service - is ultimately against the demons and the passions they try to stir in us. While soldiers must fight as commanded by their governments, provided they are not commanded either to sin or to refrain from virtuous acts despite having to take life where necessary, even they may find that it is far harder to defeat lust or greed than it

---

[188] Ephesians 6:12

is to fight a human being in a different uniform. Another man can be defeated once, and never strike again; the demons, after being repelled by our prayers and fasting, simply bide their time until the next attack. Thus one requires only a moment of duty, while the other requires a lifetime of vigilance. And there is no man more noble and worthy of honor than one who has progressed toward Christian perfection.

Warfare, though recognized by the Church as a temporary and necessary evil to maintain the peace of society, has always been rebuked by Christians if seen as a positive in and of itself. Recall that the *Basis of the Social Concept* clearly stated that the Church cannot support either "civil war" or "aggressive external war."[189] Neither of these, if viewed purely as the catalyst for human improvement, is acceptable for Orthodox Christians.

Though Mussolini always advocated for war against Italy's enemies, it must be said that he strove to keep it strategic and necessary in terms of how he ran the country: "I have always said - and those who have always followed me in these five years of hard struggle can now remember it - that violence, to be useful in settling anything, must be surgical, intelligent and chivalrous."[190]

He wrote of the Fascist Blackshirts that "I restrained our own violence to the strict limit of necessity. I enforced that view-point with lieutenants and with the rank and file. At times they obeyed me with regret and pain. They

---

[189] *III. Church and state | The Russian Orthodox Church*. (2021). Mospat.ru. https://old.mospat.ru/en/documents/social-concepts/iii/
[190] Mussolini. Page 168.

were thinking of companions treacherously murdered. But they always submitted to my orders against reprisals."[191] When his footsoldiers desired vengeance, Mussolini stopped their hands and kept them in line. It should also be noted his attempts at peace with the Left failed: "In 1921 I tried a political agreement and truce with our adversaries under the protection of the government. The utter incomprehension of the Socialists and Liberals was enormous. My gesture, prodigal and generous, created solely by me, served only to raise new fogs, miasmas and equivocations. The truce had been signed by the Socialists but not the communists. The latter continued the open struggle, helped in every way by the Socialists themselves. A generous experiment in pacifism had been quite useless."[192]

The communists not only continued their violence, but ramped up their campaigns of murder and terrorism; they set off a bomb in Milan's Diana Theater, killing 20 people and mangling 50 more. In response, the Fascists burned down the headquarters of the left-wing *Avanti* newspaper.[193] It was only after Fascists began to fight back against communist violence that they made inroads into Italian politics, as the public started to voice support for those trying to save Italy from communism.

Lastly, let us examine Mussolini's views on education. Once a teacher, he took an immense interest in the schools of Italy and the reformation of its curricula among other

---

[191] Ibid. Page 95.

[192] Ibid. Pages 95 and 96.

[193] Ibid. Page 100.

changes. One of his biggest problems with Italian schooling was that it produced "stock patterns of human beings who ended for the most part by taking tasks in bureaucracy. They lowered the function of the public service by dead and not living personnel."[194] He attributed this in part to the low wages teachers were paid, leading to their indifference or even abandoning their careers in search of more lucrative prospects.

Mussolini's reorganization of the school system, collectively referred to as the Gentile Reform as he named the program after Minister of Public Instruction Giovanni Gentile, included not just higher pay for teachers but also the imposition of stricter discipline on them; the closing of school admission to those whose merits did not warrant acceptance; the equal testing of those in both state-funded and independent schools; an intentional promotion of rivalry between state and independent schools in order to raise the level of each via competition; the directing of schools toward a "broad humanistic culture;"the introduction of a "purely humanistic and philosophical school" for teachers and, among other changes, the reintroduction of Latin in all schools except for the "elementary and introductory schools." Mussolini, commenting on the purpose of all this, wrote that "I have willed that, in collaboration with the universities, departments of Fascist economics, of corporative law, and a whole series of fruitful institutes of Fascist culture, should be created. Thus a purely academic and scholastic world is being permeated by Fascism, which is creating a

---

[194] Ibid. Page 207.

new culture through the fervid and complex activity of real, of theoretical and of spiritual experiences."[195]

By way of contrast, let us attend to the wisdom of St. Justin Popovic: "Education without sanctity, without sanctification by the Holy Spirit, education without the perfecting and completing of man by the God-man, education without God, was invented by Europe in its humanistic idolatry. It is immaterial whether this idolatry was manifested in the divinizing of the Pope or of culture, science, civilization, technology, politics, or fashion. The chief aim in all this is to organize man, society, and the world without God, without Christ. The same goes for education, whose chief aim is to educate man and mankind without Christ our God. To this end, humanistic education devoted itself to the creation of a new man. The plan for such a man is classically plain and simple: neither Christ nor anything pertaining to Him can have any part in this new man. So Europe got to work: it started creating man without God, society without God, mankind without God."[196]

St. Justin further encouraged his audience to "ask what the goal of education is, if it is not the enlightening of man, the illumining of all his abysses and pits, the banishing of all darkness from him. How can man disperse the cosmic darkness that assails him from all sides, and how can he banish the darkness from his being without that one light, without God, without Christ? Even with all the light that it is, man without God is but a

---

[195] Ibid. Pages 206-211.

[196] Popović, J. (2009). *Man and the God-man*. Page 61.

firefly in the endless darkness of this universe. His science, his philosophy, education, culture, technology and civilization are but tiny candles that he lights in the obscurity of earthly and cosmic events…Under its tragic influence, European humanistic education has created a conflict in us between Church and school, which has always spelled catastrophe for our Orthodox people. Under its influence, even the man of our nation and faith has begun to become mechanized and robotized."[197]

Finally, St. Justin proposed that "There is only one way to avoid this final catastrophe. Which was is that? To adopt theanthropic education and introduce it in all schools, from the lowest to the highest, in all education, national and state institutions, from the first to the last. Theanthropic education radiates, illumines and enlightens by the only inextinguishable light in all worlds: Christ the God-man. This light cannot be extinguished or overcome by any darkness, even that of Europe. It alone banishes all darkness from man, society, nation, and state. It is the only true light, illuminating every man to the core, and revealing to us in everyone our immortal, divine, and eternal brother. It teaches us that the problems of the person, of society, of the nation and of mankind can be easily and clearly understood and solved only when the person, society, nation, and mankind are viewed in the context of Christ the Theanthropos. The main direction and characteristics of theanthropic education can be formulated thus:

1. Man is a being that can be perfected and completed

---

[197] Ibid. Page 65.

in the most ideal and realistic way by the God-man;

2. The perfection of man by the God-man is achieved by means of the evangelical virtues;

3. An enlightened man sees in every other man his immortal and eternal brother;

4. Every human activity - philosophy, science, trade, agriculture, art, education, and culture - receive their everlasting value when they are sanctified and given significance by the God-man;

5. True enlightenment is achieved by a holy life according to Christ's Gospel;

6. The saints are the most perfect educators; the more holy a man's life, the better an educator and enlightener he is;

7. Education is the second half of the God-man's heart, the Church is the first;

8. In the center of all centers, of all ideas and activities, there stands the God-man and His theanthropic collective: the Church."[198]

May God grant the wisdom, discernment and vision to all leaders that He gifted to the great St. Justin. May all who teach others always remember that all subjects are subject to Christ. May all students in this world who sense the emptiness of secular education find their way to the Church and their fulfillment in God. Amen.

---

[198] Ibid. Pages 65 and 66.

Mussolini and the Jews

"Let us hope that Italian Jews will continue to be smart enough not to provoke anti-Semitism in the only country where it has never existed."[199] *- Benito Mussolini*

The Jewish community of 20th century Italy lived in a complex, multifaceted situation; the state of any given Jewish family depended largely on where its members lived and to which social and religious class they belonged. Jews in the Roman ghetto - the oldest Jewish community in the entire Western world - were generally dirt-poor and highly religious. Jews in the higher social classes, with professions ranging from fur trader to banker to intelligentsia, tended to be "culturally Jewish" without giving much thought to the spiritual principles of the faith. The Jewish community in Turin, one of those middle- to upper-class communities, contained a number of both Jewish Fascists and Jewish anti-Fascists.

Many conservative-minded Jews saw themselves primarily as Italian, and subsequently supported Mussolini and the Fascist Party because those forces held the Communists at bay. For example Ettore Ovazza, a Jewish veteran of World War I who joined Mussolini's Blackshirts afterward, even participated in the March On Rome (with 230 other Jewish Fascists)[200]. Like many

---

[199] Sarfatti, M. (2007). *The Jews in Mussolini's Italy : from equality to persecution.* The University Of Wisconsin Press. Page 59.

[200] *History of the Jews in Italy.* (2023, March 19). Wikipedia.

others Jews in the early years of Fascism, Ovazza supported Mussolini's government both ideologically and financially. In return for all his help to the nation, Ovazza was well-received by both King and Duce; the latter even presented Ovazza with a signed photograph of himself.

From 1922 to 1945 - the period of Fascism's rule in Italy - there were between 40 and 50 thousand Jews in the country (about 1/1000th of the population).[201] At peak enrollment, nearly an entire third of Italian Jews above the age of 21 were members of the Fascist Party - though Michele Sarfatti noted in The Jews in Mussolini's Italy that the proportion of anti-Fascists was also higher among the Jewish population than among Italian Gentiles.[202]

Unlike Hitler and Codreanu, whose ideas you'll read about shortly, Mussolini began his campaign with no malice against Jews. As noted by Alexander Stille in his book Benevolence And Betrayal, "Italian fascism was in power for sixteen years before it turned anti-Semitic in 1938. Until then, Jews were as likely to be members of the Fascist Party as were other conservative-minded Italians."[203] Julius Evola agreed, noting that - regarding what is commonly called the "Jewish Problem" in nationalist literature - "There are few or no references to this problem in Mussolini's early writings."[204]

---

https://en.wikipedia.org//wiki/History_of_the_Jews_in_Italy

[201] Sarfatti. Page ix.

[202] Ibid. Page 17.

[203] Stille, A. (2003). *Benevolence and betrayal : five Italian Jewish families under fascism.* Picador. Page 12.

[204] Evola, J., & Morgan, J. B. (2013). *Fascism viewed from the Right.* London Arktos Media Ltd. Page 94

Indeed, the word "Jew" is not found a single time anywhere in Mussolini's autobiography.[205] Evola continued: "One can only cite an old article that mentions a well-known theme, that the Hebrew, subjugated and deprived of the usual means to compete directly in the modern world, had recourse to the indirect means constituted by money, finance and intelligence (in the profane sense) to exercise power and for self-affirmation. In addition, in an article from 1919, Mussolini wondered whether Bolshevism, which was supported in its origins by Jewish bankers in London and New York and counted (at that time) numerous Hebrews among its leaders, did not represent 'Israel's revenge against the Aryan race.'"[206]

Beyond that, Mussolini's only other early mentions of Jews were in vaguely-worded warnings issued out of his concern that some of them may have been more loyal to their faith community than to Italy: "In November 1928 the Fascist dictator posed a direct question to Jews: 'Are you a religion or are you a nation?' There was no lack of responses, with those appearing in the press coming largely from anti-Zionist Fascist Jews. Of the three Jewish organizations attempting a reply, the Community of Venice declared that it 'distinctly separated its own thought and action from the thought and action of anyone who did not place his country in the forefront;' the Italian Zionist Federation stated that 'there has never been any dispute, nor can there be one, between loyalty to the

---

[205] Mussolini, B., & Richard Washburn Child. (2006). *My autobiography : with "The political and social doctrine of fascism."* Dover Publications.
[206] Evola. Page 94.

whole Jewish tradition, of which the idea of Zion is a central part, and love of Italy;' and the Consortium of the Communities reaffirmed that 'Italian Jews, whether Zionist or not,' were patriotic in equal measure…The 'clarification' the dictator sought concerned first of all the issue of the incompatibility, in his opinion, of simultaneous allegiance on the part of Italian Jews to the nation and to the Zionist movement."[207]

Mussolini's thoughts on this topic were consistent, as even in 1922 - the night before the March on Rome - Fascist leadership announced that "a Jewish question does not exist in our country and let us hope that there never shall be one, at least not until Zionism poses Italian Jews with the dilemma of choosing between their Italian homeland and another homeland."[208] In either case, most Italian Jews seem to have considered themselves to be both Italian and Jewish with no distinction between these identities or loyalties. They had no reason to fear otherwise - at least when Fascism began - especially as Mussolini declared that "All religious faiths will be respected, with special regard for the dominant one, which is Catholicism."[209] Even as Mussolini moved to make Roman Catholicism the official state religion, including the restoration of Crucifixes in many public administrative offices, Jews under Fascism (at least in the 1920s) appear to have often had more rights and privileges than they'd had under either the Popes or

[207] Sarfatti. Pages 59 and 60.
[208] Ibid. Page 43.
[209] Ibid.

Orthodox Royal Saints.

The widespread Jewish support for Italian Fascism was understandable given that Mussolini did not consider Jews to be enemies of Italy before the late 1930s. The opponents he identified in his autobiography were subversive politicians, lying journalists, communists, socialists, traitors, anti-Fascists, those who dishonored soldiers, anyone working against the best interests of Italy, and - towards the end of the book - Freemasonry and other secret societies. Whether any particular opponent was Jewish does not appear to have been of great concern to Mussolini, and from this we can deduce that the only Jews he disliked would have been those who belonged to one or more of the categories mentioned above. Jews belonging to those groups were disliked in equal measure by the Jewish members of the Fascist Party. Even as late as 1932, Mussolini told the biographer Emil Ludwig that "Anti-Semitism does not exist in Italy... Italian Jews have always conducted themselves well as citizens, and as soldiers they fought bravely. They occupy high positions in the universities, in the army, in banks."[210]

However, by the following year, Mussolini's tune had begun to change. Though he publicly distanced himself from Hitler's racial policies, he also quietly began to remove Jews from high positions in his government - and by 1934, he had begun to support the idea of a Jewish homeland in Palestine which European Jews could move

---

[210] Ibid. Page 62.

to as citizens of a new Jewish State.[211]

Mussolini's position towards the Jews evolved in parallel with his increasing concern about race in general. For the first 16 years of his rule, Mussolini often spoke of the "Italian race" or "Aryan race" but without any corresponding legislation meant to either promote his race or diminish any other. That changed in 1938, when the Fascist regime published its 'Manifesto of Race' or 'Aryan Manifesto' and one of its news organs, *The Defense of the Race*, began to inspire public support for new racial policies.

Evola commented that this change was borne of three primary factors, the least important of which related to Jews and Judaism. He wrote that "the Jewish problem in Italy was never a particularly hot issue, and Mussolini's stance towards it in 1938 had a more political than ideological character. In fact, there had been a notable increase in reports by Italian diplomats and other sources of information about the growth of militant anti-Fascist hostility demonstrated by Jewish elements abroad, especially in America, that was connected (or not) with Italy's alliance with Germany. So Mussolini was finally compelled to react, and the Jews in Italy, who, apart from a few exceptions, had not given any special indications of anti-Fascist sentiments (there were Jews among the *squadristi*, the Fascist toughs) ended up suffering the consequences of the attitude of their non-Italian co-religionists because of measures that, however, can in no way be compared with the German ones, and very often

---

[211]   Ibid. Pages 67 and 68.

remained on paper and were not enforced."[212]

The second factor, according to Evola, was Italy's conquest of Ethiopia and the plethora of new issues that resulted. He believed that Mussolini's policies in this regard were no different from what other European nations implemented upon close contact with non-White nations, primarily in regard to mixed-race marriage (or "miscegenation"). He wrote that Mussolini "did nothing more than follow what was already traditional before the rise of the democratic ideology, with its principle of the so-called 'self-determination of peoples,' which was proclaimed by Whites, and then boomeranged against them, provoking the emergence, demands and uprising of colored peoples, until the Europeans themselves became infected with the psychosis of anti-colonialism."[213] It is interesting to note Evola's observation that the same ethnic nationalism which was later turned against Whites began with Whites imposing the same against other groups.

Lastly, in a sentiment which echoes the ideas of Corneliu Codreanu, Evola wrote that Mussolini's new racial policies were meant to create a new kind of Italian man: "Mussolini thought - and he was not mistaken - that the future of Fascism and the nation depended not so much on the transmission of ideas and institutions as much as on a formative action that causes a selected 'type' to arise. Creating 'a new way of life' and 'a new type of Italian' had been a need felt by Mussolini from the very

---

[212] Evola. Page 94.

[213] Ibid. Page 96.

beginning of the regime - and we saw that during a period in which there can certainly be no talk of Nazi influence, because Hitler had not yet attained power in 1929."[214]

Mussolini's view of race, at that point, was far more in line with Evola's perspective than with Adolf Hitler's (which we will discuss in a future chapter). Evola never believed in the "biological reductionist" view of race, but rather wrote that races were "groups that are formed with sufficiently stable characteristics in relation to a given culture and tradition, defined especially by a mode of being, by an 'interior race.' We can start out with the people of Israel, that originally was not a single pure and homogeneous race, but was instead an ethnic compound united and formed by a religious tradition, and which continued all the way to the United States, where an easily recognizable type was rapidly born from a rather unlikely ethnic mix because of the climate of a given culture, or rather pseudo-culture (this situation allows us to glimpse much greater possibilities when this process instead involves a real culture with a traditional character)."[215]

Evola's understanding of race - as an interior unity shared by members of different ethnic groups - is a far cry from the materialist view that race comprises nothing but DNA. In this paradigm, it would make more sense to speak of an "Orthodox Christian race," composed of numberless ethnicities around the world, than to view an

---

[214] Ibid. Page 99.

[215] Ibid.

Orthodox Russian and an Orthodox Ugandan as belonging to different races - while still, of course, acknowledging the obvious differences of ethnicity and culture and blood.

Before we contrast Mussolini's later anti-Jewish laws with those of the Orthodox Royal Saints, let us allow Evola to complete his thought on the matter: "the 'Manifesto' affirmed that the concept of race 'is a purely biological concept' and, apart from the absurd term 'Italian race,' asserted that 'the population of Italy today is of Aryan origin, and its civilization is Aryan,' neglecting to indicate exactly what 'Aryan' was supposed to mean. In fact, this Aryan character was reduced to something negative and problematic, and consisted of not being Hebrew or from a colored race, with no positive counterpart, nor any specification of a higher criterion to establish the comportment, style, worldview, or predispositions of character and spirit of the person who was to be called Aryan. The foreign influence here is clear, since it is specified that Fascist racism should be of 'Nordic-Aryan orientation.'"[216] By "foreign influence" Evola meant the obvious fact that by the time the Manifesto of Race was written, German racial ideas had permeated the Italian Fascist Party. Evola completely opposed this influence, preferring a "traditional, anti-materialist conception of the human being."[217]

In either case, the Orthodox Church has never affirmed the sort of racial understanding which Evola

---

[216] Ibid. Page 100.
[217] Ibid. Page 101.

resisted in the laws of Nazi Germany and post-1938 Fascist Italy. Our Royal Saints composed laws, and our theologians wrote Canons, far more aligned with Evola's view than Mussolini's or Hitler's - hence why (to the Saints) a Jew who was Baptized became legally and canonically considered a Christian from that point forth, and any legislation pertaining to Jews was no longer applied to him or her. With the aforementioned caveat that said conversion was sincere - and that clerics were careful to make sure it was - for all intents and purposes, that person had changed "races" in the eyes of the Church and its officials. In that sense, there was nothing different about Jews than there was about pagans or schismatics; the interior quality of a person's soul was considered more important than blood. Were this not the case, the Church would not have canonized convert Saints of every ethnicity.

When Popes had ruled the Papal States, Jews were often confined in ghettos and not allowed to leave at night. They were kicked out of their jobs, except for specific types of labor like the sale and repair of tattered clothing, and were generally not allowed to live with Christians side-by-side. It wasn't until the *Risorgimento*, when the pro-Jewish Piedmont royalty overthrew the Papal States to unify Italy under their Kingdom, that Jews began to enjoy equality with other citizens. Jewish bankers had funded several military expeditions, and King Carlo Alberto liberated their brethren wherever his armies conquered. By the time Mussolini was made Prime Minister in 1922, Jews had only enjoyed full citizenship privileges for about half a century in Italy. Those Jews who supported Mussolini must have assumed the situation would not change. Not only did it change, but by the end of Mussolini's life Jews in Italy were far worse off than they had been even under the rule of the Popes. These changes unfolded over a series of years, with intensifying persecution as time went on.

Though Fascist racialism began more due to the conquest of Ethiopia than any other factor, that incident - and the problems which ensued - seem to have caused Mussolini's government to consider more carefully its handling of Jews as well (who were increasingly thought to be a foreign and non-Italian race). In order to bring the Jewish community more in line with the rest of Italy, an 1936 ordinance in Tripoli demanded that Jewish shops remain open on Saturdays, which Jews consider to be a day of rest (sabbath) on which it is forbidden to work. The Jewish store owners refused the order, leading to several floggings, an imprisonment, and the revocation of a dozen business licenses.[218] This incident, though unusual for its time, proved to be a harbinger of things to come. However, there was very little in the way of formal policy changes during this period and - as noted by Sarfatti - "It is not always clear if the policies fixed upon in 1936 were from the very beginning directed against all Jews...It is not even always clear at this point to what extent the proponents of an *undifferentiated* anti-Semitism were still working out or had already reached a racist orientation, nor the degree to which this was *national* in scope, and

---

[218] Sarfatti. Page 102.

whether it was of an 'esoteric-traditionalist' or 'biological' type."[219]

By 1937, tension both against and within the Jewish community had reached such a high degree that a May issue of Mussolini's paper *Il Popolo d'Italia* "demanded that Italian Jews 'either declare themselves to be unequivocally enemies (let it be repeated: enemies) of international Judaism - masonic, subversive, and especially anti-Fascist...or they should renounce Italian citizenship and residence.' Reacting to this attack, representatives of the new Committee of Italians of the Jewish Faith met in Florence on 30 May and approved a resolution in which they declared themselves to be 'unequivocally enemies of any sort of Jewish or non-Jewish, masonic, subversive, international' and they 'they had nothing in common' with Zionism."[220] Even as the country began to more closely monitor and scrutinize Jews, those with nationalist and Fascist sympathies believed - wrongly, as it would turn out - that constant declarations of their loyalty to Italy would keep them safe from increasing persecution. At this time, Mussolini was still publicly announcing that Jews had nothing to fear in Italy.

At the same time as things began to heat up against Jews, Italy's laws against race-mixing with Africans became more and more crystallized overseas. In fact, Africans were considered a separate race from Italians even before the Jews were - but shortly after the official

---

[219] Ibid. Page 108.

[220] Ibid. Page 113.

laws against miscegenation came into effect, Jews were also defined as a distinct race. The 1938 Manifesto of Race "affirmed the existence of 'human races' and especially of a 'pure Italian race,' defined as being 'of Aryan origin' and belonging to an 'Aryan civilization.' It argued unequivocally that 'the concept of race is a purely biological concept,' and it proclaimed that 'Jews do not belong to the Italian race' and that, consequently, there were to be no mixed marriages with them."[221] Recall from the chapter on *Church Canons* that while the Church always forbade marriages between Jews and Christians, these were considered spiritual and *not* racial categories. As we have discussed, a Jew who converted to Christianity was considered Christian in view of such Canons. While the 1938 Fascist ban on mixed marriage may have superficial similarity to such rules, they were built on a different foundation and imposed for a very different reason.

By November of 1938 - despite all that Jewish Fascists had done for Italy - including Ettore Ovazza's founding of a newspaper meant specifically to denounce Zionist and anti-Fascist Jews - all Jews had been expelled from the Fascist Party. Shortly afterward, the Italian government began to monitor and keep racial records of entire extended families and children. As the record-keeping began, certain Jews were marked as "discriminated," in a positive sense, from the rest of the Jewish community; the families of those killed in combat for the Fascist military, or with special merits in the political field for example,

---

[221]   Ibid. Page 128.

were for a short time considered to deserve special consideration in light of the coming anti-Jewish laws. Temporary privileges included being allowed to work as journalists, pharmacists, or lawyers - though with the caveat that they could not work for public institutions. Though thousands of these "discriminated" statuses were given out at first, they were all rescinded within the next few years and all Jews were treated the same as the rest. By October of 1938 Mussolini had begun considering the revocation of all Jewish citizenships in Italy, but limited these revocations for the time being only to foreign-born Jews who had attained citizenship after 1918.[222]

Over the next few years non-discriminated Jews lost more and more rights in Italy and were expelled from all major public offices. Mussolini decided to deport all foreign Jews but, given that they couldn't get citizenship in all the neighboring countries, began interning them in camps in 1940. On February 9th of that year, Mussolini told Dante Almansi (President of the Union of Italian Jewish Communities) that eventually, all Jews would be removed from the country except for those who had not only been baptized but had "a Christian Aryan spouse and Christian children."[223]

At the same time as the Fascist government began to round up and deport foreign-born Jews in Italy, it also began rescuing Italian Jews who lived in other countries from Nazi persecution. Perhaps this was simply a sign of the confusing nature of the times and how frequently

---

[222] Ibid. Page 138.
[223] Ibid. Pages 145 and 146.

things changed, but "in the course of 1942 [Italy] was confronted with the German decision to deport Jews to the East, including citizens of neutral and allied states who had not been repatriated promptly. Since the Fascist government, at the time, was not in sympathy with the Nazi extermination policy and wished to protect the national interests represented by these dispersed Jews, it resolved, sometime between the end of 1942 and the beginning of 1943, to arrange for their evacuation... roughly 1,800 Italian Jews were evacuated, of whom almost two-thirds came from France."[224]

At around the same time, however, Italy was making plans to expel all Jews from its territory in general. Mussolini's downfall stopped these apparently contradictory and schizophrenic measures from all coming to pass, but the plan "to expel most Italians 'of the Jewish race' assumed voluntary expatriations within predetermined periods, ten years for the 'discriminated' persons, five for the 'nondiscriminated,' and one for propertyless members of this final group. Those who failed to leave would be escorted to the border or, if departure was impossible, would be interned in 'labor colonies for works of public interest.' In 1941, when emigration was no longer possible, the government put this final alternative into effect and in 1942 established 'forced labor' programs."[225]

At the tail end of Fascism, in 1943, the "Aryanization" of the Italian economy had seen Jews pushed out of a

---

[224] Ibid. Page 146.

[225] Ibid. Page 147.

massive number of employment fields and businesses - including their own. Beginning in 1938 they'd been pushed out of entertainment, shipyards, electric companies, photography, commercial sales, garbage collection, taxi services, and many other businesses which served the public. Jewish businesses were simply stolen and handed to non-Jewish Italians, or in some cases, were sold to them at extremely cheap prices. Jews sent to interment camps lost their businesses automatically and were given to new non-Jewish owners instead.[226]

Once Germany successfully took over northern Italy, and Mussolini was reinstated to power as the puppet leader of the Italian Social Republic, German anti-Jewish laws became the law of the land: "on January 4 1944, Mussolini issued a decree…ordering the heads of provinces, as prefects were now called, to proceed 'immediately' to the confiscation of all property belonging to persons 'of the Jewish race,' including businesses, land and buildings, bank deposits, furniture, bedding, and clothing. The measure applied to both foreign Jews and to Jews who were 'Italian citizens;' in fact, the latter were designated as the principal targets of the new law."[227]

It is not clear whether Evola's theory - that most of these measures, at least in the Fascist era before that of the Italian Social Republic, were implemented primarily as pro-Gentile Italian policies rather than explicitly anti-Jewish ones - was an accurate assessment either some or all of the time. In either case, stealing from one race to

---

[226] Ibid. Pages 151-153.
[227] Ibid. Pages 188 and 189.

favor another is obviously not something the Church has ever accepted, and our previous chapter on *Imperial Laws* demonstrated conclusively that our Royal Saints would have actively punished those Christians who engaged in such behavior. When the Royal Saints themselves went astray and behaved in ways not becoming a Christian, they were rebuked and corrected by holy Bishops. Neither of these situations - of Saints leading the nation or clergy overseeing their behavior - was the case in Fascist Italy.

Germany

"I do not know what horrified me most at that time: the economic misery of my companions, their moral and ethical coarseness, or the low level of their intellectual development."[228] *- Adolf Hitler*

Describing the "social, democratic, and liberal political forces of the parliamentary Weimar Republic," Evola wrote in <u>Notes on the Third Reich</u> that "their inadequacy, weakness and inconsistency became as increasingly obvious as their inability to master the social chaos that was the inevitable consequence of Germany's defeat, the collapse of the previous regime, the disastrous clauses of the Versailles Treaty, and the growing unemployment. This situation led to a situation where Marxism and, in part, Communism too, gained a more significant foothold in the post-war period than in all preceding German history."[229]

Codreanu, upon visiting Berlin in 1922, described the scene in the following words: "The wounds left by the war just ended in defeat were still bleeding. Material misery blanketed both Berlin and the rest of the country alike. Lately the Ruhr valley, an important center of riches, had been occupied too. I was witnessing the vertiginous and catastrophic downfall of the mark. In the workingmen's quarters, lack of bread, lack of foodstuffs, lack of work.

---

[228] Hitler, A. (1999). *Mein Kampf*. Houghton Mifflin. Page 30.

[229] Evola, J. (2013). *Notes on the Third Reich*. Arktos. Page 17.

Hundreds of children were accosting passers-by, begging. The fall of the mark also threw the German aristocracy into the same misery. People who had money, in a few days were left penniless. Those who sold their land and real estate holdings, being attracted by the mirage of high prices, became impoverished in the course of a few weeks. Domestic and foreign Jewish capitalists closed colossal business deals. Those possessing strong currency became owners of huge buildings of 50 apartments for only a few hundred dollars. Speculators combed through the entire city, scoring formidable coups."[230]

Thus you can plainly see that, similar to the conditions of Italy and Romania after World War 1, Germany was badly ravaged. It is in such vacuums, and in such desperate times, that people often turn toward and support whoever promises to improve their miserable lot. We, in the modern era, often look back at such situations and wonder how these nations could possibly believe what they did; I ask in response, is it any different than you feel now? Do you not feel the sting of living in an occupied nation, of treacherous politicians imposing exorbitant taxes to spend on bribery and gifts for each other and their foreign counterparts, watching the rich get richer while you and those you love suffer under the incompetence and malice of a ruling class that sees you as its enemy? Are your feelings so different from what the impoverished and betrayed soldiers of World War 1 felt towards their own governments at the time?

When he found a book about the Franco-German War

---

[230] Codreanu, C. (2015). *For My Legionaries.* Black House Publishing. Page 108.

of 1870-71 in his father's library, young Adolf immediately developed an interest in the military. His father, a self-made man who became a farmer once he retired, wanted his son to become a civil servant like himself. Hitler described this as a major point of contention between the two of them, and wrote that he was bored to tears at the thought of sitting in an office and working for someone else.

He wanted to become a painter, but after failing the Academy of Art exam in Vienna he was told his skill more truly lay in architecture instead. He described his upbringing as a relatively rough one, always on the brink of going hungry, painting to pay his bills while studying architecture and politics in his free time. He believed that he was going to be a famous architect some day.

One of many groups with whom Hitler disagreed (including his parents, teachers, and coworkers) was the Social Democrats, who promoted an ideology he was exposed to at work. Though he disagreed with their doctrine, his time as a laborer allowed him to realize just how deeply Marxism had taken root among the Viennese masses - specifically because the Social Democrats supported trade unions and "the working man," at least in that one aspect, whereas the other parties did not. The workers performed the simple calculus that if the Social Democrats were the only party working to help them, then that's the party to which they should belong. This was the method by which the Marxists in Vienna got their "feet in the door" of the working class, a victory from which other (and more subversive) campaigns could be launched. As Hitler described the phenomenon, "Less and less attention was paid to defending the real needs of the working class, and finally political expediency made it seem undesirable to relieve the social or cultural miseries of the broad masses at all, for otherwise there was a risk that these masses, satisfied in their desires, could no longer be used forever as docile shock troops. The leaders of the class struggle looked on this development with such dark foreboding and dread that in the end they rejected any really beneficial social betterment out of hand, and actually attacked it with the greatest determination." [231]

In other words, Marxists gave their working-class victims occasional benefits while never allowing them to develop full autonomy and stand on their own, in which case they would have no further use for Marxist doctrine or the politicians who espoused it; the men claiming they were helping the working class were, in reality, primarily responsible for keeping it in a state of perpetual misery and hence, dependent upon their Marxist rulers for sustenance. We in the modern United States should be familiar with this dynamic by simply observing the forces at play in our own times and cities.

Even before World War I, Hitler believed that the situation in Germany was on a downwards spiral; he wrote long passages about the growing disparity between rich and poor, as well as the fact that the German economy was being internationalized via the stock exchange rather than remaining focused on local finance.

---

[231] Hitler. Page 49.

He also believed that the education system emphasized the collection of rote knowledge in lieu of character growth and strength, resulting in the German masses having crippled wills and possessing book knowledge without any wisdom. Lastly, he lay the blame for Germany's weakness on the press which, as today, served as nothing but a multi-headed mouthpiece for the forces of national destruction. Nothing was ever done to diminish their power or enact meaningful consequences against the worst members of the media; they were simply allowed to continue lying, harming their own audience for the benefit of international Marxism, without ever once being stopped or held accountable. Every once in a while, a particularly egregious member of the pre-War German media would be jailed for a couple of weeks or months - but even in those cases, they'd be let out quickly and "the media" as such would remain a powerful institution.

In any case, Hitler did not see anyone proposing meaningful solutions to the problems he'd encountered and so he decided to enter the political realm himself. Hitler's first foray into politics was with a group he called the "Social Revolutionary Party." He formed it with a small handful of other veterans after World War 1, whom he met in civic-thinking courses that returning soldiers were forced to take. During a set of lectures by economist Gottfried Feder, who would later become a prominent National Socialist, Hitler decided that "The fight against international finance and loan capital became the most important point in the program of the German nation's struggle for its economic independence and freedom."[232] At that time, the future National Socialist program was still mostly theoretical and developing in Hitler's mind.

After a particularly effective speech he gave while still a student in one of his courses, Hitler was promoted to the post of an educator instead. In that role, he was assigned not only to teach, but also to investigate a new group that was calling itself the "German Workers' Party." He had a neutral opinion of the group at first, finding it similar to the many other new political organizations springing up in light of Germany's problems. But it was there that he became familiar with Anton Drexler, leader of the Munich section of German Workers' Party, after a Party member gave Hitler a pamphlet explaining Drexler's transition from Marxist to nationalist beliefs. It should be noted that not every detail Hitler shared about his political journey in <u>Mein Kampf</u> is truthful, as for example when he lied about being one of the founding members of said Party, and so we must keep in mind that his autobiography is at least in part propaganda meant to endear him to his audience.

According to Hitler, he ended up attending the next Party meeting, as they'd sent him a letter welcoming into the organization. He wasn't pleased with what he felt was a manipulative attempt to get him to join, and decided to tell them in person. Once he got there, he was disappointed by the organization's near-total lack of structure, literature, and form...but the longer he thought about it, the more he realized that it could be the perfect

---

[232] Ibid. Page 214.

slate on which to imprint his own political stamp. Its lack of organizational maturity was just what he needed, as he had already decided to reshape the Party in order to essentially transform it into a vehicle of his own ideas.

According to Hitler, the "tiny" group gained traction through notes given out, advertisements in a Munich newspaper, and his appeals to former Army comrades. But since Marxists were often violent towards nationalist groups, many members of the German Workers' Party were afraid of letting their views and membership be known in public. In one of Hitler's speeches at Party meetings, he encouraged them to welcome the fight as part and parcel of their self-sacrifice for the German ideal. It was during those meetings, and during those speeches, that Hitler first began to realize the true power of his oratory skill. He was able to get entire crowds "electrified" and felt he was the only Party member capable of wielding words with such force. As the group grew, they needed larger and larger halls for meetings. The Party size began to multiply.

On February 24, 1920, nearly 2,000 people had gathered to hear a Party speech in Munich. The Party's program of 25 theses was read to the crowd, who cheered and applauded for each point they heard. Meetings began to expand in terms of both frequency and audience size, until halls with thousands of seats were being filled every time a speech was given. When Marxists sent agents into the meetings, in order to disrupt them by violence, members of the Party would react with equal force and throw such people out to restore order in the meeting halls. Eventually, the small groups initially used to maintain peace in those meetings became the infamous SA (Brownshirts) of the Nazi Party.

On August 1, 1921, Hitler became chairman of the Party. His first order of business: transferring all power and responsibility into his own hands by eliminating decision-making committees. He had believed from the beginning that one person should be elected and then given full power and responsibility, as that eliminated the bloated time-and-money-wasting efforts of committees and parliaments. Such groups could take years to make the kind of simple decisions that might take a single leader one day.

The Party was dissolved in November 1923, after a failed Nazi coup to overthrow the government. That incident, called the Beer Hall Putsch or Munich Putsch, led to the imprisonment during which Hitler wrote <u>Mein Kampf</u>. Upon beginning his prison sentence in Landsberg am Lech fortress, he decided to take the opportunity of his confinement to put down all his thoughts about National Socialism on paper. While acknowledging that people were generally more moved by the spoken than the written word, he nevertheless thought it would be helpful to his followers if they had his doctrine written out, point-by-point, to help them understand its tenets and show them where he hoped it was heading.

The program worked; after more than a decade of political activity and propaganda, Hitler was elected Chancellor of Germany on January 30, 1933.

Hitler and the Church

"With the appearance of Christianity the first spiritual terror entered into the far freer ancient world."[233]
- Adolf Hitler

When studying Adolf Hitler's engagement with Christianity, we must address the topic in two parts. Firstly we must examine Hitler's private beliefs on the topic, shared far more often with his inner circle than with the audiences to whom he spoke and wrote. Secondly, we will grapple with official Nazi policy towards Germany's Roman Catholic and Protestant organizations. There are places where these subjects overlap, particularly as it appears that over time Hitler became less and less restrained about sharing his thoughts on Christianity with the world. There are also areas in which his private and public beliefs remained largely distinct. In this chapter we will analyze both aspects of the topic, beginning with Hitler's individual beliefs as best we can discern from his writings, his speeches, and comments on the topic from those with whom he privately shared his thoughts.

If you were to search online for what Hitler believed about religion, you would quickly come across a range of incompatible positions; various sources typically describe him as an atheist, a Christian, a pantheist, or an occultist. Each voice brings forth evidence which appears convincing

---

[233] Hitler, A. (1999). *Mein Kampf*. Houghton Mifflin. Page 454.

at first - but when viewed in light of equally-persuasive evidence from opposing voices, the topic quickly becomes muddled and obscured. Hitler would say one thing in private, then another in public, then another thing in public that contradicted his earlier statement, more or less ad infinitum throughout his career. This question has been the subject of innumerable inquiries, and the results have led me to agree with Richard Weikart that, due to the almost total lack of consistent clarity with which Hitler spoke on the topic - and the near-century of debate which has followed - it is very likely that Hitler deliberately obscured his religious beliefs when he found it politically expedient to do so.[234] The other possibility (perhaps equally likely) is that neither Hitler as an individual nor the Nazi Party as a whole had a meaningful or coherent religious outlook.

To try and figure out what Hitler believed in we will study his statements on various aspects of religion which are directly relevant to Christianity. Specifically, we will look at his thoughts on God, Jesus, miracles, anthropology, Scripture, the Church, and the afterlife. We will begin with his thoughts on theology in general, as separate from his views about Jesus, as there is no indication that Hitler believed that Jesus is God. It's true that he once referred to Jesus as his "Lord and Savior,"[235]

---

[234] Weikart, R. (2016). *Hitler's religion : the twisted beliefs that drove the Third Reich*. Regnery History. Page xxix.

[235] Dawkins, R. (2010, September 22). Ratzinger is an enemy of humanity. *The Guardian*. https://www.theguardian.com/commentisfree/belief/2010/sep/22/ratzinger-enemy-humanity

but we will examine the nature of his meaning in due time. Before we can address that, however, we must analyze the foundation which gave birth to all of Hitler's other views.

Hitler never made a secret, either privately or publicly, of his belief in absolute social Darwinism; throughout his career he constantly appealed to the "struggle for existence" which can be observed in all forms of organic life. In 1944, he began a speech to army officers by asserting that "Among the processes that are essentially immutable, that remain the same throughout all time, and that only change in the form of the means applied, is war. Nature teaches us with every gaze into its workings, into its events, that the principle of selection dominates it, that the stronger remains victor and the weaker succumbs. It teaches us that what often appears to someone as cruelty, because he himself is affected or because through his education he has turned away from the laws of nature, is in reality necessary, in order to bring about a higher evolution of living organisms."[236]

As this was a consistent theme through his career, he had outlined nearly two decades earlier that he believed humanity itself was subject to these same natural laws: "You are the product of this struggle. If your ancestors had not fought, today you would be an animal...the earth has been acquired on the basis of the right of the stronger."[237] Thus we can see that Hitler not only believed in Darwinian evolution, but also that "the stronger" had

[236] Weikart. Page 236.
[237] Ibid. Page 234.

a "right" to take from those whom said stronger could dominate. In this manner, so he believed, the strong would continue to improve and make progress while the detritus of humanity died off. This sort of forced evolution - at the expense of those who could not win a physical struggle for survival and replication - formed the foundation of Hitler's worldview and as the justification for his moral compass. He made this rather explicit in <u>Mein Kampf</u>, outlining his views on eugenics: "Those who are physically and mentally unhealthy and unworthy must not perpetuate their suffering in the body of their children......it is a crime and hence at the same time a disgrace to dishonor one's misfortune by one's own egotism in burdening innocent creatures with it."[238] Though framed as a moral argument meant to prevent a child's painful life, it's clear from the overall context (and Hitler's use of the word "unworthy") that he also sought to remove certain "defects" from the German population as a whole.

Weikart summarized Hitler's position well: "Hitler believed that whatever promoted evolutionary progress was morally good, and anything that hindered progress or led to biological degeneration was reprehensible. In his view, any moral system, code, or commandments must be judged according to how it contributes to the biological advancement (or regression) of humanity."[239] As will be demonstrated throughout this chapter, all forms of religious or spiritual concepts for Hitler were filtered

---

[238] Hitler. Page 404.

[239] Weikart. Page 247.

through this lens of "evolutionary progress." Thus, we can say that Hitler's "God" was not the Personal God of Christianity, Who creates and loves all human beings made in His image, but rather closer to a deification of nature and the laws which he believed to be immutable.

Immediately we run into several problems when it comes to the Christian paradigm. To begin with, there is no indication that Hitler believed the value of an individual human being had any more or less value than the life of an ant or a blade of grass. There is no sense in his work that humanity is special - apart, of course, from his concept of the "Aryan" or Nordic race - or that there's any distinction between human life and plant or animal life. Nazi propaganda openly emphasized this lack of distinction with posters displaying birds eating their prey, or a man chopping weeds out of his garden, as analogies for how the "superior" races ought to treat those they considered to be inferior. Hitler openly spoke of his disdain for individual life, assigning it no particular value beyond a person's utility to his race: "If I want to believe in a divine command, it can only be: to preserve the species! One should also not value the individual life so highly at all. If its continuance were necessary, it would not perish."[240] We will examine the principles deduced from this foundation - namely, the "rights" to kill and steal in service of one's tribe - later. For now, however, let us continue with our examination of Hitler's beliefs regarding nature and the subsequent adherence to its laws which he preached throughout his career.

---

[240] Ibid. Page 255.

Having established that Hitler's view of "nature" was a materialistic and subsequently limited one, let us also consider the fact that his faith in "science" necessarily led to a rejection of the Christian worldview. In 1941 he claimed that "Today no one who is familiar with natural science can any longer take seriously the teaching of the church. What stands in contradiction to natural laws cannot be from God."[241] Statements like this rest upon the presupposition that the science of his day was complete, that it had accounted for all that could be measured and known by man, and that anything not matching up to what *was* known then must necessarily be incorrect. We can challenge this presupposition on two main points: firstly, that science is constantly changing as new discoveries are made, and secondly, that what can be measured by human instruments is not the totality of creation.

Criticizing the view of miracles put forth by secularists and atheists, Hitler's contemporary Archbishop Averky wrote that "They assert that miracles are impossible and unfeasible as they contradict the firmly established existing laws of nature. Can miracles really be regarded as violating the laws of nature? In order to answer this question, we must first be resolutely convinced that all the laws of nature are to a certainty well known to us. Is that really so? Scientists are constantly discovering new laws of nature hitherto unknown, with every new discovery causing astonishment and, at times, completely overturning our previous conceptions of nature. What

---

[241]   Ibid. Page 48.

appeared yesterday to be absolutely impossible and implausible from the standpoint of science, today becomes incontrovertible fact...Likewise, miracles can be viewed not as violations of the laws of nature, but rather as the manifestations of laws of nature that are as yet not known or understood by us. Additionally, supreme among all laws of nature is the will of the One Who created nature - God's will, which governs all laws of nature according to His own discretion and in accordance with His all-Good Providence. Miracles are not 'anti-natural,' but rather 'super-natural,' because they transcend the laws of nature that are known to us."[242]

Thus we see the Orthodox view of nature as compared to that of a materialist; the materialist is not necessarily wrong for wanting to understand and live by the laws of nature. He is wrong, however, in his approach to nature itself; both as to contemporary scientism's ability to understand it and, on a deeper level, his inability to discern between nature as originally intended by God and the fallen state of the world which is presently our arena for salvation. The materialist looks at death, disease, competition for resources, extinction, and war - thinking to himself that this is simply *nature*, it's *how things are*, and that one must adapt himself to it for the best chance of survival and reproduction. Utterly absent from his thought is that human sin is the cause of everything he's observed, that life did not originally exist in a state of corruption and suffering, and that one day the cosmos

---

[242] Taushev, A. (2014). *The Struggle for Virtue*. Holy Trinity Monastery. Pages 52 and 53.

will not just return to its original Paradise, but greatly exceed the joy and peace at first experienced by Adam and Eve, as all of creation is Transfigured into the eternal Kingdom of God. Without the Christian phronema as passed down by the Holy Fathers, a man cannot comprehend what he sees. In that sense Hitler was perhaps not even unusual, differentiated from other secularists only in his playing out each of his presuppositions to its logical conclusions, and attaining by the desperation of a suffering nation the power and resources to put his beliefs into practice.

Scaling down from Hitler's worldview to his specific beliefs, we must examine what he said and wrote about the God-man Jesus Christ. It is true that Adolf Hitler spoke about Jesus several times - an observation never far from the lips of atheists trying to make Christianity look bad - and that fact leads us to consider the following questions: Firstly, what did he *mean* by "Jesus?" Was he speaking of the Christian Jesus, the God-man and eternal Logos incarnate, Who came to harrow Hades and reopen the Gates of Paradise? Secondly, given his public praise of Jesus, what did Hitler think of His commandments? After all, wouldn't someone who believes in Jesus as a great figure also seek to follow His teachings? Let us begin with the first question to discern *what sort of Jesus* Hitler so admired.

When describing Jesus Christ as his "Lord and Savior" as mentioned earlier, Hitler clarified that he meant *as a fighter*. More specifically, Hitler consistently described Jesus as a blonde-haired and blue-eyed Aryan warrior, likely the son of a Roman soldier. [243] As observed by Weikart, Hitler portrayed Jesus in <u>Mein Kampf</u> as a "whip-wielding anti-Semite who was crucified for opposing Jewish materialism."[244] Thus, the Jesus that Hitler so admired was essentially one created in his own concept of an Aryan warrior. Nowhere did Hitler ever express belief in the Virgin Birth, the Incarnation of a Divine Person, or the Resurrection of Jesus Christ the God-man. Given that we have already seen Hitler denying that there's anything particularly special about a human life - including, we may deduce, that every individual has an immortal soul and is created in the image and likeness of God - it should not be a surprise to find that he likewise denied the concept of an afterlife.

According to Walter Schellenberg, an SS officer who knew Hitler personally during the war, "Hitler did not believe in a personal god. He believed only in the bond of blood between succeeding generations and in a vague conception of fate or providence. Nor did he believe in a life after death. In this connection he often quoted a sentence from the *Edda*, that remarkable collection of ancient Icelandic literature, which to him represented the profoundest Nordic wisdom: 'All things will pass away, nothing will remain but death and the glory of deeds.'"[245] Hitler mocked the Christian concept of an afterlife in a 1942 Table Talk as well, asserting that he found the Muslim version of paradise more exciting but it was a

---

[243] Weikart. Page 80.

[244] Ibid. Page 81.

[245] Ibid. Page 49.

moot point in either case since life ends with death.[246] Goebbels himself confirmed this opinion in his diaries, asserting that Hitler believed in an afterlife only in the sense that a man lived on through his children and those he influenced. This view was so common in Nazi propaganda that Pope Pius Xi criticized it in his 1937 encyclical, writing that "'Immortality' in a Christian sense means the survival of man after his terrestrial death, for the purpose of eternal reward or punishment. Whoever only means by the term, the collective survival here on earth of his people for an indefinite length of time, distorts one of the fundamental notions of the Christian Faith and tampers with the very foundations of the religious concept of the universe, which requires a moral order."[247]

Hitler stripped Jesus of His divinity, seems to have denied His miracles, and ignored the Commandments he didn't like. Essentially, he combined Arianism with Aryanism to create a new "Jesus of his imagination."[248]

As far as what Hitler believed about God, he appeared to have no clear conception of what the word meant; on one page he wrote of "the living God," on the next "the goddess of eternal justice."[249] He appealed to "Fate" - always with a capital "F" - several times throughout <u>Mein Kampf</u>. For example, Hitler lost both his parents while still a teenager trying to figure out his path to success in

---

[246]   Ibid. Page 50.

[247]   Ibid. Pages 53 and 54.

[248]   Ibid. Page 85.

[249]   Hitler. Pages 14 and 15.

life. He hated the idea of working an office job and, when he came down with a serious lung disease, Hitler was ecstatic to hear the doctor tell his mother that he should never work in that kind of environment. After the death of his father, Hitler was equally excited when his mother gave him permission to attend the Academy of Art in Vienna. She died shortly thereafter, leaving a mostly-penniless young Adolf to strike out for Vienna on his own. Describing the experience as an adult, he wrote: "When my mother died, Fate, at least in one respect, had made its decisions."[250]

It seems Hitler saw Fate as a sovereign entity with its own goals and plans. Soon after, he described himself in the arms of the "Goddess of Suffering."[251] Frequent comments like these lead me to conclude that whatever happened throughout his life, he either credited to (or simply invented) some mystical force which in his mind deserved said credit. He never described any of these forces or "gods" in any detail beyond naming them as responsible for various events in his life. He varyingly wrote of Nature, the gods, Providence, the Almighty Creator, Fate, and God - with equal superficiality in each case. It seems that he picked and chose between various deities not even as an expression of genuine pagan belief, but rather out of convenience to emphasize various points. As far as I have been able to glean from Mein Kampf, he was not particularly devoted to any deity or force beyond German racialism and the Reich.

---

[250] Ibid. Page 19.
[251] Ibid. Page 21.

Further, Goebbels noted in his diaries that "The Führer is deeply religious, but entirely anti-Christian. He sees in Christianity a symptom of decay."[252] He didn't mention precisely what Hitler *did* believe, but Goebbels was sure it wasn't Christianity. Similarly Alfred Rosenberg, a close confidant of Hitler's, wrote in his memoirs after the war that "What his own beliefs were he never told me in so many words."[253] Rosenberg did believe, however, that when Hitler referred to "God" or "the Almighty" he was referring more to an impersonal sense of fate than to any notion of a Personal God as Christian perceive Him.[254] Thus we may conclude that, in regard to Hitler's private beliefs, his occasional use of Christian language did not express a genuine belief in Christianity.

Now that we've analyzed Hitler's own pseudo-theology, we may proceed to how those beliefs affected his public policy towards various Christian organizations. I have been unable to find any comments made directly by Hitler about Orthodox Christianity, which appears to have had little to no presence in Germany or Austria during his lifetime; both Hitler and his mentor Dietrich Eckhart rather used the phrase "both denominations" to refer to the Roman Catholicism and Protestantism with which they were clearly more familiar. National Socialism did encounter Orthodoxy eventually, specifically in the occupied territories of Russia and Czechoslovakia, and we will discuss these interactions shortly. For now,

---

[252] Weikart. Page 2.

[253] Ibid. Page 8.

[254] Ibid. Page 57.

however, let us study how the Nazi government engaged with Roman Catholicism and Protestantism.

By the time he wrote <u>Mein Kampf</u>, Hitler had already formulated the position towards Catholicism and Protestantism that would remain his stance until the end of his life. In that book, he asserted (without evidence) that the fighting between Catholicism and Protestantism, which he called the *Ultramontane question*, was the result of Jewish interference in German culture.[255] He did not seem to comprehend, much less care about, the long history of theological and ecclesiastical disputes. As a necessary byproduct of this belief, and his decision to focus all German anger against the singular enemy of Jewish power, Hitler remained convinced throughout his career that fighting against any particular "denomination" would be a political disaster.

After all, so the train of thought likely went, if some Germans were roused against Catholicism and others against Protestantism, then they wouldn't still possess the anger and zeal that Hitler wanted them to cultivate against the Jews. He specifically criticized Georg Von Shonerer's Pan-German Party for exactly that; though he largely agreed with Schonerer's political views, Hitler believed that his Los-Von-Rom (Away-from-Rome) Movement was a considerable factor in why the Pan-German Party failed. Instead, Hitler decided that it would make more sense to try and unify Catholics and Protestants in both their anger against Jews (rather than each other) and, ultimately, their loyalty to Germany and

[255] Hitler. Page 571.

National Socialism. With this concept in mind, Hitler's behavior towards both "denominations" comes into a perfect clarity.[256]

Thus we should not be surprised to discover that Hitler often publicly preached religious neutrality, giving lip service to Christianity and its leaders in Germany while also keeping them on a short leash. Though he promised to defend religious institutions, and declined from publicly commenting on Christian doctrine or theological points, Hitler also made clear his belief that there exists a "clear division between politics, which have to do with terrestrial things, and religion, which must concern itself with the celestial sphere."[257] His meaning went far beyond the separation of Church and State, as he indicated countless times with his threats towards Christian leaders who he felt were not properly loyal to the Nazi Party; what he meant amounted to "believe whatever you want, but if you're not on board with National Socialism then I'm going to punish you for it."

In 1941 he said, very explicitly: "I don't concern myself with articles of faith, but I will not tolerate it, if a cleric concerns himself with earthly matters. The organized lie must somehow be broken, so that the state is absolute lord."[258] Needless to say, this is not a genuine religious liberty and none of the Royal Saints you studied in a previous chapter shared his belief; neither did any of them refer to religion as a "lie." The rulers of the

---

[256] Weikart. Page 5.

[257] Ibid. Page 10.

[258] Ibid. Page 12.

Michael Witcoff

terrestrial and celestial spheres ought to work together for the well-being of man, providing for both his worldly and spiritual needs. None of our canonized Emperors put something like a political party above theology, as their holistic Orthodox view of a human being prevented them from splitting a man down the middle.

While encouraging Germans to put aside their confessional differences, Hitler formulated a more politically-useful version of the faith that he referred to as "Positive Christianity." Though his new faith often stressed the supposed triviality of theology and doctrine, he occasionally injected content into the movement that certainly put it at odds with traditional Christianity. For example, he said in a 1922 speech that "The Christian religion is created only for the Aryans; for other people it is absurd."[259] Such comments betray that Hitler saw Christianity as more of a racial tool than the Transfiguring Faith which God wishes all men to possess. St. Paul wrote in **Galatians 3:28** that *"There is neither Jew nor Gentile, neither slave nor free, nor is there male and female, for you are all one in Christ Jesus."*

Though this verse is sometimes interpreted to mean something other than its intention, the obvious context is that those Baptized into the Holy Orthodox Church share in a Faith, and a way of life, which transcends worldly boundaries. If Jews and Gentiles are both part of the Faith, then clearly Christianity is not "only for the Aryans;" rather, we affirm with St. Jerome that "When one has once put on Christ and, having been sent into the

---

[259] Ibid. Page 75.

206

flame, glows with the ardor of the Holy Spirit, it is not apparent whether he is of gold or silver. As long as the heat takes over the mass in this way there is one fiery color, and all diversity of race, condition and body is taken away by such a garment."[260] St. Augustine of Hippo, commenting on the same verse, added that "Difference of race or condition or sex is indeed taken away by the unity of the faith, but it remains embedded in our mortal interactions, and in the journey of this life the apostles themselves teach that it is to be respected... For we observe in the unity of faith that there are no such distinctions. Yet within the orders of this life they persist."[261]

Thus we observe the balanced view of the Orthodox Church: that race and sex, while real and meaningful in our worldly affairs, are ultimately abrogated within the Church by virtue of all its members being united to Christ. The New Testament and Church Fathers did not teach that race doesn't exist, as is sometimes speculated; rather, they taught that these things ought to be respected to the correct degree and that ultimately, within the Church, they cease to be a meaningful distinction. If Christianity had been "created" only for one race, as Hitler believed, then certainly the Apostles and Fathers were unaware of it.

Like Mussolini, Hitler signed a Concordat with the

---

[260] *Jerome on Galatians 3:28.* (n.d.). Catena Bible & Commentaries. Retrieved March 2, 2023, from https://catenabible.com/com/584233c025973d7a18c66790
[261] *Augustine of Hippo on Galatians 3:28.* (n.d.). Catena Bible & Commentaries. Retrieved March 2, 2023, from https://catenabible.com/com/584233c025973d7a18c66792

Vatican. That Concordat, often called the Reich Concordat, was ratified in 1933 after Hitler formally became the head of Germany. As noted by Joseph Biesinger his essay *The Reich Concordat: The Church Struggle Against Nazi Germany*, "Before Hitler was appointed Chancellor on 30 January 1933 National Socialism had been criticized by episcopal authorities as pagan and totalitarian. The German bishops had warned Catholics against Nazism on numerous occasions as far back as 1920 and as recently as February 1931 when the Bavarian bishops had forbidden Catholics to support the party and condemned its pagan ideology."[262] However, Hitler's becoming the official Head of State supplied a challenge to the Vatican in that their policy was always to cooperate with the government in order to secure their own existence while following the Biblical principle of obedience to State authority.

The issue was further complicated by Hitler's early affirmations of his intentions to defend Christianity, as his first radio address to Germany in February 1933 "promised to make Christian morality and family the basis of German society and pursue amicable relations" with the Vatican.[263] Over the next couple of months, Roman Catholic bishops dramatically reversed their previous condemnations of National Socialism (while some still expressed reservations) and they revoked their prohibition of Catholics' ability to support the Nazi Party;

[262] Coppa, F. J. (1999). *Controversial concordats : the Vatican's relation with Napoleon, Mussolini, and Hitler*. Catholic University Of America Press. Page 122.
[263] Ibid. Page 124.

after a meeting of all German bishops in early June of that year, they released a pastoral message celebrating the "national awakening" and encouraged support of the new regime provided that Catholic confessional schools and other organizations were protected and allowed to exist.[264]

As per the Concordat, this was the arrangement agreed upon by Cardinal Pacelli and Franz von Papen. Nearly 2/3 of the Treaty's Articles pertained directly to the protection of the religious institution, which included the right of Roman Catholicism in Germany to teach, publicly defend its ideals, operate Catholic schools, and run Catholic Youth associations. Unfortunately for the Vatican, a caveat was added that these platforms must remain apolitical - a term left so vague by the Reich that it freely persecuted Roman Catholic organizations at the first sign that they defended Christian morality when and where said morality conflicted with Nazi policies. Catholics who were found belonging to other political parties were regularly harassed, beaten, or even imprisoned; this seemed especially harsh in Bavaria, where before the Concordat was ratified "over one hundred priests were imprisoned. Some were only mishandled, but some were half beaten to death. The headquarters of Catholic Associations was also attacked. The most dramatic action by the Bavarian Nazi leadership occurred between 25-28 June when almost two thousand Catholics associated with the Bavarian People's Party, which had refused to dissolve itself, were rounded up

---

[264] Ibid. Page 127.

and imprisoned. In this group were over 150 priests...
Although attacks against Catholic organizations had
begun before the Concordat was signed, they intensified
afterward."[265]

Article 31 of the Concordat had been left ambiguously
unresolved in terms of specifics - and it appears this was
deliberate on the part of Nazi leadership - to such a
degree that "No list of organizations had been included
for either of the two categories: the religious
organizations, which were to be provided with total
protection, and social and professional organizations,
which were to have protected rights if and when they
were merged into state organizations."[266] The result of all
this was that the Reich persecuted Catholic organizations
whenever and wherever it saw fit: though Reich Youth
Leader Baldur von Schirach forbade dual membership in
Catholic youth associations and the Hitler Youth the
month before the Concordat was signed, even afterward
pressure from the government drove young people away
from the former and toward the latter. In 1935, for
example, seventeen hundred Catholic Youth members
had their uniforms confiscated by German authorities
upon returning from their visit to the Pope. Further, "The
Hitler Youth Law of 1 December 1936 officially
coordinated Catholic youth organizations into the Hitler
Youth, but it was not until 6 February 1939 that the
Catholic Young Men's Association (JMV) was finally
dissolved by the Gestapo. It was formally ended by the

---

[265] Ibid. Page 143.

[266] Ibid. Page 144.

law of 25 March 1939 which made membership in the Hitler Youth compulsory."[267] Thus we can see that, in perfect alignment with Hitler's apparent desire to slowly corrode Christian influence rather than declare outright war against it, his agreements with the Vatican looked more like "death by a thousand cuts" than genuine cooperation between Catholicism and the State.

The National Socialist battle against Catholic schools applied a similar tactic: "Members of the Nazi Party demanded that parents explain why their children attended Catholic schools. Parents were not permitted any official recourse. Over one hundred such incidents were noted by [Cardinal] Pacelli. This strategy proved to be so successful that between 1933 and 1937 the percentage of Catholic families in Munich that sent their children to Catholic schools 65% to 3%. Six hundred teaching nuns were declared redundant and dismissed. Catholic teachers in state schools were pressured into resigning from confessional associations."[268]

Campaigns of harassment and subterfuge of this sort seem to have been regular violations of the Concordat, which eventually caused Catholic clergy to begin speaking out against these abuses; in 1934, Cardinal Bertram met with the Pope and shared his long list of grievances. After explaining the many ways in which the Reich was not honoring their arrangement, Bertram also predicted an overt clash with the government over its 1933 sterilization law. Further complicating the matter,

---

[267] Ibid. Pages 145 and 146.
[268] Ibid. Page 148

bishops had no real way to have these issues addressed and resolved unless the Hitler government decided to honor them. The Vatican had no meaningful leverage over the Reich, and too much public criticism simply resulted in the State declaring that Catholics were being disloyal; this, subsequently, was perceived as a Vatican violation of their vow to be apolitical and resulted in further persecution of Catholicism. Cardinal Faulhaber met with Hitler in 1936, hoping to resolve these issues. After the war, Faulhaber had described Hitler's "dark radiance" and declared that he had "looked Satan in the face."[269]

By 1937, enough Catholic clergy had complained that an encyclical published that year "forcefully protested the many violations of the Concordat, reviewed the principles of the Catholic faith, Christian ethics, and the importance of the natural law versus the interests of the state, and condemned the arbitrary 'revelations' of Alfred Rosenberg and the exponents of the 'so-called myth of blood and race'...Hitler concluded that Catholicism had declared war on the Nazi ideology and there no longer was any hope of compromise."[270] His revenge against the Vatican was a five-stage plan including "expropriation of [Catholic] assets; dissolution of religious orders and monasteries; restriction on entrance to theological studies; prohibition of education by clergy; and elimination of clerical celibacy."[271]

---

[269] Ibid. Page 155.

[270] Ibid. Page 157.

[271] Ibid.

Within a couple of years, "Private schools were abolished or taken over by the state. In the spring of 1939 the denominational schools were converted into interdenominational ones and members of religious orders were denied the right to serve as teachers. Even crucifixes and religious pictures were requested to be removed from classrooms in Oldenburg and Bavaria, which led to mass protests and criticism by the Bavarian bishops on 26 July 1941."[272] Overall, "During the period 1933-1945 the Nazi regime used coercive measures against one-third, of 7,155, of the secular clergy, and one-fifth, of 866, of the clergy of religious orders - a total of 8,021 clerics. It is estimated that about one-third, or 34.5 percent, of the total offenses prosecuted (22,703) involved criticism of the regime, political unreliability, and behavior hostile to the state."[273]

As his political career continued and Catholics vocalized more of their opposition, Hitler became less restrained about his anti-Christian vitriol. In 1941 he expressed his admiration for Julian the Apostate, a pagan Emperor who sought to overthrow Christianity and - ironically - wanted to help Jews rebuild Solomon's Temple. In July of that year, Hitler's mask came off completely and he described Christianity as "the greatest blow to strike humanity," further stating in December that it "leads to the destruction of humanity" and "is unadulterated Bolshevism in a metaphysical

---

[272] Ibid. Page 159.

[273] Ibid. Page 169 and 170.

framework."[274] In that same month, he told a group of district officials that "There is an insoluble contradiction between the Christian and Germanic-heroic worldview. However, this contradiction cannot be resolved during the war, but after the war we must step up to solve this contradiction. I see a possible solution only in the further consolidation of the National Socialist worldview."[275] Perhaps he couldn't help himself but try and speed up this long-term plan; perhaps his belief in himself as Europe's messiah had completely displaced any room for a Savior in his heart.

Regarding when and where Christianity "went wrong," the memoirs of Hitler's associate and confidant Otto Wagener provide us with an interesting tidbit. According to Wagener, Hitler once expressed his belief that the National Socialists were the *true* Christians all along; Hitler is credited in Wagener's work with the comment that "We are the first to exhume these teachings! Through us alone, and not until now, do these teachings celebrate their resurrection!"[276]

In the same spirit which possesses many other reformers, Hitler appears to have believed - similarly to the founder of Mormonism Joseph Smith - that the institutional Christian Church immediately fell into a "great apostasy" and that the *real* teachings of Jesus were being handed to him, directly by divine revelation or some other supposed mechanism, so that he alone could

---

[274] Weikart. Pages 99 and 101.

[275] Ibid. Page 94.

[276] *Religious views of Adolf Hitler - Wikiquote*. (2018). Wikiquote.org. https://en.wikiquote.org/wiki/Religious_views_of_Adolf_Hitler

restore the "truth" that was "lost." Both Mormonism and National Socialism, together with the other Protestant sects and individual "reformation and restoration" movements, deny what Jesus Christ Himself taught us in **Matthew 16:18** when He told St. Peter that He *"will build My church, and the gates of Hades shall not prevail against it."* To assert that the gates of Hades overthrew the Church is to deny the Word of God and to call Him a liar. May He have mercy on all who don't realize what they've implied - and especially on those who do.

But regardless of how Hitler and the National Socialist regime treated Protestants and Roman Catholics, the crux of the issue for us is their engagement with the Orthodox Church. Though I've been unable to find any comments from Hitler or his officers on the Orthodox Church in particular, Orthodoxy teaches and believes that Christ speaks His mind through the Saints. Thus, if we can find Saints commenting on Hitler and National Socialism - or engaging with Nazi Germany in a different way - we may conclude that even if Hitler had no particular thoughts about Orthodoxy, Orthodoxy had particular thoughts about him. That leads to the question of whether we find Saints either supporting Hitler, opposing Hitler, or even if there were Saints on both sides of this equation. If we only find Saints on one side, we may rest assured that the Church has revealed God's perception of this situation. To my knowledge, of the Saints who engaged with Nazism, only St. Nikolai Velimirovic once made a statement in support of Adolf Hitler; however, even he ended up in the Dachau concentration camp for reasons that still seem shrouded in mystery. As far as my research has revealed, every other Saint who commented on the topic opposed Hitler - though if you discover evidence to the contrary, feel free to let me know so that future editions of this book can reflect all available data on the topic.

In exploring the Orthodox relationship to Hitler, I have found several canonized Orthodox Saints who were Martyred during the Nazi regime; by glorifying these Saints and raising them up as examples of holiness, the Church seems to have revealed that God was not with the National Socialists. Let us take a brief look at each.

The first Saint executed by Hitler's regime was St. Gorazd of Prague, a Bishop of the Czechoslovakian Church. According to his entry on OrthoWiki: "With the conquest of Czechoslovakia by the Nazis in 1938, the Church was placed under the Orthodox Metropolitan in Berlin, Germany. Assigned as ruler of Czechoslovakia was Reinhard Heydrich, who was reputed to be designated successor to Adolf Hitler. On May 27, 1942, a group of Czech resistance fighters attacked and killed Heydric[h] as his car slowed down on a curve near the Cathedral of Ss. Cyril and Methodius in Prague. In making their escape the group found refuge in the crypt of the Cathedral. When Bp. Gorazd found out a few days later, he recognized the serious position this placed on the Czech Orthodox Church and before he left for the consecration to the episcopate of Fr. John (Gardner) in Berlin he asked that the resistance fighters move elsewhere as soon as possible. However, on June 18, the

Nazis found out the hiding places after a betrayal by two members of the resistance group, and the all members of the group were killed.

Reprisals came quickly. The two priests and the senior lay Church officials were arrested. Bp. Gorazd, wishing to help his fellow believers and the Czech Church itself, took the blame for the actions in the Cathedral on himself, even writing letters to the Nazi authorities. But, on June 27, he was arrested and tortured. On September 4, 1942, Bp. Gorazd, the Cathedral priests and senior lay leaders were executed by firing squad. The reprisals went much further as the Nazis conducted widespread roundups of Czechs, including the whole village of Lidice, then summarily killed the men and placed the survivors in forced labor camps. The Orthodox churches in Moravia and Bohemia were closed and the Church forbidden to operate. Metropolitan Seraphim courageously refused to issue any statement condemning Bp. Gorazd. It wasn't until the end of the war that the Orthodox Church in Czechoslovakia would function again."[277]

Further Saints I've found that were canonized for opposing the Nazi Regime are Saints Maria of Paris and her associates Yuri Skobtsov, Elie Fondaminsky, and Fr. Dimitry Klepinin. Though she turned to atheism and Bolshevism earlier in her life, St. Maria eventually embraced Christianity and became a nun. She and her contemporaries helped hide Jews from Nazis in Paris, sheltering and protecting them how and where they

---

[277] *Gorazd (Pavlik) of Prague - OrthodoxWiki*. (n.d.). Orthodoxwiki.org. Retrieved April 30, 2023, from https://orthodoxwiki.org/Gorazd_(Pavlik)_of_Prague

could. For their efforts, the group was arrested by the Gestapo and sent to die in concentration camps - where St. Maria was Martyred on Holy Saturday of 1945.[278]

Lastly, another Orthodox Christian who opposed Hitler's regime was the New-Martyr St. Alexander Schmorell. Born in Russia, of half-Russian and half-German ethnicity, Alexander Schmorell moved to Munich with his family after Bolshevism took root in his home country. He was only four years old at the time.

In Germany he continued to study the Orthodoxy of his youth and attend Divine Liturgies, usually accompanied by the nanny who moved with the family. The Schmorell home became a major attraction for other Russian immigrants in Munich, and was often visited by artists who appreciated the values that Alexander's parents cultivated in their house. Beyond the cultural appeal of being around the well-educated Schmorells, Russian refugees also began to seek them out for aid. It was provided generously and they became known as a great help to the displaced and fearful searching for a better life. Eventually, the Schmorell home was used as a secret repository for books from a nearby monastery that Hitler shut down.

After his compulsory service in the German army - where he realized that the propaganda he'd been fed did not align with the horrors he witnessed on the ground - Alexander decided to study medicine so that, in case a full-fledged war broke out, he could save lives instead of

[278] *Maria (Skobtsova) - OrthodoxWiki*. (n.d.). Orthodoxwiki.org. Retrieved April 30, 2023, from https://orthodoxwiki.org/Maria_(Skobtsova)

take them. Thus he enrolled in the University of Munich and was conscripted into a military medical unit, where he met the other students who would later form the White Rose resistance group. Though the future St. Alexander was the only Orthodox member of the White Rose, the Protestants and Catholics who filled the rest of the ranks also saw National Socialism as opposed to their Christian beliefs. Beyond their ideals of freedom to practice religion, the students were bound together by a shared love of art, literature, poetry, and music. Alexander shared his love of Dostoevsky with the others, who saw in the Grand Inquisitor of "Brothers K" an archetype resembling Hitler. Even before there were plans to formally resist the German regime, the White Rose circle sought solace in such endeavors as a way of relieving the torment they felt under Hitler.

By 1942, the White Rose group decided to become more active in resisting Hitler. According to Elena Perekrestov, author of <u>Alexander Schmorell: Saint of the German Resistance</u>: "Their aim was to make people aware that Hitler did not have the support of the entire German population; to reach out to others who were in opposition to the regime and thereby strengthen them; and to convince the undecided to overcome their hesitation and join the ranks of opposition. In this way, they hoped to foster popular resistance to the National Socialist regime within Germany and, if possible, to shorten the war. The latter, Alexander would state in his interrogation, they saw as the best possible solution for both Germany and Russia. Their method was to write and disseminate

leaflets by which they sought to stir up their apathetic
countrymen."[279] These leaflets, which encouraged passive
resistance and loyalty to Christian values, were then
mailed out across Munich (largely to the intelligentsia
and other people of means and influence). Notably, they
also contain the first documentation of the massacres
inflicted on Jews and Poles in German-occupied territory.

The leaflets also encouraged "sabotage in armament
plants, war industries, and every scientific or intellectual
field that would aid in continuing the war; sabotage of
newspapers and publications that help to disseminate 'the
brown lie;' sabotage at all gatherings, rallies, and public
ceremonies that promote National Socialism."[280] After
returning from the Russian front, the students multiplied
their efforts; they not only began copying and printing
their leaflets by the thousands, but they traveled around
Germany mailing them to far more cities than just
Munich. This had the combined effect of making their
network seem larger while temporarily diverting
attention from their base.

The first members of the White Rose to be caught were
Hans and Sophie Scholl, who were seen by a University
custodian pushing leaflets off a baluster and into the
school atrium below. The custodian chased them down
and turned them into the Gestapo. After a brief show trial
adjudicated by Roland Freisler - a Nazi loyalist and judge
notorious for handing out death sentences like candy - the

---

[279] Perekrestov, E. (2017). *Alexander Schmorell, Saint of the German resistance*. Holy
Trinity Publications, The Printshop of St Job of Pochaev. Pages 54 and 55.
[280] Ibid. Page 59.

Scholls and a third collaborator, Christoph Probst, were beheaded by guillotine at Stadelheim Prison.

After becoming aware that the regime was looking for him, as a result of raids on both the Scholl and Schmorell homes that revealed incriminating evidence, Alexander sought refuge among friends who were not connected to the White Rose circle. Unfortunately the Gestapo was a step ahead of him and he was apprehended at one of the homes he hoped to hide in. He was questioned for two straight days and nights, and fearlessly told his interrogators who he was, what he believed, and what he'd done. The only lie he told them, in the hope of keeping any more friends out of trouble, was that he and Hans had acted alone.

Charged by the People's Court with high treason against National Socialism - a "crime" to which he readily confessed - Alexander was sentenced to death. A couple friends of his devised an elaborate plan, by which he could escape from prison and go home to his family, but he turned it down. He did not want anyone else to potentially suffer for his sake, and chose to face death full of trust in God and hope in eternity instead. Months passed while Alexander's family appealed the sentence, and this petition eventually reached Hitler himself - who personally rejected the appeal for mercy. On July 13, 1943, Alexander Schmorell was likewise beheaded at Stadelheim.

Fifty years later the Gestapo files on his activities - and the White Rose circle as a whole - became public knowledge in Munich and around Europe. His gravesite is close to the parish he attended, and many Russian Orthodox Christians in Germany began to venerate his memory. Though the fall of Nazi Germany did not result in the idealistic goals the White Rose hoped for, they nonetheless resisted Hitler for the right reasons - their Christian faith and desire for humanity's suffering to lessen - and for his execution by a anti-Christian regime, St. Alexander Schmorell was canonized by ROCOR on the day of the Synaxis of the Holy New Martyrs and Confessors of Russia in 2012. He is commemorated on July 13th, the day of his death. According to Perekrestov, "Metropolitan Onuphry likened St. Alexander's denunciation of National Socialism (expressed both in the White Rose leaflets and in his interrogations) to the daring feat of St. John the Baptist, who had denounced the king, Herod, for unlawfully marrying his brother's wife Herodias. Beheading was the retribution he suffered for his audacious words."[281]

Of note, St. Alexander did not just oppose the Nazis; he opposed the communists who ruined Russia as well. Thus St. Alexander opposed both Bolshevism and National Socialism as the materialistic and soul-destroying ideologies they were, walking instead the Royal Path of Orthodox service to mankind. May St. Alexander of Munich and all others killed for the Truth pray that God may grant us the courage He granted to them.

The confusing impression left on those who personally knew Hitler seems the inevitable result of a soul being

---

[281] Ibid. Page 153.

ravaged by dark forces which, by way of his heresy and war against Christian humility, Hitler welcomed into his life with open arms. One further gets the impression that Hitler was a man who consciously understood the importance of not raging publicly against Christianity - as that would hinder his political agenda, at least early on - but was unable to stop himself from doing so both privately and even publicly on occasion. His inconsistencies betray a man who was not a deep spiritual thinker, but rather one whose pseudo-theology was subject to constant morphing in service of whatever rhetorical point he wanted to make to an audience or, ultimately, his own political agenda.

While we can agree with certain of Hitler's policies in a superficial sense – such as his banning of degenerate "art" or closing of Masonic lodges – the logic underlying these actions did not align with Christian reasoning. For example, Hitler saw Freemasonry as a subversive and corroding force (and it is certainly both of these things). However, the Orthodox position – as outlined at length in my book <u>On The Masons and their Lies</u> – is that Masonry is not just an anti-nationalist current, but a secretive and Luciferian religion whose main tenets are hostile to Christianity. Hitler, being unconcerned with Christian dogma or doctrine except insofar as their usefulness to his cause, would not have been interested in these aspects of the Fraternity – and may even, in some respect and had he studied it deeply, have supported those elements of its worldview which are most in conflict with our own.

His deeply-seated belief in his own fate, and the goals

and strategies that he felt destined to implement and achieve, seem much closer to his true "spirituality" than any words he chose to use in a given speech or essay. Perhaps the mess that we observe, the story of a man calculating his statements on theology for material gain, is why Blessed Seraphim Rose wrote that "Hitler, indeed, was the absurd man par excellence, passing from nothingness to world rule and back to nothingness in the space of a dozen years, leaving as his monument nothing but a shattered world, owing his meaningless success to the fact that he, the emptiest of men, personified the emptiness of his time."[282]

As is now evident, God has judged Adolf Hitler by raising up as Saints the men and women who opposed him for Christ. I suspect this clear denunciation of National Socialism will stir up angst among those who still imagine they can believe in both our Faith and Nazi ideology, and I hope and pray that the outcome of this internal struggle will result in peace and clarity for their souls. It is one of many points at which, if you're journeying into the heart of Orthodoxy from a particular political standpoint, you will have to choose between your own reasoning and what God has revealed through the Church. For my part I am satisfied that, as Hitler's private secretary Martin Bormann wrote in 1941, "National Socialism and Christianity are irreconcilable."[283]

---

[282] *Subhumanity – The Philosophy of the Absurd*. (2015, November 20). Deathtotheworld.com. https://deathtotheworld.com/articles/subhumanity-the-philosophy-of-the-absurd/

[283] Shirer, W. L., & Rosenbaum, R. (2011). *The Rise And Fall Of The Third Reich : A*

Hitler and the State

"The great masses of the people in the very bottom of their hearts tend to be corrupted rather than consciously and purposely evil."[284] *- Adolf Hitler*

Hitler laid out his vision for the Reich on the very first page of <u>Mein Kampf</u>: "Germany-Austria must return to the great German mother country, and not because of any economic considerations. No, and again no: even if such a union were unimportant from an economic point of view; yes, even if it were harmful, it must nevertheless take place. One blood demands one Reich....Only when the Reich borders include the very last German, but can no longer guarantee his daily bread, will the moral right to acquire foreign soil arise from the distress of our own people."[285] It is interesting to note that as early as the very first page of his autobiography, Hitler was already hard at work justifying the "morality" of theft.

Though couching it in the polite language of a desire to "acquire foreign soil," there is no mistaking the message that if Germans wanted or needed something and someone else had it - regardless of whether those other people also needed the resource in question - Hitler decided it was a "moral right" to take said resources away from them. Fundamentally, I fail to see how this

---

History Of Nazi Germany. Simon & Schuster. Page 240.

[284] Hitler, A. (1999). *Mein Kampf.* Houghton Mifflin. Page 231.

[285] Ibid. Page 1.

approach differs from the Bolshevik justification of killing the rich in order to give their money to the poor.

Hitler wrote that his nationalism was largely cultivated under the tutelage of a professor in the German equivalent of high school. This teacher, so Hitler wrote, taught him to hate the Austrian Hapsburg dynasty which he perceived as ignoring the needs and rights of ethnic Germans. More specifically, he hated that the Hapsburgs "Czechized wherever possible" and complained of Austria's "Slavization."[286] All this led to his formulation of the opinion which he claimed only deepened with age and time: "That Germanism could be safeguarded only by the destruction of Austria, and, furthermore, that national sentiment is in no sense identical with dynastic patriotism; that above all the House of Hapsburg was destined to be the misfortune of the German nation. Even then I had drawn the consequences from this realization: ardent love for my German-Austrian homeland, deep hatred for the Austrian state...Thus, at an early age, I had become a political 'revolutionary.'"[287]

Studying social problems in Vienna, Hitler decided that "Social activity must never and on no account be directed toward philanthropic flim-flam, but rather toward the elimination of the basic deficiencies in the organization of our economic and cultural life that must - or at all events can - lead to the degeneration of the individual."[288] Rather than following a plan of Just War,

[286] Ibid. Page 15.

[287] Ibid. Page 16.

[288] Ibid. Page 30.

or attempting to solve these "basic deficiencies" by normal means, the young Hitler decided instead that only "applying the most extreme and brutal methods against the criminals who endanger the state" would suffice; he further lamented that others appeared less committed to these methods than he was, adding that "Only when an epoch ceases to be haunted by the shadow of its own consciousness of guilt will it achieve the inner calm and outward strength brutally and ruthlessly to prune out the wild shoots and tear out the weeds."[289] Needless to say, you will not find such words used by our Saints. You will not find them encouraging people to overcome a guilty conscience in order to be brutal and ruthless more calmly, nor will you find them running to "the most extreme and brutal methods" as their first attempt at solving problems.

After identifying Marxism as the root of Austrian degeneration at the time, and more specifically the Social Democrats as its main proponents and propagators, Hitler dedicated himself to studying their dogmas in his free time. He described heated tirades from all his coworkers, who often repeated Marxist slogans and doctrines, forcing him to learn more about the topic simply so that he could argue with them. The more he learned about it, according to him, the more clearly he understood its dangers: "I understood the infamous spiritual terror which this movement exerts, particularly on the bourgeoisie, which is neither morally nor mentally equal to such attacks; at a given sign it unleashes a veritable barrage of lies and slanders against whatever

---

[289] Ibid.

adversary seems most dangerous, until the nerves of the attacked persons break down and, just to have peace again, they sacrifice the hated individual."[290] Finally, he decided that he had to oppose fire with fire by designing a new doctrine with which he could fight back against Marxist degeneracy and lies.

Like the other nationalists included in this book, Hitler disliked democracy and saw it as the eternal companion of Marxism: "The Western democracy of today is the is the forerunner of Marxism which without it would not be thinkable. It provides this world plague with the culture in which its germs can spread."[291] He considered parliamentarianism as insufficient for proper governance as well, blaming the lack of individual responsibility incurred by consensus-government as the cause of this problem; subsequently, he decided that a government led by one man would lead to someone taking responsibility when things went wrong, rather than simply offloading the fault onto the other members of the group. In of itself, this critique of democracy and approval of Monarchy is not at odds with the Christian view.

As opposed to Western democracy, Hitler preferred a "truly Germanic democracy characterized by the free election of a leader and his obligation fully to assume all responsibility for his actions and omissions. In it there is no majority vote on individual questions, but only the decision of an individual who must answer with his

---

[290] Ibid. Page 43.

[291] Ibid. Page 78.

fortune and his life for his choice."[292] That leader, in his view, ought to rule over a state which exists not for its own sake but rather for the sake of the people contained within in it - in this case, a state composed only of Germans whose right to citizenship was determined by blood and ability. He elaborated that National Socialism "in its nature and inner organization [is] anti-parliamentarian; that is, it rejects, in general and in its own inner structure, a principle of majority rule in which the leader is degraded to the level of a mere executant of other people's will and opinion."[293]

Describing his concept of the State, Hitler wrote that "It is not a collection of economic contracting parties in a definite delimited living space for the fulfillment of economic tasks, but the organization of a community of physically and psychologically similar living beings for the better facilitation of the maintenance of the species and the achievement of the aim which has been allotted to this species by Providence."[294] It should be noted that in his book, Hitler often (and incorrectly) used the word "species" to refer to what is usually called "race" or "ethnicity."

In one of many passages which seem to indicate a begrudging admiration for Judaism - if not envy for its power to organize and support its ethnic preservation - Hitler wrote that "The Jewish state was never spatially limited in itself, but universally unlimited as to space,

---

[292] Ibid. Page 91.
[293] Ibid. Page 344.
[294] Ibid. Page 150.

though restricted in the sense of embracing but one race. Consequently, this people has always formed a state within states."[295] Blind to the spirituality which at least in theory binds Jews together, he continued that "It is one of the most ingenious tricks that was ever devised, to make this state sail under the flag of 'religion,' thus assuring it of the tolerance which the Aryan is always ready to accord a religious creed. For actually the Mosaic religion is nothing other than a doctrine for the preservation of the Jewish race. It therefore embraces almost all sociological, political, and economic fields of knowledge which can have any bearing on this function."[296] Reading Mein Kampf, I often got the impression that Hitler looked to world Judaism as a model of a successful (if, at the time, borderless) State and sought to implement several of its techniques while adapting others to his own German cause. If one were to switch out the words "German" and "Jew" in Mein Kampf, it could be mistaken for a Zionist manifesto.

Hitler's "folkish" worldview prioritized the perspective that Germans alone were "the last race capable of culture;"[297] hence, the purpose of a German State was not simply to help Germans, but to retain a certain level of "culture" among the human population in general. By preserving Germans as a people, so his logic went, there would always be a race on Earth which was capable of producing the creative genius he perceived as

---

[295] Ibid.

[296] Ibid. Pages 150 and 151.

[297] Ibid. Page 392.

the sole possession of Germans. He took issue with the fact that before Christianity, Germans were barbaric and worshiped trees; he claimed that if those ancient Germans had only lived in a different region, they "would have grown into radiant bloom just as happened, for example, with the Greeks."[298] These words seem to undermine his general perspective that only Germans were truly capable of cultural achievement. In either case, he believed that true civilization would disappear if he did not create a State just for Germans.

To that end, once Hitler moved to Munich, he began to consider what he perceived as the gravest issue facing the potential future of the German Reich: that 900,000 new Germans were born every year and that - at some point - there wouldn't be enough resources to keep them healthy and strong. He pondered a number of potential correctives, including artificially limiting the birth rate (which he discarded on the grounds that it would make the race weaker) and increasing food production via better farming technology (which he believed would work, but only up to a point at which the needs of the German population would outweigh the food able to be produced).

He concluded that the best way to ensure the future health of a growing German population was to conquer new territory and the soil it contained, thus adding new farmland to what was available for producing food. More specifically, he wanted to focus Germany's military energy on taking territory from the Russian landmass.

---

[298] Ibid. Page 393.

Thus, from the very beginning - before gaining any political power - Hitler's perspective was solidified as one of non-negotiable German expansion, specifically by military force.

He justified this expansion, along with the death toll and theft it would entail, by writing that "The right to possess soil can become a duty if without extension of its soil a great nation seems doomed to destruction. And most especially when not some little nigger nation or other is involved, but the Germanic mother of life, which has given the present-day world its cultural picture. Germany will either be a world power or there will be no Germany. And for world power she needs that magnitude which will give her the position she needs in the present period, and life to her citizens."[299] Thus, in order to make Germany a "world power," the destruction of other nations and their people was not just moral, but "a duty" and "a right." Needless to say, this sort of limitless adventurism and contempt for human life are not aligned with the Christian concept of Just War or any principles we find in *Basis of the Social Concept*.

One of Evola's many critiques of Hitler and his movement was that Hitler defined "German" in a way, and insisted on rules for citizenship, which were far removed from the traditional European understanding of these terms: "According to the views expressed by Hitler in *Mein Kampf*, becoming a 'citizen,' a real member of the Reich, would require a further validation, based, in addition to race, on physical health and then on an oath of

---

[299] Ibid. Page 654.

allegiance, solemnly sworn and shown to the *Volksgemeinschaft*, the community of birth. Only then would the applicant receive a 'certificate of citizenship,' which would be 'like a bond that unites all classes and covers every abyss.' Hitler goes so far as to affirm that 'being a street cleaner in a Reich like this would signify a greater honor than being a king in a foreign state.' With these words and others like them that attest a completely plebeian spirit, Hitler offered as much as was needed so that any German who was not born from the mixture with 'non-Aryan' or Jewish blood could raise his head."[300]

In order to implement these ideas unilaterally, and enact what he mistakenly referred to as a "Germanic democracy" despite its lack of resemblance to traditional Prussian Monarchism (and more closely resembled dictatorship in the worst sense of the word), Hitler dissolved all other political parties and passed the Enabling Act in 1933 - which made him accountable to no one and criminalized all opposition. Though Evola believed that such measures were sometimes necessary in the middle of the severest national emergencies, he criticized Hitler for maintaining this dynamic all the way until his defeat in 1945 - and though Hitler presented his ideas as continuations and evolutions of the First and Second Reich, Evola continually pointed out the ways in which National Socialism departed from these more traditional styles of government.

Elaborating on his critique of Hitler's pseudo-traditionalism, Evola added that "The most negative

---

[300] Evola, J. (2013). *Notes on the Third Reich*. Arktos. Page 50.

aspect of Hitlerism is represented by the fundamental and fatal part that the radicalism of an irredentist ethnic nationalism played in it. It was a true *idée fixe* for Hitler, and drove him into adventures that were at first successful but in the end led to catastrophe because of his lack of a sense of limits and realistic possibilites. All Germans had to be united at any prince into a single Reich, the Third Reich, and under a single *Führer*. Hitler believed that this was literally a mission entrusted to him by Providence. The ideology of the *Volk*, which we discussed earlier while indicating its antecedents, here fused with the ideology of modern anti-traditional nationalism. It is anti-traditional especially in regard to Germany, because in neither the First nor the Second Reich do we encounter anything resembling such an infatuation. This was not the basis on which Prussia or Frederick the Great conducted their wars."[301]

Elsewhere he added: "Judged straightforwardly, the Third Reich presented itself in terms of a popular dictatorship, since power was in the hands of a single individual lacking any superior chrism, drawing the principle of its 'legitimacy' uniquely from the *Volk* and its consensus. This is the essence of the so-called *Führerprinzip*. It was supposed to relate to a tradition from the times of the ancient Germani, with the chief and his followers united by a bond of fidelity. In all this, several important issues were forgotten, however. First, at that time this bond was established only in an emergency or in view of definite military ends and, like the dictatorship in

---

[301] Ibid. Page 80.

the early Roman period, the character of *Führer* (*dux* or *heretigo*) did not have a permanent character. Second, the 'followers' were the heads of the various tribes, not a mass, the *Volk*. Third, in the ancient German constitution, in addition to the exceptional instances in which, in certain circumstances as we have mentioned, the chief could demand an unconditional obedience - in addition to the *dux* or *heretigo* - there was the *rex*, possessed of a superior dignity based on his origin.

All this we have already established in our discussion of the 'dyarchy' that was established in Fascism by the coexistence of the monarchy, which we have seen as positive. As for Hitler, he nourished a fundamental aversion to the monarchy and, as we have noted, his polemic against the Habsburgs, for instance, was of an unparalleled vulgarity. For Hitler, the *Volk* alone was the principle of legitimacy. He was established as its direct representative and guide, without intermediaries, and it was to follow him unconditionally. No higher principle existed or was tolerated by him. Therefore it is perfectly correct to speak of a consolidated populist dictatorship employing the tools of a single party and the myth of the *Volk*. Not only the ancient German traditions, but also the very concept of Reich and, as we shall see, the concept of race were brought by Hitler to the level of the masses, which implied their degradation and distortion."[302] I believe that we as Christians can agree with Evola that the origin of leadership must be something higher than the approval of a given race or group of people; it must have

---

[302]   Ibid. Page 34.

its roots in the spiritual realm which for us, means God and His Providence. By materializing and desacralizing the concept of leadership, Hitler brought the notion of divine Monarchy down to the level of merely human dictatorship.

Thus Evola concluded that "Everything gravitated around a man with exceptional abilities for captivating, transporting, arousing and fanaticizing the people, while he himself presented under more than one aspect the traits of a possessed person, as if an extraordinary force were acting through him, giving him lucidity and iron logic in action, but depriving him of every sense of limit. These are the character traits that differ strikingly between Hitler and Mussolini. In Mussolini, the outstanding traits were those of a person who maintained control and a certain distance when exploiting opportunities. Naturally, in a system gravitating to this degree around a *Führer* like the Third Reich, a stable future was not conceivable. Constitutionally it was possible to have a type of tribunate of the people. In reality, however, had the war not ended in military defeat, a vacuum would have appeared after Hitler's death, since it would not have been possible to bring to power, in a continuing succession, men possessing Hitler's exceptional individual qualities, which alone assured him power and made him the center of the system's gravity. The *Führer-Staat* would necessarily have had to yield to a different order. As long as Hitler lived and fortune was on his side, his galvanizing power succeeded in holding everything together and inspiring unbelievable achievements up to the last hour, up to the edge of the abyss. The complete ideological collapse of Germany after 1945, however, when that tension failed - not comparable to the one that followed its defeat in the First World War - shows how superficial was the effect of his magnetic action on the masses in spite of the power of 'myths' and the strict totalitarian organization."[303]

Needless to say, genuine Christian leadership - whether ecclesiastical or civil - does not suffer any of these defects. The leadership of a Christian man revolves not around himself, but around Christ. The Eternal and Almighty God-Man Christ is his guide, his Master, *his* leader, Who *"is the same yesterday and today and forever"*[304] and, as such, acts with an unfailing consistency down through the generations of those who follow Him.

A faithful Orthodox King who passes away ideally leaves his kingdom to another faithful Orthodox King; they follow the same moral law and the same Symphonic model of cooperation with the Church. In the same way, a faithful Orthodox Bishop ideally leaves his flock to another faithful Orthodox Bishop; they likewise follow the same moral law, the same Symphonic model of cooperation with the State, and the same Holy Canons as passed down the Saints and Fathers who have left them for us as guides to Church organization. These Canons and principles are neither created by, nor rooted in, the imaginations or inclinations of mortal men; they cannot pass away, they cannot be uprooted, and the systems

---

[303] Ibid. Pages 35 and 36.
[304] Hebrews 13:8

cannot fall apart if followed with true faith by those to whose care they are entrusted.

Hitler and the Jews

"The Jewish religion doctrine consists primarily in prescriptions for keeping the blood of Jewry pure."[305]
- Adolf Hitler

Before addressing Hitler's view of Judaism and his government's policies toward Jews, we must first look to his model of the world in general and understanding of race more specifically. In addition to essentially deifying fallen nature and fervently believing in social Darwinism, Hitler also - according to Himmler - had also been a "convinced adherent for a long time" in what was called the World Ice Theory.[306] Popularized by Viennese engineer Hanns Hörbiger in 1913, the World Ice Theory posited that the basic substance of the cosmos was ice, and that after millions of years of conflict between ice and fire, the civilization of Atlantis emerged from an ancient ice age. Germans, in Hörbiger's view, were the descendants of those ancient people.

It should be noted that he did not arrive at this view from any sort of scientific hypothesis and testing; rather, he claimed to have had an epiphany, while looking at the moon, by which he "realized" the moon was made of ice and led him down the path of formulating his theory. In 1942, Hitler professed that Hörbiger should be "honored

---

[305] Hitler, A. (1999). *Mein Kampf*. Houghton Mifflin. Page 306.

[306] Weikart, R. (2016). *Hitler's religion : the twisted beliefs that drove the Third Reich*. Regnery History. Page 181.

along with Ptolemy and Copernicus in the observatory that he planned to build in Linz, because the World Ice Theory was a major scientific discovery."[307] For a man who took great pride in his supposed loyalty to truth and facts, Hitler did not seem overly concerned with either the history or the science on which he claimed his views were grounded.

The same phenomenon can be observed in his understanding of the term "Aryan," which he seemed to believe was an ancient reference to a specific Germanic genetic group. Evola took him to task for this misunderstanding in a number of his books, explaining at length how empty the word was as presented by National Socialism and Hitler himself. For example, in a passage from <u>Notes on the Third Reich</u>, Evola wrote that "no thought was given to defining in positive, even spiritual, terms the concept of 'Aryan.' It implicitly allowed every German to think that he was preeminently the 'Aryan' to whom was attributed the creation and origin of every higher culture. This was the incentive for a baleful arrogance that was more than nationalist (and completely foreign to the traditional Right)."[308]

Later in that book, Evola described this approach as "a 'naturalism' that denied every true transcendence. Let it be enough to think that it condemned, as of a spirit that is not Aryan but 'Levantine,' the distinction between body and soul, since racism postulates and presupposes their indissoluble and substantial unity. Then there were those

[307] Ibid.

[308] Evola, J. (2013). *Notes on the Third Reich*. Arktos. Page 52.

who drew from this denial the logical consequence by denying true immortality and conceiving of an 'immortality of the stock.' We see here how the slogans of a certain racial propaganda does violence to what clearly results from any serious investigation of the traditions of 'Aryan' (Indo-European) cultures, because these cultures recognized transcendence and made it the reference point for ethical virtues to which these National Socialist ideologues gave a value that was purely human and basically naturalistic."[309]

As mentioned in a previous chapter, Hitler often used the word "species" to refer, incorrectly, to "race." Further, he spoke and wrote of human beings as if mankind were not fundamentally different from any other type of creature; not only did he look to the animal world's territorial expansion and might-makes-right dynamic as models for human activity, but his spiritual views (or lack thereof) gave him a very incomplete understanding of what a human being *is* to begin with. In his Foreword to Notes On The Third Reich, E. Christian Kopff noted that "Evola's objections to National Socialist views of race were based on a principled objection to biological reductionism, which he argued was a materialist vision that ignored the reality that, unlike thoroughbred dogs or horses of different breeds, humans are soul and spirit (or character and openness to the transcendent) as well as, actually much more than, body, flesh and bones. After the Second World War, Evola denounced in the strongest terms the practical results of Nazi racism, not only for the

---

[309] Ibid. Page 63.

terrible loss of life involved but also for its subversion of the rule of law on the basis of a misuse of modern science, which Evola distrusted on principle."[310]

Though the Christian and Evolian perspectives have a different beginning and a different end, this is one of several areas in which our respective criticisms of National Socialism overlap. The Orthodox Church professes that man is a composed of body and soul - sometimes presented by Saints as a tripartite composition of body, soul and spirit, whereas in other Saints the spirit is an aspect of the soul - and not simply a biological machine. In his book <u>Orthodox Psychotherapy</u>, Metropolitan Hierotheos Vlachos taught that "Man is made up of body and soul. Each element alone does not constitute a man. St. Justin, the philosopher and martyr, says that the soul by itself is not a man, but is called 'a man's soul.' In the same way the body is not called a man but is called 'a man's body.' 'Though in himself man is neither of these, the combination of the two is called man; God called man into life and resurrection, and he did not call a part, but the whole, while is the soul and body.'"[311] By a denial of the reality that God imbued each man with an immortal soul, regardless of his ethnicity or any other bodily factor, Hitler and his ideological kin likewise denied the teachings of Christ and the Holy Fathers.

Hitler claimed in <u>Mein Kampf</u> that he gave no real thought to Jews at all until he began to study Marxist

---

[310]   Ibid. Page 8.

[311]   Hierotheos Vlachos, & Williams, E. (2017). *Orthodox psychotherapy : (the science of the fathers)*. Birth Of The Theotokos Monastery. Page 106.

doctrine in depth. Even then, the connection between Marxism and Judaism was, for him, tenuous at best and not a topic of which he had any real grasp: "Not withstanding that Vienna in those days counted nearly two hundred thousand Jews among its two million inhabitants, I did not see them...For the Jew was still characterized for me by nothing but his religion, and therefore, on grounds of human tolerance, I maintained my rejection of religious attacks in this case as in others. Consequently, the tone, particularly that of the Viennese anti-Semitic press, seemed to me unworthy of the cultural tradition of a great nation. I was oppressed by the memory of certain occurrences in the Middle Ages, which I should not have liked to see repeated."[312] He further asserted that he had no memory of hearing the word "Jew" as a child at home, and recalled that even in Vienna he considered them to be simply Germans with a different religion.

Hitler described his "transformation into an anti-Semite" as a great internal war between his feelings and his sense of reason. Dr. Karl Lueger, the anti-Jewish mayor of Vienna and leader of the Christian Social Party, was a man Hitler first hated but gradually came to admire. During this period, Hitler began to read anti-Jewish newspapers and pamphlets, but described himself as repulsed by their tone and unscientific arguments: "The whole thing seemed to me so monstrous, the accusations so boundless, that, tormented by the fear of doing

---

[312] Hitler. Page 52.

injustice, I again became anxious and uncertain."[313] Despite his purported hesitance to see Jews as anything other than Germans, and his dislike for the tone of the local anti-Jewish press, he claimed to have gradually begun to notice differences between the Germans and the Jews of Vienna. Along with his beginning to notice a difference in appearance and character, Hitler wrote that it was really the attitude of the Zionists - along with the fact that even non-Zionist Jews seemed to be their allies - that began to persuade him that Jews were not true Germans: "The so-called liberal Jews did not reject the Zionists as non-Jews, but only as Jews with an impractical, perhaps even dangerous, way of publicly avowing their Jewishness. Intrinsically," he wrote, "they remained unalterably of one piece. In a short time this apparent struggle between Zionistic and liberal Jews disgusted me; for it was false through and through, founded on lies and scarcely in keeping with the moral elevation and purity always claimed by this people."[314]

Eventually, he found himself asking the following question: "Was there any form of filth or profligacy, particularly in cultural life, without at least one Jew involved in it?" He continued that "What had to be reckoned heavily against the Jews in my eyes was when I became acquainted with their activity in the press, art, literature, and theater...I now began to examine carefully the names of all the creators of unclean products in public artistic life. The result was less and less favorable for my

---

[313] Ibid. Page 56.

[314] Ibid. Page 57.

previous attitude toward the Jews. Regardless how my sentiment might resist, my reason was forced to draw its conclusions. The fact that nine tenths of all literary filth, artistic trash, and theatrical idiocy can be set to the account of a people, constituting hardly one hundredth of all the county's inhabitants, could not simply be talked away; it was the plain truth."[315]

Once he became familiar with the core doctrine of Marxism, Hitler described having attempted what many others have as well: pointing out to those espousing Marxism's tenets that it was bad for the population and having very negative effects. He was often struck by the fact that this had no bearing on their beliefs whatsoever. As this process continued - his trying to point out the errors of Marxism and other peoples' doubling-down in response - he eventually reached a point of anger that would last for the rest of his life.

"The more I argued with them," Hitler wrote, "the better I came to know their dialectic. First they counted on the stupidity of their adversary, and then, when there was no other way out, they themselves simply played stupid. If all this didn't help, they pretended not to understand, or, if challenged, they changed the subject in a hurry, quoted platitudes which, if you accepted them, they immediately related to entirely different matters, and then, if again attacked, gave ground and pretended not to know exactly what you were talking about. Whenever you tried to attack one of these apostles, your hand closed on a jelly-like slime which divided up and poured

---

[315] Ibid. Pages 57 and 58.

through your fingers, but in the next moment collected again. But if you really struck one of these fellows so telling a blow that, observed by the audience, he couldn't help but agree, and if you believed that this had taken you at least one step forward, your amazement was great the next day. The Jew had not the slightest recollection of the day before, he rattled off his same old nonsense as though nothing at all had happened, and, if indignantly challenged, affected amazement; he couldn't remember a thing, except that he had proved the correctness of his assertions the previous day. Sometimes I stood there thunderstruck. I didn't know what to be more amazed at: the agility of their tongues or their virtuosity at lying." [316]

As his life went on and his involvement in politics increased, Hitler began to blame all of Germany's problems on Jews. In a strange case of what one might describe as "telling on himself," Hitler wrote in several Mein Kampf passages - beneath very thinly-veiled arrogance and braggadocio - about his ability to understand the masses and what made them tick; he even went to great lengths describing the precise propaganda techniques which he was using on the same audience for which his autobiography was intended. Perhaps he described these calculations in order to make himself seem more intelligent, or perhaps his estimation of the masses' collective intelligence was so low that he thought they wouldn't understand what they were reading anyway. In either case, Hitler was often criticized for pitting all of his anger and vitriol against the Jews and the

[316] Ibid. Page 62.

Jews alone - which, if we read between the lines, it seems likely he knew was not entirely accurate.

For example, he admitted in <u>Mein Kampf</u> that "To achieve any success one should, on purely psychological grounds, never show the masses two or more opponents, since this leads to a total disintegration of their fighting power...In general the art of all truly great national leaders at all times consists among other things primarily in not dividing the attention of a people, but in concentrating it on a single foe. The more unified the application of a people's will to fight, the greater will be the magnetic attraction of a movement and the mightier will be the impetus of the thrust. It belongs to the genius of a great leader to make even adversaries far removed from one another seem to belong to a single category, because in weak and uncertain characters the knowledge of having different enemies can only too readily lead to the beginning of doubt in their own right."[317]

So whether or not Hitler truly believed the Jews were to blame for all Germany's problems, he decided to focus all the anger of the masses against Jews as a way to rally their energy and keep them his loyal subjects. He feared that if he presented too complex an issue, their energy would disperse and they would become confused and less useful. Needless to say, false accusation for the sake of political expediency - and the consequences such slander can (and did) have on countless innocent people who were not involved in Marxism or cultural subversion - are not Christian concepts. By focusing the anger of the

---

[317] Ibid. Page 117 and 118.

population upon all Jews as a group, he caused harm to those which, in many cases, he must have known had done nothing wrong.

Hitler further acknowledged focusing on one category of enemies because he felt that to be more thorough would introduce too much "objectivity" to make his future subjects useful. He feared that "Once the wavering mass sees itself in a struggle against too many enemies, objectivity will put in an appearance, throwing open the question whether all others are really wrong and only their own people or their own movement are in the right."[318] One has to wonder why Hitler believed in the superiority of the "Aryan" masses when he consistently displayed such a low opinion of them. His own words make it sound as if he played them like puppets, considering them far too stupid to either think for themselves or follow him without being ruthlessly manipulated.

Evola criticized this aspect of Hitlerism for a number of reasons, perhaps not realizing that Hitler himself quite consciously chose to ignore reality in favor of gaining and maintaining political power: "Hitler over and over again attributes to the Jew the cause of every evil. He truly believed that the Jew was the only obstacle to the creation of an ideal German national society, and he made this obsession an essential ingredient in his propaganda. Apart from Marxism, for Hitler all Bolshevism has been the creation and tool of Judaism. The same holds true for Western 'capitalist plutocracy' and the Masons. These are

---

[318] Ibid. Page 118.

all theses of which he should have recognized the one-sided character early on. We may wonder whether Hitler, in his 'fixation,' was not the victim of one of the tactics of what we have elsewhere called the 'occult war,' a tactic consistent with turning all our attention to concentrate on only one particular sector where the fighting forces are acting, while distracting our attention from other sectors where their activity can continue almost undisturbed."[319] As we have seen, Hitler was not the victim of this dynamic; rather, he was its very conscious perpetrator. Evola continued: "When I say this, I do not mean that there is no Jewish problem, on which we shall dwell in a moment. As Hitler professed it, however, displaying attitudes that had long been part of the so-called 'German Movement,' anti-Semitism had the character of an obsessive fanaticism. It was the sign of a lack of inner control, and it is because of that that there is a stain that is difficult to remove from the Third Reich. The common error that racism and anti-Semitism are regarded by many people as synonyms also has its principal origin in Hitlerism."[320]

Once Hitler decided that Jews were the category on which he'd pin all of Germany's problems, the question then arose of what he planned to do about it. To begin with, in a typical Hitlerian inversion of Christian principles, he wrote that "Blood sin and desecration of the race are the original sin in this world."[321] For a Christian,

---

[319] Evola. Pages 54 and 55.

[320] Ibid. Page 55.

[321] Hitler. Page 249.

the phrase "original sin" can refer to one of two aspects of our faith: firstly (and more commonly) to the first sin committed by Eve and then Adam - in which they submitted to Satan's temptation and turned their backs on communion with God - and secondly, to the mystery of how this event has affected all the rest of mankind. Though a study of this topic is beyond the scope of <u>Fascism Viewed From The Cross</u>, "blood sin and desecration of the race" - by which Hitler meant intermarriage and miscegenation - cannot be found in Genesis or the Fathers as an explanation of humanity's fall from grace. As one might expect - especially as Hitler described himself as someone "who appraises the value of men on a racial basis"[322] - he subsequently enacted laws meant to keep those who married other races from becoming citizens of his German Reich. In fairness, such laws were not uncommon; many American States had laws preventing marriage between Whites and other races at the time.

Evola wrote, describing Hitler's plan for Jews, that "In the beginning of the Third Reich, anti-Semitism was restricted to boycotting Jewish businesses and the direction seemed to be heading toward a sort of apartheid. Since Jews were not considered members of the *Volksgemeinschaft*, the German ethnic-national community, but only citizens of a non-Aryan race, almost like a foreign guest (for Hitler, Jews were not Germans of another religion confession, but a people apart), the goal was for Jews to live apart, have their own businesses,

---

[322] Ibid. Page 659.

professions, schools, and so on, separated from Aryan society, and were to be prevented from carrying out an activity that was held to be parasitic, materialist, miserly and underhanded. The government left open the possibility that those Jews who did not like this policy should abandon the Reich, without taking with them all the property they had acquired, however. The truth was - a matter generally suppressed - that for a large number of other nations, they were also undesirable elements, and obtaining an entry visa was very difficult...In general, the ideal solution of the Jews' problem was seen as setting them free by assigning them a land."[323]

At this point we do not encounter anything particularly reprehensible as interpreted through the *Imperial Laws* of the Royal Saints, with the exceptions of property theft and the fact that this segregation in the Third Reich was based on race and not religion - a concept which, as you've seen, is not found in the Royal Saints at all. These are major and noteworthy exceptions, and highlight that even if certain Nazi policies appeared acceptable through the lens of Christian history, they were built on a different foundation and had only superficial similarity. Regardless, the peaceful separation of communities - particularly when enacted to prevent conflict between them - does not strike me an inherent violation of Christian principles.

However, Evola continued, "Serious persecutions in the Third Reich began with reprisals that were organized in response to the 1938 assassination of a German

---

[323] Evola. Pages 55 and 56.

diplomat from the embassy in Paris, vom Rath, by a Jew who wanted to make a political statement. Aside from the devastations and excesses that resulted **[Kristallnacht, or the Night of Broken Glass]**, it furnished the excuse for the promulgation of harsh anti-Jewish laws that had the backlash effect of exacerbating the campaign abroad against the Third Reich beyond all limits. Added to this spiral was a further spin that in part involved Fascist Italy as Germany's ally because, as we have said, this campaign was one of the causes that drove Mussolini to take rather moderate anti-Semitic measures in retaliation. The physical liquidation of Jews, however, has to be seen as taking place in the period of the war in the territories occupied by Germany, because estimates say that in Germany itself at the start of hostilities there remained only about 25,000 Jews **[modern historians estimate the number to be somewhere between 160,000 and 245,000]**. For these massacres, about which the greater part of the German people learned only later, no justification or excuse can be accepted."[324]

As recorded in the minutes of the 1942 Wannsee Conference, the plan for Jews by that part of the war was to simply deport them all from Germany and its conquered territory into the "General Government," which was the occupied part of Poland. The document uses the phrase "final solution of the Jewish Question," often identified as an implicit call for the total genocide of European Jews, though the wording in the document itself vaguely states that the Conference's goal was to

[324] Ibid. Page 57.

create a plan which would "cleanse German living space of Jews in a legal manner."[325]

Thus we see observe a vicious cycle between the Marxist influence disproportionately propagated by Jews in Germany, Germany's subsequent repression of Jewish interests, and the organs of international Jewry increasingly waging various kinds of war against Germany, back and forth until Hitler's defeat in 1945. Any reasonable and accurate assessment of World War 2 must take the actions of both sides of this conflict into account. Regardless, with Hitler's attempt to build a blood-pure "Aryan" Reich came the subsequent laws and policies which not only harmed other races, but also - through his eugenic policies - even those of the "right" bloodline who were not considered healthy or fit enough to be citizens in his new German state.

As you learned in a previous chapter, Hitler adamantly denied that Judaism contains any spiritual content and instead chose to perceive it as a strictly racial preservation system disguising itself as a religion. For that reason, Hitler mocked the very sentiment which both Orthodoxy and his native Roman Catholicism have always taught in regard to Jews who convert to the Christian faith. He hated the notion that a Jew converting to Christianity might resolve, to quote Dr. E. Michael Jones, that "revolutionary spirit"[326] which sets a soul against Christ. Hitler complained that "If the worst came

[325] *The Wannsee Conference Protocol. (n.d.). Writing.upenn.edu.*
https://writing.upenn.edu/~afilreis/Holocaust/wansee-transcript.html
[326] Jones, E Michael. (2008). *The Jewish Revolutionary Spirit.*

to the worst, a splash of baptismal water could always save the business and the Jew at the same time."[327] Unable to grasp the transcendent reality of Christ, Hitler saw attempts to convert Jews as as one of the Christian Social Party's greatest failures. He believed that Jews should be persecuted based on race instead, without regard to the real Sacramental change enacted by Holy Baptism.

While the Fathers and Canonists of the Orthodox Church were careful at times to ensure that Jewish converts were genuine, and not pretending to convert for material reasons such as to escape from debt, one cannot find in any of their writings that belonging to a particular race makes a person incapable of embracing Christ and being saved.

---

[327] Hitler. Page 120.

Romania

"In those hours the life and death of the Romanian people was at stake."[328]
- Corneliu Zelia Codreanu

One of the difficulties of using Codreanu's own writings for this section is that, as noted by Lucian Tudor in his introductory essay to For My Legionaries, Codreanu wrote his magnum opus specifically for Romanians who understood the whole context and history of the various situations he described. Tudor noted that as a result, "the average, modern reader living outside of Romania will most likely not have an adequate knowledge of Romanian history and culture necessary to comprehend the causes and consequences of many of the events and philosophical concepts written about"[329] in the book.

Since I do not speak a word of Romanian, and subsequently have no way of reading any non-translated books about the country, I have done my best to piece the situation together based on what I've been able to glean from Codreanu and those who commented on his work. This is an admitted weak spot in my understanding - but ultimately no different from the fact that I also did not live in either Italy or Germany before, during, or after World War 2. Tudor's essay was extremely helpful, as he

---

[328] Codreanu, C. (2015). *For My Legionaries*. Black House Publishing. Page 65.
[329] Ibid. Page 35.

wrote it specifically for non-Romanians who wanted to better understand <u>For My Legionaries</u>. As such, I will relate some of his thoughts to you so that you may better understand Codreanu and the situation in Romania.

As Tutor described, "The history of Romania is dominated by struggles related to two goals: (1) independence from foreign control, and (2) the unification of all territories composed of majority Romanian people. This is because for much of its history, ever since the Middle Ages, Romania was divided into three sections: Transylvania, which was ruled by Hungary ever since the eleventh century, and the kingdoms of Moldavia (equivalent to modern-day northeastern Romania and the current country of Moldavia) and Wallachia (equivalent to the southern half of modern-day Romania)."[330] Moldavia united with Wallachia in 1859 and after World War 1, the whole region finally became united under what Codreanu refers to as "Greater Romania." This is important because Codreanu lived in a time when a young nationalist's role models were various rulers of those three territories, and/or combinations thereof, who expelled threats from their lands and protected the people from foreign conquest.

Furthermore, most Romanians during Codreanu's life were peasants and farmers. After World War 1, according to Tudor, "an agrarian reform was undertaken which involved arranging for the boyars (traditional nobles who functioned as large landowners) to relinquish much of their agricultural land and redistribute it to the peasants.

---

[330] Ibid. Page 36.

This involved roughly ninety-two percent of Romania's arable land. This reform was thus expected to make the peasants more productive, and as a result also more able to pay what they owed for receiving the land. While one might assume that such a reform would benefit the peasants, it ironically did just the opposite. The peasants, who now became small landowners, lacked the proper equipment and capabilities to make full use of the land. They were also unable to sell whatever agricultural products they produced in order to cope financially. Thus, they were forced to agree to financially difficult deals and gradually fell into debt as a result."[331]

This poorly-done agrarian reform turned Romania from a stable society into a largely unstable one, with both peasants and boyars having their livelihoods diminished as a result. A number of political parties cropped up to try and help with the situation, but none of them was particularly effective. The failure of the reform and subsequent political attempts to fix it led to a scenario in which, as Tudor described, "the only people who benefitted from the agrarian reform and the situation it created were capitalists and speculators."[332] Thus Romania found itself in a similar situation to both Italy and Germany after World War 1: far worse off, with the masses living in misery, without a meaningful political solution in sight.

Tudor's essay next examined Romania's situation in terms of Nationalism, Anti-Semitism, Monarchism,

---

[331] Ibid. Page 38.
[332] Ibid.

Economic Theory, and Political Values. As an
understanding of each of these aspects will help you
comprehend the rest of this chapter, I will briefly relate
the most relevant sections. After acknowledging that
modern readers may find Codreanu's nationalist
sentiments difficult to grasp, Tudor explained that - as
opposed to the egalitarian or internationalist view that
human ethnic groups are largely just interchangeable skin
colors without meaningful differences between them -
"Romanian nationalists recognized that humans are not
merely a collection of disconnected individuals, that they
are in fact affected and united by the collective groups
they belong to, such as ethnicity or nationality, and that
these groups are sacred and need to be preserved with
necessary measures...it is natural and healthy for
different ethnic groups to exchange cultural products and
ideas between themselves, but an ethnic group must
moderate such interactions so as to not allow foreign
groups to dominate their culture."[333]

This sentiment is in line with Section II. 3. of *The Basis
Of The Social Concept* which, as a reminder, states
that "Christian patriotism may be expressed at the same
time with regard to a nation as an ethnic community and
as a community of its citizens. The Orthodox Christian is
called to love his fatherland, which has a territorial
dimension, and his brothers by blood who live
everywhere in the world. This love is one of the ways of
fulfilling God's commandment of love to one's neighbor
which includes love to one's family, fellow-tribesmen and

---

[333] Ibid. Pages 39 and 40.

fellow-citizens. The patriotism of the Orthodox Christian should be active. It is manifested when he defends his fatherland against an enemy, works for the good of the motherland, cares for the good order of people's life through, among other things, participation in the affairs of government. The Christian is called to preserve and develop national culture and people's self-awareness."[334] Tudor noted that Codreanu's book often used the term "nation" not in the modern Western sense of a State or territory marked by boundaries, but in the more classical Eastern European sense of meaning an "ethnos" or ethnocultural structure. And though Codreanu sometimes used the word "race" in a biological sense, Tudor explained that "while Codreanu and many Legionaries believed that racial constitution in the biological sense had some importance to national identity, race was only a background, and ethnic groups and peoples were thought of as being primarily spiritual and cultural entities."[335]

In that context and as regards Codreanu's opposition to Judaism, Jews had been granted Romanian citizenship in 1879 as a condition of the Treaty of Berlin - which Romania had to submit to in order to be recognized as an independent state. After becoming citizens, Jews gradually came to outnumber Romanians in University classrooms, winning a wildly disproportionate number of future high-level jobs. Naturally, this angered many

---

[334] *II. Church and nation | The Russian Orthodox Church.* (n.d.). https://old.mospat.ru/en/documents/social-concepts/ii/
[335] Codreanu. Page 41.

Romanians who felt that a foreign minority was becoming the dominant power in their homeland. We will study this phenomenon, and the reaction it provoked, in greater detail shortly.

Tudor also wrote that "Codreanu was an ardent, lifelong supporter of the Romanian monarchy, along with many other Romanians, to the point where he made Monarchism a key feature of his Legionary ideology."[336] As you'll read about soon, the Legionaries believed in the institution but disliked the actual King, effectively demonstrating a proper understanding of the difference between principle and contingent. They did not allow their disappointment in King Carol to turn into some kind of revolutionary political movement which, in many other European countries, often led to the bloody overthrow of the royal house and the institution of the Monarchy as a whole.

Economically, Codreanu was a Third Positionist. Tudor explained that the "key idea behind Third Position economics is to create a society in which people of all classes, occupations, and social positions are spiritually united and live in a cooperative and harmonious manner. This concept accordingly rejects both the notion of class warfare present in Marxist thought as well as the sort of unrestricted competition and economic expansion favored by capitalists, which leads to workers becoming prey to blind economic forces...The reasoning behind the formulation of this kind of system is that neither Marxism - which advocates only the rights of the workers - nor

---

[336] Ibid. Page 43.

Capitalism - which advocates only the rights of the financially and economically powerful - are sufficient for creating worthy societies to live in." [337]

Third Positionism expresses itself in a multitude of forms, taking various shapes throughout various movements and countries. It was the foundational idea of the medieval guild system, and was subsequently around long before Fascism. National Socialism is another example of a Third Positionist movement, but Codreanu's version was what he called "National-Christian Socialism" due to the importance of religion and faith (which was lacking from Hitler's understanding of the concept). He further noted that one should not mistake National-Christian Socialism for simply being a Christian version of German National Socialism; instead, it is a simply a national version of what might be called Christian Socialism. Later in this chapter, I have reprinted the official "Creed Of National-Christian Socialism" in full. All of these currents coalesced into Codreanu's movement, the Legion of St. Michael the Achangel, in order to help bring Romania out of its situation after World War 1.

In his Foreword to <u>For My Legionaries,</u> Kerry Bolton wrote that Codreanu "found Iasi to be rife with Bolshevik agitation among the workers and chaos in the workplace. Demonstrations of 10,000 to 15,000 filled the streets every day; 'starved workers, maneuvered by the Judaic criminal hand from Moscow, [who] paraded the streets while singing the *Internationale* [the Bolshevik anthem], yelling:

---

[337] Ibid. Page 45.

'Down with the King!', 'Down with the Army!', and
carrying placards on which one could read 'Long live the
communist revolution!', 'Long live Soviet Russia!'
Codreanu saw in this bolshevization of the masses not the
possibility of a Romanian people's revolution, but the
prospect of a total Judaization of Romania and the
liquidation of its peasantry. It was this urgent need for a
movement that would not only thwart Bolshevism but
that would also reconstitute Romania as a strong nation
predicated on the necessity of a social and ultimately a
spiritual ethos, that prompted Codreanu to establish a
movement that would capture the zeal of the working
masses and the peasantry."[338]

Codreanu loved Iasi and considered it the center of
Romanianism in general. Many war veterans - proud
nationalists - joined the University around the same time
as Codreanu. He described them as being divided
between the school's Letters and Law departments, and
noted that they were vastly outnumbered by Jewish
students from Basarabia. Those Jewish students, he
noticed, tended to be communist agitators. Politically and
ideologically, most professors aligned with the
communists as well.

In the fall of 1919, Codreanu attended a meeting of
"The Guard Of The National Conscience," a new
nationalist group led by Constantin Pancu. Codreanu was
endlessly impressed by Pancu, who he described as a
lifelong blue-collar worker of Herculean strength and
size. From the moment of that first meeting onward,

---

[338] Ibid. Page 4.

Codreanu said that he spent half his time fighting at school and the other half fighting for Pancu,

Pancu's rallies eventually began to gather up to ten thousand people per event, at which Codreanu began to give speeches to the crowd. The rallies expanded beyond Iasi, and the movement began to circulate its own newspaper as well. Codreanu wrote that fights between the Guard and the communists began to occur nearly every day.

The Guard gained serious attention in Iasi after taking over the Nicolina railway facility. It was brimming with communists - over four thousand, by Codreanu's estimate - and the surrounding area was the base of communist resistance in the region. The Guard rerouted a train (containing all their men) into the station, and then Codreanu scaled the building and replaced the communist flag with the Romanian one. It was the first major sign that communists could be defeated, their efforts scaled back by men more serious than the politicians.

In 1923, Codreanu and a large group of students and peasants barged their way into the office of Ion Bratianu, the Prime Minister of Romania. They demanded two things: that deforestation by Jewish companies be halted immediately, since their precious forests were being ripped down around them, and that Romanian schools and universities have *numerus clausus* implemented so that the number of Jewish students was kept in proportion with the Jewish population. They were worried - justifiably, given the enrollment numbers - that

Jewish students were pushing Romanian students out of their own schools. Since universities were essentially training grounds for the next generation's elite, Codreanu and his movement realized that filling the schools with Jews instead of Romanians would lead to being ruled by Jews even more overtly than they were already experiencing. Romanians wanted to live with, attend school with, and be led by other Romanians.

Bratianu responded that he'd look into deforestation, but told the group that *numerus clausus* was asking too much. He told them that no other country in Europe had it, and that if they could find a single example to the contrary, he would implement it in Romania as well. They came up with no examples, and the matter was discarded.

In response, Codreanu and Ion Mota (one of his top supporters) formed a plan to enact vengeance against the politicians who they perceived as failing both the student movement and Romania as a whole. Mota wanted to go out in a blaze of glory, willing to sacrifice his life - if it came to that - for an act of violence that would take out as many of his enemies as he could manage. Codreanu agreed that death or imprisonment were not meaningful impediments to their overall goal: terrifying traitors to the Romanian cause into behaving more properly in the future. They chose as victims six cabinet Ministers, high-profile rabbis, and a number of bankers and press moguls in Bucharest. The list of targets contained both native Romanians and Jews.

Codreanu, Mota, and the rest of the group left Iasi for

Bucharest shortly afterward...but before they were able to carry out their plans, they found their house surrounded by police. The whole group was arrested, their weapons were confiscated, and each member was interrogated as to the plan's details. They were charged with a "conspiracy against State Security" and sentenced to hard labor.

It was in Vacaresti Prison that Codreanu decided to name his movement after St. Michael the Archangel. The prison Church had an icon of the angel near the door, and Codreanu described that icon as bringing him tremendous joy and peace during his troubles. The group found such inspiration in that icon that, just before their trial and facing an unknown extension of their sentences, they had several copies of the icon made by a painter in the prison. One of the copies was a full six feet tall - an exact replica of the original in every way.

After being transferred from Focasni to Turnul-Severin for trial, Codreanu walked into the prison courtyard and noted the following: "Around noon I noticed massed before the prison gates over 200 small children between 6 and 7 years of age, who upon seeing me pass by began waving their tiny hands at me, some using handkerchiefs, some using caps. They were school children who heard I had come to Turnul-Severin and was there in prison. Those children were to be there daily from then on to show me their sympathy. They waited for me to pass, to wave their tiny hands...At that time everybody was feeling Romanian and saw in our fight a sacred struggle for the future of this country. They were aware of my misfortunes and saw in my gesture a gesture of revolt for human dignity, a gesture that any free man would have made."[339] Codreanu stated that even his prosecutors began to soften up as a result of this national outpouring of support.

He wrote that for his trial, the Tribunal's president "received 19,300 signatures of lawyers wishing to defend me, from all over the country" and that during the trial, the "theater was full to capacity, and around it outside, over 10,000 people were waiting."[340] It was an event that captivated the entirety of Romania. When it came his turn to speak during the trial, Codreanu simply said: "Gentlemen of the jury. Everything we have fought for was out of faith and love for our country and the Romanian people. We assume the obligation to fight to the end. This is my last word."[341]

The jurors returned from their deliberation wearing nationalist ribbons on their lapels. Codreanu was acquitted, hoisted upon the shoulders of his supporters in the courtroom, and carried outside to the cheers and shouts of the Romanian crowd that loved him and his movement completely.

The Legion Of Michael The Archangel was officially founded on June 24th, 1927. The group was mainly composed of the original Vacaresti prisoners, plus a few other students who dedicated themselves to the cause. Codreanu had realized that the "old guard" had lost sight

---

[339] Ibid. Page 243.

[340] Ibid. Page 244.

[341] Ibid. Page 246.

of the mission and, having degenerated into an irreconcilable schism, could no longer form the core of the movement. When asked what the Legion's program was, Codreanu responded that "This country is dying of lack of men, not of lack of programs; at least this is our opinion. That, in other words, it is not programs that we must have, but men, new men...In these critical times, the Romanian nation has no need of a great politician as many wrongly believe, but of a great educator and leader who can defeat the powers of evil and crush the clique of evil-doers. But in order to do this he will first have to overcome the evil within himself and within his men."[342]

---

[342] Ibid. Page 292 and 293.

Codreanu and the Church

"God sees and will reward."[343] - *Corneliu Codreanu*

As with Mussolini and Hitler, we must examine Codreanu's engagement with Christianity on multiple levels; unlike with the former two, however, we must add a layer to the Codreanu section simply because he lived in an Orthodox country and dealt directly with Orthodox clergy. While I have yet to find a single quote from the Orthodox Church on Benito Mussolini, and the consensus of the Saints rebukes Adolf Hitler, Codreanu's movement was intertwined with Orthodoxy from the very beginning. As we will discover clergy on both sides of the issue - some supporting him and some in opposition - we must carefully examine the situation as best we can discern. Before we get there, however, we can look to Codreanu's own writings and legacy in order to determine both his personal beliefs about the Faith and how he perceived his interactions with official Church organs.

There is no doubt in my mind, based on what I've read from Codreanu and those who knew him, that he genuinely believed in the Orthodox Christian Faith. What exactly that *meant* to him seems to have evolved over time - especially during his final incarceration in Jilava Prison - but I have not found a single comment from those who knew him which implied or explicitly stated that

[343] Codreanu, C. (2015). *The Prison Notes*. Page 58.

Codreanu professed one belief in public and another behind closed doors. You learned in previous chapters that Mussolini and (especially) Hitler professed a belief in God which ultimately was subjugated to political ideology when and where the two paradigms came into conflict; in Hitler's case, he was simply biding his time until the war ended before he planned to openly campaign against Christianity. By way of contrast, Julius Evola was impressed with the depth of Codreanu's spiritual vision and faith, which did not appear to have been calculated or political. Codreanu's sincerity shines through most especially in The Prison Notes, a collection of journal entries he wrote leading up to his murder.

In order to understand The Prison Notes, and the change in Codreanu displayed throughout its entries, the Introduction by Faust Bradesco offers the following very useful overview: "In order to understand fully the meaning and importance of this short work, two phases must be identified. 1. *The despair of the hunted man*, who feels the hatred all around him and suffers a moral torture. During this first phase, there is no depth to the text: just short notes and repetitions. One has the distinct impression that it is a question of points to be returned to at a later time, of the milestones of a suffering man who hopes to regain his freedom. Such is his state of mind until his shameful and unjust condemnation. 2. Then, *the bursting forth of Christian enlightenment*, when his soul finally realizes the importance of the spiritual change through the approach to and communion with the Godhead. This is the phase where his inner transformation is effected, when he grasps fully the greatness of the divine presence in the life of a man and society. The sentences are more detailed, as if he felt that he would never have the time to look at them again and to blend them into a maturely considered and structured whole. It urges on his death; he says so. But, as time passes, and as his thoughts bring him towards a metaphysical and spiritual understanding of human perfection, he is overwhelmed by peace, brought on not by mere wisdom, but by the purely theological. The spiritual sense of life - social, political, or quite simply human - advocated by Legionary doctrine, is no longer a potentiality, something to be brought into being. It is an actual fact, and of its nature holy. The three theological virtues, Faith, Hope and Charity, which also make up the essence of Legionary doctrine, opens up into the 'New Man' (understood and put into relief by the Iron Guard) the path of *moral perfection, right reason* and *spiritual improvement*."[344]

An example from each of these two periods will help illuminate the concept and demonstrate that, like other victims of communist imprisonment and torture, Codreanu's spirituality was accelerated - and ultimately fulfilled - by suffering. The stark realities of prison and death showed him what mattered and what didn't, unlocked the Gospels, and helped him endure the pain with a Christian spirit and attitude.

For the first phase, let us read his entry on April 24th, the day of Holy Easter (or Pascha) in 1938. From within

---

[344] Ibid. Page 8.

the confines of his filthy and soul-crushing cell, he wrote that "My mother is alone once again! A son-in-law dead in Spain, a widowed daughter with two children. Me, in prison. Four other children, also in prison or about to be arrested. One amongst these also has four children without anything to eat. My father, gone to Bucharest to pick up his pension before the holidays, never returned. He was arrested and taken to an unknown place. Nobody knows his fate. At home, mother is waiting for us to celebrate Easter with her. The joys of an old mother are so few; she can rarely get all of her children together at once! At our home, at Easter, it is a desert. None of those awaited are present. Not one soul comes near my mother. All the neighbors avoid her and, out of fear, do not even approach the house. A heart beats, alone, and seeks after us in the prisons, running from cell to cell to find us, to comfort us, to embrace our suffering bodies. But what to do, when no one tells you anything and when you receive no news? O mother, who cries alone in a corner of the house and who no one sees, know that we, too, cry for you, on this Easter day, each of us in our cell!...For the first time in my life, I will celebrate the Resurrection without light - in darkness. Alone."[345]

His pain was evident, both in body and soul, and he proceeded with an entry on Page 23 that he never knew if anyone would read: "I spent two other Easters in prison, in Focsani in 1925 and in Galata in 1929. Never, however, was I so sad, racked by so much pain, crushed by so many thoughts. I take my missal and set myself to read. I

---

[345] Ibid. Pages 18 and 21.

pray to God for everyone. For my wife, so tried and afflicted; for my mother, whom the Husi police have surely visited once again and terrified; for my father, whom only God knows in which cell he is passing this night; finally, too, for my brothers, who are in the same situation as me. Then, for the Legionary fighters, old and young, these heroes and martyrs of the Legionary faith, torn from their houses and taken to who knows what prison. How much sadness and how many tears there will be today in hundreds of Romanian families! I pray then for all the dead. Grandparents and relations, then for the friends who loved me and helped me in this life. I see all of them, each in turn. Here is Mr. Hristache, and, finally, Ciumeti appears to me with a group of Legionary martyrs who fell at that time. At their head - immense - I see his image as a painting - old, 500 years old, with his long hair and his crown upon his head: Stephen the Great, Prince of Moldavia. I pray for him, too. He helped me in so, so many battles." Thus we see a man in great pain, trying to endure it and reign in his thoughts of sadness and defeat with prayer and hope in God.

However, there are scattered hints throughout his final journals which indicate that his faith developed in an especially powerful way near the end of his life. Of special note is his entry on June 15th, 1938, after learning that he'd been convicted of the fabricated charges against him: "When I had finished reading the *Gospels*, I understood that I found myself here, in prison, because of God's Will; that, despite not being guilty of anything from a legal standpoint, He was punishing me for my sins and putting my faith to the test. That reassured me. Peace came upon the torment of my soul, like a quiet evening in the countryside comes down upon the worries, the agitations and hatreds of the world." After commenting on some of his favorite passages from the Epistles of St. Paul, he concluded - after a lifetime of both physical and spiritual battle - that "We concern ourselves more with the struggle between ourselves and against other men. And hardly with the struggle between the commandments of the Holy Ghost and the desires of our earthly nature. We are taken up with and love the victories over other men, and not the victories over Satan and sin. All the great men of yesterday and today: Napoleon, Mussolini, Hitler, etc., were taken up above all by these victories. The Legionary Movement is an exception, in concerning itself also, however insufficiently, with the Christian victory in man for his salvation. Yet not enough!"[346]

Such sentiments mark a major change from his earlier, more zealous attitude toward defending himself from his persecutors; though he believed and taught that Legionaries should be ready to die for their cause, it seems that he also struggled with not wanting to strike back when he was struck: "I carried on myself a revolver which I intended to use at the first, slightest provocation; nobody was to budge me from that resolve."[347] He further described being beaten by a policeman and the feelings which it brought up in him: "The following day I told my

---

[346] Ibid. Pages 52-54.

[347] Codreanu, C. (2015). *For My Legionaries*. Black House Publishing. Page 213.

father what befell me. 'Leave him in peace' he said. 'Do not do anything. Two slaps on the face of such a person, just dirties your palms. The time of his justice will come, rest assured. They are probably ordered to provoke you. But you must control yourself and try not to go out alone any more.' I accepted his advice. But it seems that a man who was beaten and did not retaliate is no longer a man. He feels ashamed, dishonored. I carried this dishonor like a big boulder on my heart."[348] Thus we can see Codreanu's spiritual growth over time, from a young man whose pride was wounded by self-control to finally accepting a Christlike embrace of persecution.

I do have to note that, at one point in <u>The Prison Notes</u>, Codreanu referred to the Roman Catholic Anthony of Padua as a Saint: "Hour after hour, my flesh dries up on me. However, my faith in God grows in my heart. I pray each day to the Holy Virgin and St. Anthony of Padua, thanks to whose miracles I escaped death in 1934."[349] It is unclear whether he was referring to the Theotokos or Anthony in the final part of this sentence, but in either case Anthony of Padua is not considered a Saint by the Orthodox Church. He made one more mention of this on Page 39 of that book, writing that "I open the book of prayers of St. Anthony at random," and there are no other references to Anthony in the remainder of Codreanu's corpus. These two vague references provide no insight into how Codreanu became exposed to the prayerbook - for example whether it was given to him

---

[348] Ibid. Page 207.

[349] *The Prison Notes*. Page 33.

in prison or whether he had it beforehand - or how exactly Anthony of Padua became known to him by 1934. It is certainly possible that he was exposed to Anthony via his contacts with the Greek-Catholic priests who supported the Legion. In either case it does not appear from these comments that he was trained or well-read in ecclesiology, and they certainly do not come off as if he were making a comment on Eastern Orthodox - Roman Catholic unity or anything beyond a simple but (in this case) misguided piety.

Earlier in his career, Codreanu outlined what he saw as a distinction between a Christian's duty to forgive personal enemies and the need to punish enemies of the nation. His overall approach was to avoid violence whenever possible: "we will follow the path of the country laws, not provoking anyone, avoiding all provocations, not answering any provocation." However, this policy did not extend to traitors of Romania, several of whom the Legion planned to assassinate: "those who have tortured you for your faith in the Romanian people, you will not forgive. Do not confuse the Christian right and duty of forgiving those who wronged you, with the right and duty of our people to punish those who have betrayed it and assumed for themselves the responsibility to oppose its destiny. Do not forget that the swords you have put on belong to the nation. You carry them in her name. In her name you will use them for punishment - unforgiving and unmerciful. Thus and only thus, will you be preparing a healthy future for this nation."[350]

---

[350] *For My Legionaries*. Page 459.

While our Royal Saints certainly executed enemies of the State, the fact remains that Codreanu was not in a formal position to do so and lacked the government authority which Scripture tells us is needed to *"bear the sword."*[351] However, given that the authorities and organs of the State coordinated against him as strongly as they could, and that those who should have been using their power responsibly to maintain Romania's health were instead selling out to foreign interests and betraying the people over whom they ruled, we must leave it to God to judge what little violence the Legionaries carried out under Codreanu.

In addition to his personal faith and views, Orthodoxy appears to have been a key element of Codreanu's Legionary movement. They named themselves "the Legion of St. Michael the Archangel" after devoting themselves to an icon of him, and Codreanu noted that "The icon appeared to us of unsurpassed beauty. I was never attracted by the beauty of any icon. But now, I felt bound to this one with all my soul and I had a feeling the Archangel was alive. Since then, I have come to love that icon. Any time we found the Church open, we entered and prayed before that icon. Our hearts were filled with peace and joy."[352]

He further taught, on Page 322 of <u>For My Legionaries</u>, that "The legionary believes in God and prays for the victory of the Legion. It should not be forgotten that we are here on this earth by God's will and the blessing of the

---

[351] Romans 13:4

[352] *For My Legionaries.* Page 189

Christian church. Before the altars of our churches, the
entire Romanian Nation on this earth has assembled,
times without number, in periods of flight and
persecution - women and children and old people - aware
that this is the last possible place of refuge. And today
too, we are ready to assemble - we, the Romanian people -
round the altars as in former times of great danger and to
kneel to receive God's blessing."

Describing the beginnings of Legionary life, Codreanu
put "faith in God" at the top of the list: "All of us believed
in God. None of us was an atheist. The more we were
alone and surrounded, the more our preoccupations were
directed to God and toward contact with our own dead
and those of the nation. This gave us an invincible
strength and a bright serenity in the face of all blows."[353]

Strict ascetic discipline was a core teaching for his
Legion, and he always taught his men not to lower
themselves to the level of their enemies: "Teach your
children not to use treachery either against a friend or
against their greatest foe. Not only will they not win, but
they will be more than defeated, they will be crushed.
Nor should they use treachery against the treacherous
person and his treacherous ways, for if they should win,
only the persons change. Treachery will remain
unchanged. The treachery of the victor will be substituted
for that of the defeated. In essence, the same treachery
will rule the world. The darkness of treachery in the
world cannot be replaced by another darkness but only
by the light brought by the soul of the brave, full of

---

[353] Ibid. Page 289.

character and honor."[354]

Evola wrote in his essay *Nationalism and Ascesis: The Iron Guard* that "the religious element constitutes the central core of Romanian Legionarism, which has derived from it a need to create a new man by means of specific ascetic practices. Many a reader will thus be surprised to discover that over 600,000 men - for this is roughly the number of Codreanu's followers - systematically practice not only prayer, but even fasting: three times a week the Legionaries are asked to keep the so-called 'black fast', which consists in not eating, drinking, or smoking. Codreanu himself, during one of our conversations, explained the meaning of the above practice in the following terms: the complete supremacy of the spirit over the body must be ensured and fasting is one of the most effective means to this end; by loosening the bonds formed by the most natural, material part of man, fasting also fosters a favorable condition for evoking invisible forces - forces from on high which are evoked through prayer and ritual. And in all tests and struggles - despite what 'positive minds' may believe - these forces play a part no less decisive than that played by visible, material and purely human forces."[355]

Beyond his personal faith and the ascetic focus of his Legionary movement, we must also consider the reactions he and his men got from various Orthodox clergy. The Legion's flags were constantly blessed by local clergy, who also played a key role in helping to organize young

---

[354] Ibid. Page 288.

[355] *The Prison Notes.* Page 70.

men in the building and reconstruction projects with which they were expected to help. Many priests - by some estimates, more than a quarter of all the Orthodox priests in Romania - joined and supported the Legion.[356] Even some Romanian Uniates ended up supporting Codreanu simply because all other options had failed; he explained that "It was early in June 1930 that a wagon drawn by two horses stopped the gate of my house in Iasi. From it descended two priests, a peasant and a young man. I asked them to come in. They introduced themselves, Orthodox priest Ion Dumitrescu, Greek-Catholic priest Andrei Berinde, and the peasant Nicoara. 'We come by wagon from Maramures. We have been on the road for two weeks; we are both priests in Borsa, one Greek-Catholic, the other Orthodox. We can no longer bear to see the misfortune of the Romanians of Maramures. We wrote memorandum after memorandum which we sent all over, to Parliament, the government, cabinet ministers, the Regency, with no reply from any of them. We do not know what else to do. We came by wagon here to Iasi to ask Romanian studentry not to abandon us to our fate. We speak in the name of thousands of peasants from Maramures who have grown desperate. We are their priests. We cannot close our eyes to what we see. Our people are dying and our hearts are breaking with

---

[356] *Relationship between the Romanian Orthodox Church and the Iron Guard | Detailed Pedia.* (n.d.). Www.detailedpedia.com. Retrieved March 23, 2023, from https://www.detailedpedia.com/wiki-Relationship_between_the_Romanian_Orthodox_Church_and_the_Iron_Guard#Notes

pity."[357] By the 1930s, Orthodox seminaries had turned into "legionary strongholds,"[358]and Metropolitan Nicolae Bălan even led the prayers for a 1940 commemoration of Codreanu.[359]

However, Codreanu also noted that many clergy were against him; when he first ran for Parliament in 1931, he noted that "Of all social categories, the priest showed us the least understanding. In a country in which the crosses on Church steeples have been falling down before the politicians' masterdom, atheistic and Jewized, in a battle in which we were the only ones coming in the name of the cross - our chests bared before the pagan monster - the county's priests, excepting three or four, were against us."[360]

During Codreanu's final trial, which condemned him to hard labor despite no evidence being presented against him (while evidence in his favor was barred from being entered as testimony), the first Patriarch of Romanian Orthodoxy stood against him. That Patriarch, Miron Cristea, was Prime Minister under King Carol II in a very unusual and uncanonical set of circumstances. Commenting on this situation, Codreanu wrote on June 3rd of 1938 that "I do not know if we can refer to the statement to the youth by Patriarch Miron Cristea, in which he condemns the Legionary movement in harsh terms, in any other way. The Orthodox Church is taking

---

[357] *For My Legionaries.* Page 356.

[358] *Relationship between the Romanian Orthodox Church and the Iron Guard.*

[359] Wikipedia Contributors. (2023, February 27). *Nicolae Bălan.* Wikipedia; Wikimedia Foundation. https://en.wikipedia.org/wiki/Nicolae_B%C4%83lan

[360] *For My Legionaries.* Page 379.

an openly hostile attitude to Romanian youth...To struggle for the Church of your country, on the edge of the Christian world, when the fire which is burning the Churches nearby is spreading its flames towards us! We are struggling, we are sacrificing ourselves, we are dying, blood gushing from our breasts, to defend the Churches, and the *CHURCH* denounces us as 'a danger to the people', as 'gone astray', as 'alien to the nation'. What a tragedy in our souls!...The Church of our fathers, the Church of our forebears is hitting us! The Patriarch is also the Prime Minister, it is in his name that all these things are done and from whom so much suffering comes day after day. Lord, Lord! What a disaster! And to what trials are you subjecting our poor soul!"[361] Given that Patriarch Miron openly supported the deportation of Jews - and once greeted the King with a Roman salute[362] - it seems that his problem with the Legionaries was more about having to share power than with concrete ideological differences.

It is worth noting that Codreanu professed something along the lines of Byzantine Symphonia - if without that specific vocabulary - and acknowledged that the Legionary movement worked along parallel lines with the Church: "I have been asked whether our activity so far has followed along the same lines as those of the Christian Church. I answer: We make a great distinction between the line we follow and that of the Christian

---

[361] *The Prison Notes.* Pages 43 and 44.

[362] *Patriarch Miron of Romania.* (2023, February 10). Wikipedia. https://en.wikipedia.org/wiki/Patriarch_Miron_of_Romania

Church. The Church dominates us from on high. It reaches perfection and the sublime. We cannot lower this plane in order to explain our acts. We, through our action, through all our acts and thoughts, tend toward this line, raising ourselves up toward it as much as the weight of our sins of the flesh and our fall through original sin permit. It remains to be seen how much we can elevate ourselves toward this line through our worldly efforts."[363] He was clearly aware of the separation between worldly action and the Church, the Theanthropic Body of the God-Man Jesus Christ, which exists on a higher plane and ultimately serves a greater purpose than merely organizing the State or the temporal comfort of Christians. At the same time, he wanted to raise up his movement and its cooperation with the State to resemble the Heavenly Kingdom to the greatest possible degree.

Thus we may conclude that the Legion's engagement with Orthodoxy was a multifaceted and complex one; some clergy supported it, others fought against it, and the whole time Codreanu and his men believed they were the only ones truly fighting for Christianity. It was with great pain of heart that Codreanu wrote of his clerical resistance, maintaining up until the end of his life that the Church voices who opposed him were misguided.

---

[363] *For my Legionaries*. Page 391.

Codreanu and the State

"Masonic democracy through an unparalleled perfidy masquerades as an apostle for peace on this earth while at the same time proclaiming war between man and God."[364]
- Corneliu Codreanu

Following our outline, in this chapter we will address the three primary questions to consider as regards the State: 1. What type of government structure did Codreanu support, and *why*? 2. What did he believe was the purpose of government, and its proper role in the lives of its subjects? 3. What concrete policies did he reject, support, or hope to get passed? By studying each of these three concepts, we can compare his thoughts with those of the Orthodox Church on these topics.

In his essay *The Tragedy of the Romanian Iron Guard*, Julius Evola quoted Codreanu's thoughts on form of government: "At the head of peoples, above the elite, one finds the monarchy. I reject the republic...Not all of the monarchs were good. Monarchy itself, however, has always been good. One must not confuse the man with the institution and draw false conclusions. There can be bad priests; but can we, because of this, conclude that the Church must be abolished and God stoned to death? There are weak and bad monarchs, certainly, but we cannot renounce monarchy because of this...To each

---

[364] Codreanu, C. (2015). *For My Legionaries*. Black House Publishing. Page 393.

nation God has traced a line of destiny. A monarch is great and good when he stays on that line; he is small or bad, to the extent that he wanders away from this line of destiny or opposes it. This then, is the law of monarchy. There are also other lines that may tempt a monarch: the line of personal interest or that of a class of people or group; the line of alien interests (domestic or foreign). He must avoid all these lines and follow that of his people."[365]

This brief but illuminating passage reveals to us the depths of Codreanu's thought: he believed in the divine institution of Monarchy, realized that principles cannot be judged by contingents, and professed that a Monarch should be accountable to his people. These nuances avoid the worst sort of extremes; he neither taught his followers to blindly obey all orders from a Monarch simply because they were issued from the mouth of a King, nor to try and overthrow the institution itself and replace it with something else when the Monarch goes astray.

Evola further noted, as detailed on Pages 93 and 94 of The Prison Notes, that "While Codreanu twice served as a member of Parliament, right from the start he took a firm stance against democracy. To quote him verbatim, democracy breaks the unity of the race through party factionalism; it is incapable of continuity in terms of effort and responsibility; it is incapable of displaying authority, since it lacks the power of sanction and turns the politician into the slave of his partisans; it serves the interests of big finance; and finally, it makes millions of

---

[365] Codreanu, C. (2015). *The Prison Notes*. Page 94.

Jews Romanian citizens. In contrast, Codreanu asserted the principle of social selection and of elites. He clearly foresaw the new politics of nations striving for reconstruction, whose underlying principle is neither democracy nor dictatorship, but rather the relationship between nation and leader - potency and act, obscure instinct and expression. The leader of these new forms of government is not elected by the crowd; rather, the crowd, or nation, lends its consent to him and recognizes its own ideas in his…In such a case the leader is no longer a 'master,' a 'dictator,' who does as he 'pleases,' who leads 'according to his whims.' He is the incarnation of this unseen state of spirit, the symbol of this state of consciousness. He no longer does 'as he pleases,' he does what he 'must' do. And he is guided not by individual or collective interests, but by the interests of the immortal nation which have penetrated the conscience of the people. It is only within the framework of these interests and only in that framework that personal and collective interests find their maximum of normal satisfaction."

Commenting on the 1938 Constitution of Romania which disbanded political parties and put all power into the hands of King Carol II, Evola added his insight that "we do not wish to deny that under normal conditions, with its power and significance intact, monarchy requires no dictatorial surrogate in order to properly perform its function. This is not the case, however, in a state where traditional *fides* has been replaced by political intrigue, in which the Jewish hydra has wrapped its tentacles around the chief vital cores of the nation, and in which electoral democracy has undermined the ethical integrity and patriotic feelings of large sectors of the political world. These conditions call for a totalitarian movement of renewal, something which, through a collective drive, will prove capable of overwhelming, re-founding, transforming and elevating the whole nation, essentially on the basis of a new state of consciousness and the power of an ideal and faith. If present, the institution of the monarchy will not be brought down by a totalitarian national movement of this sort; rather, it will find strength and completeness in it, as the very example of Italy goes to show. In these terms, a collaboration between the new regime and Codreanu's national Legionary movement was deemed both desirable and possible, particularly since, as we have seen, Codreanu expressly defended the idea of monarchy and never planned to offer himself as the new King of Romania - something which even his opponents have never implied."[366]

Thus we can see the overall hope present in Romania at the time: that the government would seize power as a temporary emergency measure and work together with the Legionary movement in order to restore Romania to a state of health that would not require such authoritarian action to begin with. As you'll read about soon, this did materialize for a short time in Romania after Codreanu's death - but in a way that, as illustrated by a couple of particular incidents, departed from both Codreanu's initial vision and traditional Orthodox praxis.

---

[366]   Ibid. Pages 97 and 98.

In either case there is no ambiguity as to whether the Legionaries were Monarchists, and Codreanu summed up his thoughts on democracy by writing that "Finding truth cannot be trusted to majorities, just as in geometry Pythagoras' theorem cannot be put to the multitude's vote in order to determine or deny its validity; or just as a chemist making ammonia does not turn to multitudes to put the amounts of nitrogen and hydrogen to a vote; or as an agronomist, who studied agriculture and its laws for years, does not have to turn to a multitude trying to convince himself of their validity by their vote."[367] And further: "Not only does democracy remove the national elite, but it replaces it with the worst within a nation. Democracy elects men totally lacking in scruples, without any morals; those who will pay better, thus those with a higher power of corruption; magicians, charlatans, demagogues, who will excel in their fields during the electoral campaign. Several good men would be able to slip through among them, even politicians of good faith. But they would be the slaves of the former. The real elite of a nation would be defeated, removed, because it would refuse to compete on that basis; it would retreat and stay hidden."[368]

As to what Codreanu believed the purpose of a nation or State to be, we find hints in the second Evola passage quoted above; he desired "the unity of the race," "continuity in terms of effort and responsibility," and "displaying authority" as among the objectives that he

---

[367] *For My Legionaries*. Page 387.

[368] Ibid. Page 388.

believed a democratic system naturally hindered. Codreanu also believed that different nationalist movements emphasized different aspects of mankind, and that his was a uniquely spiritual one. Evola detailed in his essay *My Meeting with Codreanu* that "Among the various arguments of our conversation, I recall the interesting way in which Codreanu defined Fascism, German National Socialism, and his own movement. He argued that there are three aspects to each organism: form, vital force, and the spirit. The same is true of nations and so each renovation movement will develop by stressing a particular one of these principles. According to Codreanu, what prevailed in Fascism was form, in the sense of that informing power that shapes states and civilizations - something reflecting the heritage of Rome as an organizing power. National Socialism instead emphasized vital force most of all, hence the importance it assigned to race and the myth of race, and its appeal to the idea of blood and of national-racial community. The Iron Guard's starting point was instead believed to be the spiritual element. This is where Codreanu wished to begin. And what he meant by 'spirit' was something also connected to strictly religious and ascetic values."[369]

It is interesting to note that (as previously mentioned) depending on which Orthodox Saints you read, you will find a human being described as either tripartite - that is, composed of body, soul, and spirit - or as composed of body and soul, without a distinction between soul and

---

[369] *The Prison Notes.* Page 102.

spirit. Based on Codreanu's presupposition, it would seem that the tripartite division was the one taught in Romanian Orthodoxy at the time, and his extrapolation of this system to describe the emphases of various political movements is one I find fascinating and accurate. It is not that he disregarded form or vital force, as he expressed, but rather believed that the spiritual ("religious and ascetic") must take priority in order to lead man - and nations - to true fulfillment of potential. I find in this sentiment echoes of **Psalm 127:1**, in which we read from St. King David that *"Unless the LORD builds the house, they labor in vain who build it; Unless the LORD guards the city, the watchman stays awake in vain."* May those who seek change always remember Who must forever remain its foundation.

The role of God was central to Codreanu's understanding of the State; as detailed in the essay *Caught in the Romanian Storm,* he explained to Evola that "'Three elements exist: the individual, the nation, and God. The individual must be integrated within the nation. The nation, within divine law. We regard the nation as an organic whole. It includes the living and the dead, human forces as well as divine. It is both an ethnic and mystical entity. The individual must integrate himself within the laws of the nation, and the nation within the laws of God. What we are taking up here is the concept of ecumenicity found in our tradition, namely the Orthodox Christian religion."[370] Before we continue, note that Codreanu's use of the word "ecumenicity" clearly referred to the entire

---

[370] Ibid. Page 82.

Church, the Church Militant and the Church Triumphant, those struggling for salvation and those who have already attained it, and *not* to the similar word "ecumenism." The arch-heresy of ecumenism, commonly referred to as "Branch Theory" or a similar name, states that all (or at least many) groups calling themselves Christian are somehow part of the same Church and altogether form one Body of Christ. As detailed at the Orthodox Christian Information Center and elsewhere, such ruinous ecclesiology is "completely unacceptable to the Orthodox."[371] That is not what Codreanu had in mind, and the topic is beyond the scope of the present work.

Instead, Evola tells us in his essay *An Interview With Codreanu* that the Legion's understanding of the word *ecumenism* was "the positive transcendence of all internationalism and abstract, rationalistic universalism. The ecumenical idea envisages society as a unity of life, a living unity, and a way of living together not only with our people, but also our deceased and God."[372]

Further, Codreanu shared many thoughts in For My Legionaries regarding his views of what makes a State, of what sort of people a State is composed, and what its ultimate aim ought to be. Quoting from Vasile Conta, a 19th-century Romanian politician, Codreanu included the following passage in his book: "'It is a recognized fact, even by those attacking us today, that the first condition for a State to exist and prosper, is that the citizens of that

---

[371] *The Orthodox Church and the Ecumenical Movement*. (n.d.). Orthodoxinfo.com. Retrieved March 17, 2023, from http://orthodoxinfo.com/ecumenism/denverreport.asp

[372] *The Prison Notes*. Page 67.

State be of the same race, same blood, and this is easy to understand [...] bearing in mind that the same blood flows through the veins of all the members of a people, one understands that all these members will have through heredity, about the same feelings, about the same tendencies, and even about the same ideas; so that in perilous times, on unique occasions, their hearts will beat as one, their minds will adopt one opinion, the action of all will seek the same purpose; in other words the nation made up of a single race will have only one center of gravity; and the State made up of such a nation, that and only that one will be in the best condition of strength, durability and progress [...] True, this does not prevent foreigners from acquiring the citizenship of a State, provided they assimilate into the dominant nation; namely, to mix totally so that ultimately the State remain of the same single blood [...] I am not saying it is impossible for various races that would exist in some country to have sometimes a common interest, that the hereditary tendencies of one race be just as favored of those of another by the same circumstances. As long as this state of affairs lasted, both indigenous and naturalized would certainly live peacefully.

But circumstances change and with them the interest of the various races could also change; and if not today, then tomorrow; if not tomorrow then day after tomorrow the tendencies of the naturalized will be in conflict with those of the natives, and then the interest of some will be at odds with that of the others, and then the interests of some could not be satisfied without sacrificing those of the others; and then we would have a fight for existence between two races, with fierce battles that could only be ended either by the total abolishment of the State, or when one of the races is totally crushed so that again only one dominant race will remain in the State."[373]

To summarize his perspective, Codreanu affirmed (through the words of Conta) that a State ought to be composed primarily of one dominant race and the foreigners who intermarry and assimilate into the native culture and people - not because one race is superior or inferior to another, because only one of them can be Christian, or because of atavistic hatred for others. Rather, he believed that a State ought to primarily serve one group because over time, if there is no assimilation, the unity of the State will be split into trying to serve different groups of people and that eventually, those interests are likely to come into open conflict which can only be solved by either a dissolving of the State (as it was intended to exist) or the complete destruction of one race by another. While I think that on the whole world history has borne out these principles, it is important to make several notes on the nuances of the topic. To begin with, we must keep in mind that when Romanians at the time spoke of "race" they specifically meant ethnic Romanians; they were not referring to Europeans as a whole.

After all, history has demonstrated over and over that simply "being European" has never been enough to maintain a nation or a continent; some of the bloodiest wars in human history have been intra-European

---

[373] *For My Legionaries*. Pages 152-154.

conflicts, in which a German and an Englishman (for example) most certainly did not consider themselves to belong to the same group of people. We have been conditioned in the modern world to think of "White" as a collective race, and perhaps it is increasingly a unified category due to Europeans as a whole - regardless of actual ethnicity or nationality - being collectively slandered and attacked as if they were all one group of people. But historically that has not been the situation. Even in the days of the Byzantine Empire, certain European parties tended to be Arians and brutally fight against other Europeans of the Orthodox Faith. Thus we see that typically religion, and not "race" as conceived in modern terminology, was more considered the "center of gravity" for a people than mere blood similarity.

At the same time, as you learned in a previous chapter, ethnicity is not considered illusory or unimportant by the Orthodox Church. It is an acknowledged reality that on the whole, people belonging to the same ethnic group can more readily compose a State than people of many groups - especially when, as Conta noted, those groups do not assimilate but rather oppose each others' interests. One could surely argue that these concerns are worldly and ought to ideally be obliterated in Christ...but here in the fallen world, where each of us often loses the battle against our passions and attachments, certain realities must be considered in terms of how best to organize a nation.

If you will recall, Section II of *Basis of the Social Concept* explains that "In the contemporary world, the notion of 'nation' is used in two meanings, as an ethnic community and the aggregate citizens of a particular state. Relationships between church and nation should be viewed in the context of both meanings of this word…The universal nature of the Church, however, does not mean that Christians should have no right to national identity and national self-expressions. On the contrary, the Church unites in herself the universal with the national… Among saints venerated by the Orthodox Church, many became famous for the love of their earthly homeland and faithfulness to it. Russian hagiographic sources praise the holy Prince Michael of Tver who 'gave his life for his fatherland,' comparing his feat to the martyrdom of the holy protomartyr Dimitrius of Thessaloniki: 'The good lover of his fatherland said about his native city of Thessaloniki, 'O Lord, if you ruin this city, I will perish together with it, but if you save it, I will also be saved.''[374] Thus, for a leader or politician to express his belief that the State he represents ought to protect its primary ethnic group does not seem sinful or un-Orthodox…provided that his policies and actions do not transform from a love of kin and peace into a hatred of other groups.

Codreanu's approach to politics evolved somewhat as he grew older and as the circumstances in Romania changed. In the beginning, his goal was to organize a movement that would encompass all Romanian university students who wanted to bring attention to the situation and fight back against the overwhelming

---

[374] *II. Church and nation | The Russian Orthodox Church.* (n.d.). https://old.mospat.ru/en/documents/social-concepts/ii/

presence of unassimilated Jewish foreigners in the top levels of Romanian schools. These students would then hang nationalist flags where they could and try to draw in local leaders to help them. It does not seem that, at the beginning, Codreanu and his movement had specific policy changes in mind; instead, they wanted to raise awareness of the nation's problems and gather together people of like feeling across the country. In 1923 however, as you will read more about in the following chapter, Romanian politicians established a new Constitution which granted citizenship to all foreign Jews who happened to live within Romania's borders. Thus, Codreanu issued a command to his followers: "The March 28, 1923 Constitution must be abolished immediately. Protest against its promulgation. Demand free elections. Organize, in order to ensure your victory. A new Constitution must guarantee the Romanian Nation's rights of priority, as the dominant people in the State."[375] The revolution which followed this order saw the local authorities, army, press, and police unite against the Legion and arrest its leaders.

As the movement progressed to the next stage, it remained focused on changing the State by way of personal transformation rather than political involvement; Codreanu's principles, which he saw as fundamental to Legionary life, included "moral purity," "disinterestedness in battle," " enthusiasm," "faith, work, order, hierarchy, discipline," "justice," and "deeds, not words." He believed that through a life lived according to

---

[375] *For My Legionaries.* Page 148.

these concepts, "a new Romania will emerge and the long-awaited resurrection of this Romanian people, the aim of all our efforts" would almost spontaneously arise in their midst.[376] He further - at first - forbade Legionaries from joining any political parties or giving their support to a system he saw as irreparably subverted.

Remaining focused on the idea of movement rather than party, he further encouraged leaders to "refuse all offers of financing if he wishes his movement to survive... A leader who accepts the outside financing of his movement is like a man who accustoms his body to live on medication. To the extent an organism is administered medication, to the same extent it is condemned to being unable to react on its own. Moreover, when it is deprived of the medication, it dies; it is at the mercy of the pharmacist! Likewise, a political movement is at the mercy of those who finance it. These could cease their financing at any given moment and the movement, unaccustomed to living on its own, dies."[377]

Thus we see that, rather than try and organize or fundraise for a political party in the classic sense (at least at first), Codreanu believed that restoring the Christian and national feeling among a great group of people would naturally result in the goals he desired rather than engaging in the sort of political intrigue which he saw as intrinsically immoral and dishonest. Ultimately, the Legionaries formed a political party called "All For The Fatherland" in order to have their voices heard in

---

[376] Ibid. Page 304.

[377] Ibid. Pages 327 and 328.

Parliament. For Codreanu, a political party was merely the extension of a movement. It was a specific tool, with a specific purpose, to be deployed or dissolved as circumstances required. There was no notion of loyalty to a "political party" as an entity separated from spirituality. Without a spiritual foundation, and the movement it inspires, a party is simply an empty shell; it's fundamentally just a jersey worn at a sports game, with nothing separating it from that worn by the other team.

That said, there were seeds of political ideas present in even the earliest iterations of his movement. In 1920, when he helped organize what he referred to as "National-Christian Socialism" (and in For My Legionaries Codreanu noted that they created this name the proto-Legionaries had not yet heard of Adolf Hitler or German National Socialism)[378], the following adaptation of the Nicene Creed was articulated as a political formula:

"I believe in the one and undivided Romanian State, from Dniester to the Tisa, the holder of all Romanians and only of Romanians, lover of work, honor and in fear of God, concerned about the country and its people; giver of equal rights, both civil and political, to men and to women; protector of the family, paying its public servants and workers on the basis of the number of children and the work performed, quality and quantity; and in a State, supporter of social harmony through minimizing of class differences; and in addition to salaries, nationalizing factories (the property of all workers) and distributing the land among all the ploughmen.

---

[378]   Ibid. Page 71.

It would distribute benefits between owner (state or private) and workers. The former owner, in addition to his own salary should get a percentage inversely proportional to the size of his original investment; furthermore, the State would insure his original investment; furthermore, the State would insure the workers through a 'risks fund;' would provide storehouses for food and clothing for workers and civil servants who, organized in national unions will have their representatives in the administrative boards of the various industrial, agricultural and commercial institutions.

I believe in a great and strong 'father of the workers' and King of the peasants, Ferdinand the First, who has sacrificed all for the happiness of Romania and who for our salvation became as one with the people; who at the head of his troops at Marasti and Marasesti vanquished the enemy; who ever since, looks lovingly and trustingly upon the soldiers owing him allegiance, soldiers who will find their military duty to be a real school of their nation which they can finish in a year.

I believe in one tricolor surrounded by the rays of National-Christian Socialism, symbol of harmony among the brothers and sisters of Greater Romania.

I believe in one Sacred Christian Church with priests living the Gospel and for the Gospel, and who would, like the apostles, sacrifice themselves for the enlightenment of the many.

I recognize the election of the Ministers by the Chamber, the abolition of the Senate, the organization of rural police, a progressive income tax, schools of agriculture and crafts in the villages, 'circles' for housewives and adults, homes for invalids and old folks, national homes, the determination of paternity, effectively bringing the knowledge of the laws to everybody, the encouragement of private initiative in the interest of the Nation, and the development of the peasant's home industry.

I await the resurrection of national conscience even in the most humble shepherd and the descent of the educated into the midst of the tired, to strengthen and help them in true brotherhood, the foundation of Romania of tomorrow. Amen!"[379]

These types of ideas, a combination of guiding principles and specific policies, seem to have been born more out of patriotic feeling than of meetings with lawyers and politicians who could draft up the exact methods by which such ideas could be implemented. Yet despite his disdain for politicians and parties, Codreanu always believed that the Legionaries should take power via whatever legal means were available to them. Thus, when he heard that a Parliament seat was open in the county of Neamt in 1931, he mobilized his men to travel there - whether by train, horse, or on foot - in order to canvass the neighborhoods and stir up support for his candidacy. At the end of campaign season, Codreanu won 11,300 votes - over 4,000 votes more than the next highest-ranking candidate. Thus Codreanu entered Romanian political life.

---

[379] Ibid. Pages 72 and 73.

He quickly issued a list of demands which even he admitted "were not the result of some prolonged thinking or ideological search, but the result of momentary reflections over what the Romanian people needed then." Those demands included the following points:

"1. We demand the introduction of the death penalty for the fraudulent manipulators of the public funds.

2. We demand the investigation and confiscation of the wealth of those who have bled our poor country.

3. We demand that all politicians who may be proved guilty of having worked against the interests of our country by supporting shady private speculations or in any other fashion, be brought to justice.

4. We demand that in the future, politicians be barred from the administrative boards of the various banks and financial enterprises.

5. We demand the expulsion of the hordes of pitiless exploiters who have come here to drain the riches from our soil and exploit the work of our hands.

6. We demand that the territory of Romania be declared the inalienable and indefeasible property of the Romanian nation.

7. We demand that all campaigning agents be sent to work and that a single command be established, which will inspire the whole Romanian nation with one heart and one mind." After putting forth his first demand, Codreanu was interrupted by a man who told him that he was calling himself Christian but promoting an anti-Christian ideal (the death penalty). Codreanu responded that "when it is a question of choosing between the death

of my country and that of a thief, I prefer the death of the thief, and I think I am a better Christian if I do not permit the thief to ruin my country and to destroy it."[380]

Tudor summarized the Legion's view of economics and labor in the following words: "The Legion rejected both capitalism and communism as economic systems, the former because it led to exploitation of workers by the wealthy and the latter because it was atheistic and resulted in dictatorship. Instead, the Legionaries aimed for a third position - generally a type of corporatist system in which commerce would be combined with socialistic practices. In 1935, Codreanu attempted to establish a Legionary trading system: 'Legionary commerce signifies a new phase in the history of commerce which has been stained by the Jewish spirit. It is called: Christian commerce - based on the love of people and not on robbing them; commerce based on honor.' Around the same time, the 'Corps of Legionary Workers' was established to work towards fairer conditions for workers."[381] Thus we can see that as with most nationalist movements, the Legion's economic views were concerned mainly with the well-being of the working class and with protecting them from exploitation and oppression.

After Codreanu was murdered, command of the Legion was ultimately assumed by Horia Sima - a man Codreanu's father considered a traitor, and whom Sima later imprisoned. Nevertheless, after a great deal of

---

[380] Ibid. Pages 382 and 383.
[381] Ibid. Page 458.

political chaos and the expulsion of King Carol from Romania, General Ion Antonescu (whom King Carol had put in charge) came to an agreement with the Legionary movement and on September 14th, 1940, the National Legionary State was instituted. Antonescu remained in charge of the government, with Sima serving as his Vice-President. This state of affairs, while short-lived, "enjoy[ed] the enthusiastic support of most of the Romanian populace."[382] According to Tudor, "The Legionary State initiated the removal of Jews and corrupt Romanians from their various political, economic, legal, and educational positions, replacing them with trustworthy Romanians, mostly Legionaries. Although the living standards for Jews obviously declined as a result, their conditions under the Legionary State were not as harsh as some authors have claimed."[383]

It must be said that under the Legionary State, there were two episodes during which certain Legionaries seem to have lost sight of Codreanu's principles and engaged in mass murder of political prisoners and Jews. It is worth noting that Sima disapproved of the killings and in the former case, then-Minister of Foreign Affairs Michel Sturdza "pointed out that this mass execution was entirely in conflict with both the interests and the principles of the Legionary Movement."[384] The latter case, the Bucharest pogrom in which over 100 Jews were slaughtered and their property destroyed, was a horrific

[382] Ibid. Page 468.
[383] Ibid. Page 469.
[384] Ibid. Page 470.

302

deviation from anything that traditional Orthodoxy has ever encouraged or approved.

There are some who say that certain photos of the massacre's aftermath have been altered or forged, and there seems to be some evidence that the incident did not take place as it typically described.[385] Tudor claimed on Page 472 of <u>For my Legionaries</u> that the actions in Bucharest were neither entirely carried out by members of the Legion nor "even supported by most Legionaries, who were in principle against such behavior." In either case, there seems no doubt that the riot which occurred departed from both Orthodox and Legionary guidance; as you read about in a previous chapter, when such incidents occurred in Orthodox lands those responsible were always censured by the clergy.

Eventually, Antonescu initiated a successful coup against the Legionaries and assumed full control of Romania. Hitler, having allied with Antonescu, rounded up those Legionaries who had fled to Germany and imprisoned them "largely in the concentration camps of Buchenwald, Dachau, and Oranienburg, although their conditions were not as poor as those of other prisoners."[386] King Michael I of Romania, who took the crown after King Carol's expulsion, ended up betraying the Axis and aligning with the Allies instead; as a result, Hitler released the incarcerated Legionaries in order to help them establish a new government-in-exile in Vienna.

---

[385] Thorpe, C. (2012, June 13). *The Romanian Legionary Movement between Truth & Deception*. Counter-Currents. https://counter-currents.com/2012/06/the-romanian-legionary-movement-between-truth-and-deception/

[386] *For my Legionaries*. Page 473.

By 1947, however, the Legionaries in Vienna had surrendered and Romania was usurped by communists. This resulted in captured Legionaries being tried in the Nuremberg Trials, at which they were "declared *not guilty* of 'war crimes,' ' crimes against humanity,' or 'collaborationism' by April of 1947"[387] and ultimately released. From the late 1940s to the early-mid 1950s, Legionaries and other Romanian nationalists were imprisoned en masse and subjected to some of the worst torture conditions ever inflicted upon human beings. Some Orthodox Christians who suffered under these programs have left behind writings and legacies which are worthy of study; primary among them are works by and/or about Valeriu Gafencu and Fathers Roman Braga and George Calciu.

In a section of <u>For My Legionaries</u> entitled "The Final Aim of the Nation," Codreanu wrote a beautiful passage with which I believe all Orthodox Christians can agree and ought to keep in mind when reading about, interpreting, or becoming involved in politics. He thus concluded his thoughts on the State: "The final aim is not life but resurrection. The resurrection of peoples in the name of the Savior Jesus Christ...There will come a time when all the peoples of the earth shall be resurrected, with all their dead and all their kings and emperors, each people having its place before God's throne. This final moment, 'the resurrection from the dead,' is the noblest and most sublime one toward which a people can rise."[388]

---

[387] Ibid. Page 474.

[388] Ibid. Page 395.

Codreanu And The Jews

"The Jewish problem is not born of 'racial hatred.' It is born of an infraction committed by Jews against the laws and natural order in which all peoples of the world live."[389]
- Corneliu Codreanu

Nearly an entire quarter of <u>For My Legionaries</u> is a section entitled "The Jewish Problem." Codreanu wrote, at the beginning of that section, that his thoughts on the topic were derived from the ideas of his professor, A.C. Cuza, at the University of Iasi.[390]

Codreanu described, with great anguish, the gradual takeover of Romania by foreign Jews; he detailed in particular the exclusion of Romanian merchants from all major commerce centers, the closure of Churches due to the surrounding areas becoming Jewish communities, the transformation of ancient palaces into banks and - in one case -the replacement of a garden with a theater. He pointed out that this foreign invasion was illegal according to the Constitution of Romania, and despaired - in many words - over the treacherous politicians who took bribes to look the other way. "The loss of our Romanian towns has for us devastating consequences," he wrote, "for towns are the economic centers of a nation. The entire richness of the country is accumulated in them.

---

[389] Codreanu, C. (2015). *For My Legionaries*. Black House Publishing. Page 120.
[390] Ibid. Page 115.

So that whoever controls the towns control the means of subsistence, the wealth of a nation."[391] Primarily, he was concerned with the granting of citizenship to millions of Jewish foreigners; said citizenship would allow them access to the nation's levers of power and highest offices. As a student, he watched the political battle over Jewish naturalization play out - and once it was on the table at 1923 meeting of the Romanian Parliament, it was granted after less than half an hour.[392]

He further mentioned watching powerlessly as the people elected to protect the nation threw its inheritance away to enrich themselves instead. He described Romanian politicians at the time as "administrators in name only because they are nothing but supine executors of Jewish plans. These officials are supported, flattered, showered with gifts, co-opted in administrative councils, paid by the month by the Judaic economic power (Judas was paid but once); their lust for money is roused, they are urged on to luxury and vice, and when disobeying Jewish directives and stances, are purely and simply thrown out even though they be cabinet ministers. Their pay and subsidies are cut, their thieveries brought to light and shady business deals exposed, implicating them, in order to compromise them."[393] Codreanu's great fear regarding the new citizenship grant, the laxity and greed of local politicians, and Jews making up over half of Romania's elite universities was that Romanians would

---

[391] Ibid. Page 123.
[392] Ibid. Page 147.
[393] Ibid. Page 125.

no longer be served by Romanian doctors, government officials, engineers, lawyers, etc.

He opined, with great despair, that Romania was changing in educational, economic, demographic, and cultural terms. Most of all, he hated the Jewish newspapers - which he invariably described as serving no higher purpose than to corrupt the Romanians who read them. Codreanu further described "the Jewish press" as "inciting to rebellion against the Crown, against the form of government and the legal order."[394] He printed many examples in <u>For My Legionaries,</u> demonstrating these attitudes using quotes from Jewish newspapers. Hatred of the King and the institution of Monarchy as a whole were regular features of their articles at the time. Codreanu wrote that to the Romanians, "the crown always constituted a dear patrimony. As the guarantor of our unity and resistance facing any dangers, the Jews never hesitated to attack it, to insult and compromise it by any means."[395]

The assault against Godly authority, whether the King or in more modern times simply the institution of fatherhood in general, is typical of communist movements; those animating such revolutions appear to possess an intuitive understanding that Patriarchy protects the innocent from them. In order to destroy both bodies and souls, demons must firstly remove that which is most likely to help their victims: a Father figure who can guide, support, and defend those beneath his

---

[394] Ibid. Page 78.

[395] Ibid. Page 79.

protection.

The other examples Codreanu included in his book demonstrate an equally vicious hatred against the Church and the clergy. The Jewish newspaper called "The Opinion" even printed an article, in August of 1919, bragging that they had no fear of the Church's anathema.[396] The arrogant, spiteful tone of such articles goes a long way to explain Codreanu's attitude towards Jews.

He wrote: "I saw in the columns of these newspapers, at a time of great Romanian hardship, all the hatred and foxy plotting of an enemy race, settled and tolerated here by the pity and only by the pity of the Romanians. I saw how they flaunted their lack of respect for the Roman Army's glory and for the hundreds of thousands who died in its sanctified uniform; their lack of respect for the Christian faith of an entire people. No day passed without venom being poured into our hearts from each page. By reading those newspapers which crisped my soul, I came to know the real feelings of these aliens, which they revealed without reticence, at a time they thought we had been knocked to the ground. I learned enough anti-Semitism in one year to last me three lifetimes. For one cannot strike the sacred beliefs of a people or what their heart loves and respects, without hurting them to the depths and without blood dripping from their wound. Seventeen years have passed since and the wound is still bleeding."[397] After physically destroying several of the

[396] Ibid. Page 80.
[397] Ibid. Page 82.

presses that published such filth, Codreanu became a favorite target of the media.

Following the naturalization grant of 1923, and university students across the nation rising up in revolt against it, Codreanu noted that suddenly the newspapers took on a very different tone: "In 1919, 1920, 1921, the entire Jewish press was assaulting the Romanian state, unleashing disorder everywhere, urging violence against the regime, the form of government, the Church, Romanian order, the national idea, patriotism. Now, as if by a miracle, the same press, controlled by the same men, changed into a defender of the state's order, of laws; declares itself against violence. While we become: 'the country's enemies,' 'extremists of the right,' in the pay and service of Romanianism's enemies,' etc. And in the end we will hear also this: that we are financed by the Jews."[398]

Codreanu further described, in great detail, the strategy he observed being employed by each city's Kahal (or Jewish community) for taking over the local economy, politics, and industries. He prefaced his breakdown of said strategy by noting that "Whoever imagines that the Jews are some poor unfortunates, arrived here haphazardly, brought by winds, pushed by fate, etc., is mistaken. All Jews over the entire world form a great collectivity bound together by blood and by the Talmudic religion. They are constituted into a very strict state, having laws, plans, and leaders making these plans. At the foundation, there is the Kahal. So, we do not face

---

[398] Ibid. Page 169.

some isolated Jews but a constituted power, the Jewish community."[399]

Having explained the foundation of his view, he continued: "In every city or market town where a number of Jews settle, the Kahal, (the Jewish community there) is immediately formed. This Kahal has its own leaders, separate judicial set-up, taxes, etc. and holds the entire Jewish population of that locality tightly united around itself. It is here, in this tiny Kahal of market town or city, that all plans are made: How to win over local politicians and authorities; how to infiltrate certain circles of interest to them, such as magistrates, officers, high officials; what plans to use to take over such and such branch of commerce from the hands of a Romanian; how to destroy a local anti-Semite; how to destroy an incorruptible representative of local authority who might oppose Jewish interests; what plans to apply when, squeezed beyond endurance, the populace would revolt and erupt into anti-Semitic movements."[400] Finally, having set the stage for what follows, Codreanu described the Jewish plans he deduced by observing what occurred in various neighborhoods:

"I. For winning over local politicians: 1. Gifts; 2. Personal favors; 3. Financing the political machine for propaganda, leaflet printing, travel expenses, etc. If there are several bankers in town or rich Jews, each is assigned to a specific political party.

II. For winning over local authorities: 1. Corruption,

---

[399] Ibid. Page 163.
[400] Ibid. Pages 163 and 164.

bribery. A policeman from the smallest town in Moldavia, in addition to the pay he receives from the State, gets another monthly salary or two. Once he accepts a bribe, he becomes the Jews' slave and if he does not follow orders, then they use on him the second weapon: 2. Blackmail, if he does not comply, his bribe-taking is revealed. 3. The third weapon is destruction. If they realize you cannot be swayed or subjected they will try to destroy you searching well your weaknesses. If you drink, they will seek an opportunity to compromise you through alcohol; if you are a skirt-chaser, they will send you a woman who will compromise you or destroy your family; if you are violent by nature, they will send your way another violent man who will kill you or whom you will kill then go to prison; 4. If you lack all of these defects, then they will employ the lie, whispered or printed calumny, and denounce you to your superiors. In the market towns and cities invaded by jews, local authorities are either in a state of bribery, a state of blackmail, or in a state of destruction.

III. In order to infiltrate into various circles or around some highly placed people, they use: 1. Servility' 2. Boards of directors; 3. Base personal favors; 4. Flattery. Thus, all politicians are given Jewish secretaries, because they are handy at doing the shopping, shining the shoes, rocking the babies, holding the briefcase, etc., while at the same time cajoling and insinuating themselves. A Romanian is not going to be as good for he is less refined, is not perfidious, comes from the plow, and particularly because he wants to be a faithful soldier, guarding his honor, refusing to be a valet.

IV. Plans to ruin a Romanian merchant. 1. Flanking the Romanian either with one or two Jewish merchants. 2. Selling merchandise below cost, the loss being made up by special funds given by the Kahal. This is how Romanian merchants were ruined one by one."[401]

As mentioned in his preface to this description, Codreanu took special note of a strategy he believed the Kahal would use in order to crack down on resistance to its plans. That strategy, which he described as a "truly unique and diabolical"[402] one, he illustrated thusly:

"1. They will try to break the spiritual ties of the Romanian to heaven and to earth. To break our ties with heaven they will engage in widespread dissemination of atheistic theories in order to separate the Romanian people or at least some of their leaders from God; separating them from God and their dead they can destroy them, not by sword but by severing the roots of their spiritual life. To break our ties binding us to the land, the material source of a nation's existence, they will attack nationalism, labeling it 'outmoded,' and everything related to the idea of fatherland and soil, in order to cut the love thread tying the Romanian people to their furrow.

2. In order to succeed in this, they will endeavor to get control of the press.

3. They will take advantage of every opportunity to sow discord in the Romanian camp, spreading

[401] Ibid. Pages 164 and 165.

[402] Ibid. Page 166.

misunderstandings, quarrels, and if possible to split it into factions fighting each other.

4. Will seek to gain control of most of the means of livelihood of the Romanians.

5. They will systematically urge Romanians on to licentiousness, destroying their families and their moral fiber.

6. They will poison and daze them with all kinds of drinks and other poisons.

Anyone wishing to conquer and destroy a people could do it by using this system: Breaking its ties with *heaven* and *land*, introducing fratricidal quarrels and fights, promoting immorality and licentiousness, by material ruin, physical poisoning, drunkenness. All these destroy a nation more than being blasted by thousands of cannons or bombed by thousands of airplanes.

Let the Romanians look back a bit to see whether against them this system has not been used with precision and tenacity - truly a murderous system. Let the Romanians open their eyes to read the press for the last 40 years since it has been under Jewish control. Let them re-read *Adevarul* ('The Truth'), *Dimineata* ('The Morning'), *Lupta* ('The Fight'), *Opinia* ('The Opinion'), *Lumea* ('The World'), etc. and see if from each page this plan does not constantly emerge. Let the Romanians open their eyes to see the disunity in present day Romanian public life; let them open their eyes and see well.

The Jews use these plans like poison gas in a war, to be used against the enemy, not their own people. They propagate atheism for Romanians but they themselves are not atheistic, as they fanatically hold to respecting their most minute religious precepts. They want to detach Romanians from their love for the land, but they grab land. They rise up against the national idea, but they remain chauvinistically loyal to their own nation."[403]

Despite all this - and with the important caveat that he perhaps overstated the degree of unity and cohesion within the Jewish world, which in my experience tends to be more splintered and heterogeneous than his observations led him to believe - Codreanu never once preached violence against Jews. While it's true that the Legion did plan to assassinate select politicians, financiers and journalists - some of whom were Jewish - such actions were planned as targeted attacks against specific individuals. Codreanu never planned or promoted violence against Jews as a whole, and even admonished his own followers when they went against this command. In that regard, the situation was not unlike that which the ancient Church had preached: that Jews were not to harm Christians, but Christians were not to harm Jews either. And just as we found in regard to the ancient faith, these commands from the top were not always followed by those below them; if and when such incidents occurred, the leaders were quick to try and end the violence.

Codreanu even punished Legionaries who mistreated Jews against his orders. His book recounts a story from the town of Dorna-Cozanesti: "Four youths went to a Jewish tavern, ordering sardines, bread, and wine, and after they ate well, they stood up. Instead of paying their

[403] Ibid. Pages 166 and 167.

bill, one of them heroically brandished a revolver threatening the life of the Jew if he should squeal, for - he added - they were from Corneliu Codreanu's group. I punished him. Had I not done so, it would have been this youth - not the Jew from whom a can of sardines had been stolen - who would have morally destroyed himself. As a matter of fact, among legionaries, punishment cannot cause resentment, for all us are fallible. In our concept, punishment means a man of honor has to make good on his error."[404] Codreanu did not want his followers to stain their souls through such criminality or thuggish behavior. Maintaining moral uprightness among his group - especially in one's conduct against one's enemies - was a constant focus in his writings.

Instead, and despite his disdain and hatred for all things political, Codreanu always maintained that the "The only legal way to bring about nationwide measures for the solving of the Jewish problem was through political avenues."[405] He did not seek to break laws (his few planned assassinations aside), he did not seek to overthrow the government, and he did not seek to harm or kill Jews. Ideally, he wanted them deported to Palestine so that the Romanian peasantry would be able to flourish and become prosperous. By desiring a peaceful relocation of those fighting against the Church, in order that the local Christians may flourish, it does not seem that Codreanu promoted anything which goes against the Orthodox view of patriotism.

---

[404] Ibid. Pages 341 and 342.

[405] Ibid. Page 342.

Regarding how to solve what he called the "Jewish Problem," it is worth noting that evangelizing and converting Jews are absent from Codreanu's proposed solutions. Out of love for Jewish souls, I staunchly believe that preaching repentance and Holy Baptism to Jews is both a virtue and a command. This most important step, the one borne of love and a desire to obey Christ by preaching His Gospel to sinners, must always be attempted to the greatest degree possible. Where the program of repentance succeeds, there is no need for further action; a sinner embraces Christ, improves or outright ceases his bad behavior, and is now subject to canonical penalties under the Church. Such converts can be excommunicated, cut off from the Body of Christ, should they *"return to their vomit"*[406] and revolutionary ways.

In either case, part of Codreanu's lack of interest in conversion may be (and this is just speculation) that he thought of "Jew" as a racial, rather than religious, category. If so that would explain why he never formulated a plan to convert them - but is not clear from his writings whether he would have considered a Jew who was Baptized into Holy Orthodoxy to be a Jew or an Orthodox Christian. The Church has always considered "Jew" a religious category, while for most Fascists it is a racial one. It is worth noting that, in a departure from Orthodox tradition, a Romanian law passed in 1940 declared Jewish converts to be "Jews" for legal purposes – and under this law, Jewish converts to Orthodoxy could

---

[406] Proverbs 26:11

not marry native Orthodox women.

For some Romanian nationalists "Jew" appears to have been neither strictly religious or racial, but rather one of more immediate practicality; in his book Codreanu approvingly quoted from the 19th-century Minister of Internal Affairs, Mihail Kogalniceanu, who wrote that "In Romania the Jewish question is not a religious one, but a national and at the same time an economic one. In Romania, Jews not only constitute a different religious community; they constitute in the full sense of the word a nationality, foreign to Romanians by virtue of origin, language, dress, customs, and even sentiment. It is not a matter, then, of religious persecution, for if this were the case, the Israelites would face interdiction or restriction in the exercise of their cult, which is not the case. Their synagogues would not be allowed to rise freely near Christian churches; their religious instruction, the publicity of their cult, likewise would not be tolerated." Thus it became a question not of theology or genetics, but of "stopping the exploitation of the Romanian people by an alien people, the Jews."[407]

In his essay *Historical Overview*, an Appendix to <u>For My Legionaries</u>, Lucian Tudor wrote that "The Legionaries believed that nationality (i.e., ethnicity) and not race is the essential category of human types, but they recognized that because race is still a significant factor in nationality, when a national's racial type and solidarity is destroyed through excessive miscegenation, the biological background of the nation is eliminated and thus the

---

[407] Codreanu. Pages 156-158.

nation is harmed and endangered. It is crucial to grasp this concept in order to understand what race means in the Legionary doctrine, and also to avoid common misunderstandings regarding the Legionaries' view of race."[408]

In either case, Codreanu's proposed political solution was to deport the Jews of Romania to the Middle East; as he stated in his <u>Nest Leader's Manual,</u> "Romania for Romanians and Palestine for Jews."[409] In Codreanu's defense, there does not appear to have been any concerted effort by the Orthodox Church to preach Christianity to the Jews in Romania - just as there does not appear to be one, anywhere, in any country, today. Though Dr. Eitan Bar has done substantial work countering rabbinic propaganda and preaching Christ in Israel, at the end of the day he is a Protestant and does not have the fullness of the Christian Faith (which cannot be found outside of Orthodoxy). It is unfortunate that the void left by Orthodox laziness is filled instead by those outside the Church, but if God will show mercy on those who have been truly called to preach the Gospel - and thus far have failed in this high calling - then perhaps the seeds planted by men like Dr. Bar will someday be watered by Christ into Orthodox fruit as those who leave Judaism under his direction may find their way to the ancient and Apostolic Church.

Roman Catholic efforts to convert the Jews really came

[408]   Ibid. Page 454.

[409]   Thorpe, C. (2012, January 24). *The Legionary Doctrine*. Counter-Currents. https://counter-currents.com/2012/01/the-legionary-doctrine/

into focus in the 13th century and beyond, hundreds of years after splitting away from Eastern Orthodoxy, and there was simply no parallel in the Orthodox world. This heartbreaking failure on the part of our Church will have to be remedied at some point if we are serious about loving our enemies and winning them over to Christ. Given that Codreanu had likely never heard of the Western conversion campaigns, nor seen any examples of their success, it is perhaps understandable that he never attempted one himself.

A truly nonviolent movement which seeks the restoration of a Christian people has three potential options in dealing with whoever is harming them: conversion, encouragement to adapt to the local and national ways, and ultimately some type of segregation. The important thing, in all cases, is to act from a place of love; in the first case, conversion, one acts from love towards the souls of those whom are not yet Christian. In the second, one acts from love towards both his enemies and the local community; when a foreign people adapts to the ways of its new host country, they become better-assimilated and can feel more like a part of the whole than an isolated fragment at odds with everyone else. Finally, in the case of segregation – or in its most extreme form, deportation - one acts dispassionately out of love for one's neighbor and countryman.

Codreanu was also the only leader we've studied who placed a priority on the internal transformation of his people, always emphasizing the need for spirituality in returning Romania to its roots. Evola wrote in his essay

The Tragedy of the Romanian Iron Guard that for Codreanu, "It is not a matter of new parties of formulae, but of creating a new man. It is this view that gave rise to Codreanu's Legion, which is primarily a school for life for the forging of a new type displaying 'all the possibilities of human grandeur that are implanted by God in the blood of our people'…The creation of this new type of man is the essential thing, according to Codreanu; the rest is only of secondary importance and will follow as an inevitable consequence in a natural and irresistible process. Through this regenerated man, the Jewish problem will be solved and a new political order will be established, awakening the kind of magnetism that is capable of carrying crowds away, of bringing victory, and of leading the race along the path of glory."[410]

Codreanu regularly emphasized that the most direct and immediate cause of the nation's calamity was not Jews, but Romanian immorality. For example, after the granting of citizenship to Jews, he wondered "what curse on our heads and what sins condemned us Romanians to have part in such scoundrelly leaders?"[411] Gathering together with other students to protest that amendment to their Constitution, he wrote that "The first problem we had to face was to decide who were the principal guilty parties; who were most responsible for the state of misery which seized the whole country: Romanians or Jews? We unanimously agreed that the first and greatest culprits were the treacherous Romanians who for Judas's silver

---

[410]   Codreanu, C. (2015). *The Prison Notes*. Pages 91 and 92.
[411]   *For My Legionaries*. Page 151.

pieces betrayed their people. The Jews are our enemies and as such they hate, poison, and exterminate us. Romanian leaders who cross into their camp are worse than enemies: they are traitors. The first and fiercest punishment ought to fall first on the traitor, second on the enemy. If I had but one bullet and were faced by both an enemy and a traitor, I would let the traitor have it."[412] Finally, in his fullest expression of this particular sentiment, he wrote from Vacaresti prison that "A country has only the Jews and the leaders it deserves. Just as mosquitoes can settle and thrive only in swamps, likewise the former can only thrive in the swamps of our Romanian sins. In other words, in order to win over them we will have first to extirpate our own defects."[413]

Thus Codreanu touched upon a deeply Orthodox truth: that our enemies can only defeat us to the extent to which we've defeated ourselves. When we are ignorant, when we are forgetful, when we are indolent and lazy and neglectful of our souls, we give permission to the passions to strike us down. Destroyed by our faithlessness, our distractions and pride, we make ourselves into the devil's playthings. At the same time, we look for someone to blame, desperately pointing the finger at *anyone but ourselves*, as if the demons and those they animate have any real power over a man who is united to Christ. Above all, let us again keep in mind the Apostle's exhortation: "*For we wrestle not against flesh and blood, but against principalities, against powers, against the*

---

[412] Ibid. Pages 179 and 180.
[413] Ibid. Page 195.

rulers of the darkness of this age, against spiritual hosts of wickedness in the heavenly places."[414]

Those "*spiritual hosts of wickedness*" seek any crack in our armor which allows them to gain influence over us, and the same is true for our worldly enemies: they would not be doing what they're doing, causing the harm they're causing and ruining what they're ruining, if they believed in the Gospel and were Baptized. May we always keep this in mind and seek the salvation of ourselves and those around us, as salvation is the only genuine and permanent solution to the problems we often grasp only superficially. Amen.

---

[414] Ephesians 6:12

"On Fascism"

by Ivan Ilyn

"Fascism is a complex phenomenon: it is multifaceted and historically speaking, far from exhausted. Within it one finds elements of health and illness, old and new, protection and destruction. Therefore in an evaluation of fascism fair-mindedness and equanimity are needed. But its dangers must be considered in full.

Fascism arose as a reaction to Bolshevism, as a concentration of power guarding sovereignty from the Right. As leftist chaos and totalitarianism advanced, this was a healthy phenomenon, as well as necessary and unavoidable. And such a concentration will come about henceforth, even in the most democratic states: in an hour of national danger the more vigorous forces of the people will always rally to the defense of sovereignty. Thus it was in ancient Rome and the new Europe, and so it shall be hereafter.

Standing against leftist totalitarianism, fascism was correct, as it sought just socio-political reform. This quest could be successful or unsuccessful: solving such problems is difficult, and first attempts might not have made any headway. But to meet the wave of socialist psychosis - through social and consequently anti-socialist measures - was imperative. These measures had long been imminent, and waiting any further was out of the question. Finally, fascism was right since it derived from a healthy national-patriotic sensibility, without which a people can neither lay claim to its existence nor create a unique culture.

However, along with this fascism committed an entire range of grave and serious errors that defined its political and historical physiognomy and lent its very name that odious pallor which its enemies never tire from emphasizing. Therefore for future social and political movements of a similar cast, another self-designation is necessary. If someone gives his movement the former name ('fascism' or 'National Socialism'), this will be interpreted as the intent to restore all the faults and fatal mistakes of the past. These faults and mistakes comprised the following:

1. Irreligiousness: a hostile attitude toward Christianity, religions, faith and churches in general.

2. The creation of right-totalitarianism as a permanent and supposedly 'ideal' system.

3. The establishment of a party monopoly and the resultant corruption and demoralization that sprang from it.

4. Withdrawal into extremes of nationalism and militant chauvinism (national megalomania).

5. Mixing social reforms with socialism and the slide through totalitarianism to a state takeover of the economy.

6. The fall into idolatrous Caesarism with its demagoguery, subservience and despotism.

These errors compromised fascism and set against it entire religions, parties, peoples and states, ultimately leading it to an unwinnable war and destruction. The cultural and political mission of fascism failed, and the Left flooded in with ever greater force.

1. Fascism should not have held a position hostile to Christianity and any religiosity in general. A political regime that attacks the Church and religion brings schism into the souls of its citizens, undermines in them the deepest roots of justice and begins to claim its own religious significance, which is mad. Mussolini soon understood that in a Catholic country, state power needs an honest concordat with the Catholic Church. Hitler, with his vulgar godlessness, behind which was concealed equally vulgar self-deification, unto the end never recognized that anticipating the Bolsheviks, he walked the path of Antichrist.

2. Fascism could have *not created* a totalitarian system: it could have satisfied itself with an authoritarian dictatorship sufficiently strong to a) uproot Bolshevism and Communism, and b) provide religions, the press, academia, art, sectors of the economy and non-communist parties freedom of judgment by virtue of their political loyalty.

3. Never and nowhere can the establishment of a one-party monopoly lead to anything good: the best men will depart the stage, and the worst will flock to the party in droves. For the better men think independently and freely, while the worse are ready to adjust to anything in

325

order to make a career. For this reason the monopolist party lives by self-deception: beginning [with] 'qualitative selection,' it demands 'party consensus.' Making this the condition for work in any legal and political capacity, it calls men to absurdity and hypocrisy; in so doing it opens the doors wide to all manner of imbeciles, dissimulators, impostors and careerists. The qualitative level of the party breaks down, and pretenders, crooks, predators, speculators, terrorists, yes-men and traitors come to power. As a result all the shortcomings and errors of political partisanship reach in fascism their highest expression; the party monopoly is worse than party competition (a law known in trade, industry and all the creation of culture). Russian 'fascists' did not understand this. If they manage to entrench themselves in Russia (God forbid), they will compromise healthy ideas of sovereign power and fail in ignominy.

4. Fascism did not at all have to fall into 'political megalomania,' despise other races and nationalities, and proceed with their conquest and extermination. A sense of one's own dignity is not in the least arrogant hubris. Patriotism does not call for the subjugation of the Universe; to liberate your people does not at all imply overtaking and wiping out your neighbors.

5. The line between socialism and social reforms has a deep, principal significance. Stepping over this line would mean the ruin of social reform. For we must always remember that socialism is antisocial, and justice and liberation in society tolerate neither socialism nor Communism.

6. The greatest fascist error was the restoration of idolatrous Caesarism. 'Caesarism' is the direct opposite of monarchism. Caesarism is godless, irresponsible, and despotic; it holds in contempt freedom, law, legitimacy, justice and the individual rights of men. It is demagogic, terroristic and haughty; it lusts for flattery, 'glory' and worship, and it sees in the people a mob and stokes its passions. Caesarism is amoral, militaristic and callous. It compromises the principle of authority and autocracy, for its rule does not prosecute state or national interests, but personal ends.

Franco and Salazar recognized this and are attempting to avoid the aforementioned errors. They do not call their regime 'fascist.' We shall hope that Russian patriots will also reflect in full upon the mistakes of fascism and National Socialism and not repeat them."[415]

---

[415] December 27, M. H., & Comments, 2013 2. (2013, December 27). *Ivan Ilyin: On Fascism*. The Soul of the East. https://souloftheeast.org/2013/12/27/ivan-ilyin-on-fascism/comment-page-1/

Failed Nations: The Cause and Cure

"The external physical captivity of a nation is only a symbol of its preceding spiritual captivity...a nation that falls into captivity through war deserves to be enslaved through their wicked lives in the preceding peace."[416]
+ *St. Nikolai Velimirovic*

In times of desperation - when a nation has been brought so low that it becomes unrecognizable to those who live there, when its founding principles have been so subverted that it bears little if any similarity to its original intention, when its government has been occupied by hostile powers or sold off to foreign enemies - then people who love that nation, with sorrowful and angry hearts, desperately seek a solution. The worse things get and the more pressure they feel, the more alienated from their neighbors and atomized in their communities, the more heavily they're taxed and the less they have left for themselves and their families, then the more likely they become to cling to any person or ideology promising to ease their woes and restore their lives to some semblance of normalcy. While it is easy to understand and empathize with their plight - one which we ourselves may even share - this scenario nonetheless requires a great degree of caution and discernment. For it's when people are at their lowest,

---

[416] Velimirovic, N. (2018). *War and the Bible*. Diocese of New Gracanica and Midwestern America. Pages 51 and 52.

and most in need of help, that they are most likely to turn to God; the demons also know this and employ the full use of their wicked power to redirect man to false saviors instead. Thus, if we find ourselves in this situation and wish to avoid losing our souls, we must study, believe, and live by what the Orthodox Church has taught us about how to restore our land to health.

In order to learn what our Holy Faith has taught, we must - as always - turn to the Bible and the Saints. **Ecclestiastes 1:9** reminds us that *"there is nothing new under the sun,"* despite superficial appearances to the contrary. Our Prophets and Fathers have already told us the unchanging truth about failed nations: firstly, of the cause and secondly, of the cure. In his book <u>War and the Bible</u>, St. Nikolai Velimirovic stated that "Besides the Bible, there is no other book in the world that describes so many wars and gives explanation of their forecauses."[417] Armed with the Scriptures and St. Nikolai's interpretation, we will surely arrive at right conclusions.

Our Biblical analysis of these particular dynamics focuses on the Old Testament nation of Israel. By studying both its successes and failures, along with the factors that contributed to each, we may partake of God's timeless wisdom and apply His ancient teachings to modern life. Let us begin with **Judges 1:1-4**, where God outlines the bigger picture: *"Now after the death of Joshua it came to pass that the children of Israel asked the LORD, saying, 'Who shall be first to go up for us against the Canaanites to fight against them?' And the LORD said, 'Judah*

---

[417] Ibid. Page 28.

shall go up. Indeed I have delivered the land into his hand.' So Judah said to Simeon his brother, 'Come up with me to my allotted territory, that we may fight against the Canaanites; and I will likewise go with you to your allotted territory.' And Simeon went with him. Then Judah went up, and the LORD delivered the Canaanites and the Perizzites into their hand; and they killed ten thousand men at Bezek."

Notice that when the Israelites asked God who would fight for them, God responded - in the past tense - that He had *already delivered* the land to Judah. The decision about who would win the battle had *already been made*; God's sovereignty, which transcends time and space and by which He interacts with His beloved children, orchestrated the outcome of the scenario *ahead of time*. The Israelites were not told what weapons to make, how many soldiers to recruit, or what tactics to use. They were told that God had already delivered them the land, and instructed as to who would carry out His plan. His sovereignty is once again emphasized in the last sentence of the quoted passage, in which it is stated that *"the LORD delivered the Canaanites and the Perizzites into their hand."* Each step of the way to victory, God was in charge and not man. Thus we learn that a people conquers and wins when God is on their side.

In the following chapter, Israel apostatizes and loses the favor of God. After the death of Joshua, *"the children of Israel did evil in the sight of the LORD, and served the Baals; and they forsook the LORD God of their fathers, who had brought them out of the land of Egypt; and they followed other gods from among the gods of the people who were all around* them, and they bowed down to them; and they provoked the LORD to anger. They forsook the LORD and served Baal and the Ashtoreths. And the anger of the LORD was hot against Israel. So He delivered them into the hands of plunderers who despoiled them; and He sold them into the hands of their enemies all around, so that they could no longer stand before their enemies. Wherever they went out, the hand of the LORD was against them for calamity, as the LORD had said, and as the LORD had sworn to them. And they were greatly distressed."[418]

We find the same pattern in **2 Kings 21:8-12**, when God said that "Neither will I make the feet of Israel move any more out of the land which I gave to their fathers; only if they will observe to do according to all I have commanded them, and according to all the law that my servant Moses commanded them. But they hearkened not: and Manasseh seduced them to do more evil than did the nations whom the Lord destroyed before the children of Israel. And the Lord spake by His servants the prophets, saying, Because Manasseh king of Judah hath done these abominations, and hath done wickedly above all that the Amorites did, which were before him, and hath made Judah also to sin with his idols: Therefore thus saith the Lord God of Israel, Behold, I am bringing such evil upon Jerusalem and Judah, that whosoever heareth of it, both his ears shall tingle."

Now we see the other side of God's favor toward His people: when they turn from Him, He chastens them and delivers them to their enemies. When they forget Who He Is, when they forget What He's done, when they put their

---

[418] Judges 2:11-15

trust and faith in idols, then God withdraws His favor and protection. Throughout the Old Testament we see Israel fall into captivity every single time they turn away from God: first to the king of Mesopotamia, then to the king of Moab, to the Midianites, and to the Philistines. Why? Because *"The children of Israel did evil in the sight of the Lord."*[419] Whenever Israel turned its back on God, God turned His back on them. Yet we must always remember that when God turns His back on us, it's for our own good; it's because we've gone astray and He knows what will bring us back. In the words of St. Nikolai, "God knows that misfortune turns sinful people to the Truth; that is why He sends misfortune. In peace and abundance, people become godless and selfish, that is why God sends misfortune - to sober them up. It is from this that Serbs have this expression: Without distress there is no prayer to God."[420]

Thus far we have seen that God's favor is with those who love Him, and withdrawn from those who forget Him. But what about when a nation comes to its senses, repents of its errors and returns to Him? The Bible tells us that *"the LORD longs to be gracious to you, and therefore He waits on high to have compassion on you. For the LORD is a God of justice; How blessed are all those who long for Him."*[421] As the **Book of Judges** demonstrates the falls of Israel, so does it display their repentance; no matter who they've been conquered by, no matter how bad things have

---

[419] Judges 3:12
[420] Velimirovic. Page 128.
[421] Isaiah 30:18

gotten, when the nation and its leaders turn back to God they are restored to their former favor. After 8 years of captivity under Cushan-Rishathaim, we read in **Judges 3:9-11** that when the Israelites *"cried out to the LORD, He raised up for them a deliverer, Othniel son of Kenaz, Caleb's younger brother, who saved them. The Spirit of the LORD came on him, so that he became Israel's judge and went to war. The LORD gave Cushan-Rishathaim king of Aram into the hands of Othniel, who overpowered him. So the land had peace for forty years, until Othniel son of Kenaz died."* After Othniel's death, **Judges 3:12** tells us that *"Again the Israelites did evil in the eyes of the LORD, and because they did this evil the LORD gave Eglon king of Moab power over Israel."* After another 18 years of captivity to a foreign power, **Judges 3:15** tells us that *"Again the Israelites cried out to the LORD, and He gave them a deliverer - Ehud, a left-handed man, the son of Gera the Benjaminite."*

We see the same pattern all throughout the **Book of Judges**: a righteous Judge liberates Israel from its enemies, and after his death the nation falls into ignorance and forgetfulness. God hands them over for chastisement once again, and after a period of captivity they repent. Then God raises up another judge to save them, and the cycle begins all over again. The rise and fall of nations is nowhere better described.

The dynamic we can so easily and consistently observe in the Bible is one that entirely relies on God's favor or lack thereof. The size of an army, its technological prowess, and the ferocity of its soldiers only matter to the extent that He allows. There is perhaps no better example of this phenomenon than the story of St. David and Goliath; David, a humble shepherd and musician, killed the powerful Philistine giant with a slingshot. David did not have the size, strength, or weaponry which would normally have allowed such an outcome - we read in **1 Samuel 17:5-7** that Goliath" *had a bronze helmet on his head, and he was armed with a coat of mail, and the weight of the coat was five thousand shekels of bronze. And he had bronze armor on his legs and a bronze javelin between his shoulders. Now the staff of his spear was like a weaver's beam, and his iron spearhead weighed six hundred shekels."*

Even King Saul did not believe David could prevail, telling him *"You are not able to go against this Philistine to fight with him; for you are a youth, and he a man of war from his youth."*[422] But David, putting his faith in God rather than in his size or martial prowess, declared that *"The LORD, Who delivered me from the paw of the lion and from the paw of the bear, He will deliver me from the hand of this Philistine."*[423] And this despite the fact that David could not even bear the weight of bronze armor! After being mocked by Goliath for his youth and weakness, David responded that *"You come to me with a sword, with a spear, and with a javelin. But I come to you in the name of the LORD of hosts, the God of the armies of Israel, whom you have defied. This day the LORD will deliver you into my hand, and I will strike you and take your head from you. And this day I will give the carcasses of the camp of the Philistines to the birds of the air and the wild beasts of the earth, that all the earth may*

---

[422] 1 Samuel 17:33

[423] 1 Samuel 17:37

know that there is a God in Israel. Then all this assembly shall know that the LORD does not save with sword and spear; for the battle is the LORD's, and He will give you into our hands."[424] Then David slew Goliath with a stone.

The same principle is illustrated in **1 Maccabees 3:17-23**. Judas Maccabeus and his men were confronted with a far larger army, led by a pagan prince of Syria named Seron. We read in that passage that the Maccabees were afraid, asking their leader *"'How shall we be able, being so few, to fight against so great a multitude and so strong, seeing we are ready to faint with fasting all this day?' Unto whom Judas answered, 'it is no hard matter for many to be shut up in the hands of a few; and with the God of heaven it is all one, to deliver with a great multitude, or a small company: For the victory of battle standeth not in the multitude of a host, but strength cometh from heaven. They come against us in much pride and iniquity to destroy us, and our wives and children, and to spoil us: But we fight for our lives and our laws. Wherefore the LORD Himself will overthrow them before our face: And as for you, be ye not afraid of them.' Now as soon as he had left off speaking, he leapt suddenly upon them, and so Seron and his host were overthrown before him."* Neither David nor Judas had any material advantage, yet the Lord delivered victory to them both.

Thus we may agree entirely with St. Nikolai's conclusion that "the side that will win is the one that the will of God chooses. Which side will the will of God choose? This is evident in the Holy Book of God; it is evident in our current exposition; it is evident in all the

---

[424]   1 Samuel 17:45-47

wars throughout human history, only if those wars are read in the light of the Bible. Simply put: The will of God chooses victory for the side that has the clearest and strongest faith in God and keeps the law of God the most seriously. A nation that has apostatized from God and is lawless will lose war, even in their numbers are like grains of sand in the desert. And the leader of a nation who has apostatized and is lawless cannot be helped by intellect or calculation or army or culture or weaponry or diplomatic networks or eloquence or anything in the material world. But a nation that, together with its leaders, holds onto the Christ God (we are still speaking about Christian nations) will be either spared from war or will leave war victorious, regardless of their number, culture, or weaponry."[425]

We have no need to look to economics, politics, media narratives, accusations of systemic injustice, or any other worldly cause to discern why a nation has fallen; the cause is, has always been, and will always be apostasy. That fatal mistake can occur either by way of overt apostasy, explicitly turning away from God and the Orthodox Faith, by moral apostasy via weakness and the succumbing to temptation, or both. The more widespread and intense this apostasy, the more severe the chastisement from God. Every single time we sin, giving ourselves over to a wicked passion or entertaining an errant thought or movement of the will, we fall short of the high ideal to which we are called and directly contribute to our community's destruction.

---

[425] Velimirovic. Pages 122 and 123.

If we desire God's favor upon our neighborhoods and nations, we must refocus our attention from the sins of others to our own faults - for even if we were to completely eradicate the evil around us, the evil within us would still serve as a doorway for demons. Through us the same dark spirits would still manifest and take root, decaying the world around us and bringing us back into the same situation. Do you wish to know why you now live in a failed nation? Look to your own conduct, and no further.

For if we were truly living up to our calling in Christ - shedding our worldliness like the snakeskin it is, growing in God and becoming one with Him, radiating the peace and the joy and the love of Christ from every fiber of our being – then our neighbors would be begging us to share what we have with them, begging us to come to the next Divine Liturgy, begging us to teach them how we became what we are, burning with a zeal to attain God for themselves because we – *if we were truly worthy of being called Christians* - would be torches lighting up the darkness of this world, lighting a flame in the heart of every person we meet.

Instead we fall short, failing to live up to the standards we profess, and pass by our neighbors without so much as a kind word. We hide from them the very Christ in Whom the only true salvation is made possible. Why are we surprised that our nation has fallen when those who should be lifting it above its filth are just making it even dirtier instead?

Only by reorienting the nous to scan the inner world

for sin, begging God to help us locate and expel it from our souls, may we grow in the purification which serves not only *our* salvation - but the salvation of the world around us. In the immortal words of St. Seraphim of Sarov: "Acquire the Holy Spirit, and thousands around you will be saved."[426]

---

[426] Freeman, F. S. (2007, September 17). *What St. Seraphim Meant*. Glory to God for All Things. https://blogs.ancientfaith.com/glory2godforallthings/2007/09/17/what-st-seraphim-meant/

Conclusion

"Do not put your trust in princes, in human beings, who cannot save. When their spirit departs, they return to the ground; on that very day their plans come to nothing. Blessed are those whose help is the God of Jacob, whose hope is in the LORD their God." - **Psalm 146:3-5**

The Church has recognized Saints from all walks of life, with all manner of stations and attitudes. Some were canonized as warriors and Martyrs for their people, fighting and dying for the homelands they loved, while others were "ascetically divested of fatherland, race, possessions, and of the whole world altogether."[427] God upholds both as examples of pious men. Thus, rather than worry over whether we love our nation too much or not enough, let us rather keep watch over ourselves and ensure we approach the topic with dispassion.

The wisdom of St. Neilos the Ascetic is worthy of contemplation: "When the mind prays purely and without passion, the demons approach not from the left but from the right. For they suggest to it the glory of God and some form of things pleasant to the senses, in order that it might think that it has attained completely the aim of prayer."[428] He further instructed: "You should not be ignorant of this guile: at times the demons divide

---

[427] *St. John Chrysostom and the Jesus Prayer.* (2019). NewRome Press. Page 3.

[428] Saint Macarios & Saint Nicodemos. (2008). *The Philokalia.* Inst for Byzantine & Modern Greek. Pages 75 and 76.

themselves, and if you seem to be seeking help, one group will come in the guise of angels and drive away the other group, in order that you might be deceived by them into believing that they are truly angels."[429]

In his excellent book <u>Antichrist: The Fulfillment of Globalization</u>, Dr. G.M. Davis speculated that the Antichrist may apply this spiritual principle on a political scale: "Because Antichrist will be seen by many heterodox Christians as Christ come again, it seems at least possible that his reign from the temple in Jerusalem will have to occur after the defeat of a false antichrist. By defeating another who claims to be Christ, Antichrist could more plausibly claim to be fulfilling prophecy as Christ come again. By defeating another antichrist, he could more plausibly claim that he is the true savior whose supposed 'thousand-year reign' has now begun."[430] Later in that book, Dr. Davis further warned that "Popular feeling toward a man who one believes can deliver an earthly paradise will, by nature, be total, reverential, worshipful. Such a political figure then is by nature a messiah figure, an antichrist, promising salvation for his faithful who have handed over to him their votes along with their hearts and minds."[431]

Thus our main task is to remain watchful over ourselves, paying special attention to any feelings of hope or excitement that may arise within us when considering a new politician or ideology to support. We must ask

---

[429] Ibid. Page 80.

[430] Davis, G. M. (2022). *Antichrist: the Fulfillment of Globalization*. Page 63.

[431] Ibid. Page 255.

ourselves whether we are approaching the topic with sobriety, dispassionately supporting the person or system with due restraint, or whether the powers of our souls that ought to be directed toward God are being misdirected down other avenues instead.

If we find that we fall into the latter camp, let us immediately run to prayer and to holy reading, immersing ourselves in the Scriptures and Fathers; even if we continue our support for the person in question, we will at least be more discerning - having cultivated a prayerful state - and more aware of our own inner movements. By better discerning good and evil within ourselves, we more easily discern it externally. We become less likely to be fooled by leaders with Christ on their lips and blood their hands. We will not fall for the trap when Presidents hold the Bible in photos while imposing sodomite "marriage" on foreign countries. We will not make those "small" compromises in order to excuse their anti-Christian behavior, thereby giving up a part of our souls in the hope that such people may attain power.

In times of trouble, people will always seek and cling to men who promise and offer solutions. The key is to choose the Man Who Is God, lest a usurper steal His throne in our hearts.

In the name of the Father, and the Son, and the Holy Spirit.

Amen.

About the Author

Michael Witcoff is an Oblate of St. Benedict and can be found under his Benedictine title "Brother Augustine" on Twitter, Telegram, Gab, and YouTube. He was raised in a Jewish home, spent his young adulthood as a New Ager and occultist, and was eventually Baptized into the Holy Orthodox Church on Pentecost of 2018. Other titles by Michael Witcoff include <u>On The Masons And Their Lies</u>, an apologetic work demonstrating the incompatibility of Freemasonry with Orthodox Christianity, and a book of poems and essays entitled <u>Theopoetica</u>. Both are available on Amazon.com and can also be purchased directly from the author. If you learned something valuable from <u>Fascism Viewed From The Cross</u>, please feel free to leave an Amazon review letting me know your honest thoughts on the book. May God bless, keep, heal, forgive, love, and save you and yours. Amen.